IRELAN

— ☿ —

Mark Morris

Photography by Anthony Cassidy

PASSPORT BOOKS
a division of *NTC Publishing Group*
Lincolnwood, Illinois USA

Published by Passport Books in conjunction with
The Guidebook Company Ltd

This edition first published in 1995 by Passport Books, a division of NTC Publishing Group, 4255 W. Touhy Avenue, Lincolnwood (Chicago), Illinois 60646-1975, USA, originally published by The Guidebook Company Ltd. © The Guidebook Company Ltd. All rights reserved.

ISBN: 0-8442-9669-4
Library of Congress Catalog Card Number: 93-86166

Grateful acknowledgment is made to the following authors and publishers for permissions granted:

Random House Inc for *Annaghkeen* by Deborah Love © 1970 by Deborah Love; John Farquharson Ltd, London for *Some Experiences of an Irish R M* by Edithe Œnone Somerville and Martin Ross © 1983 by Edith Œnone Somerville and Martin Ross; Colin Smythe Ltd Publishers for *Gods and Fighting Men* by Lady Augusta Gregory © 1970 by Lady Augusta Gregory; Curtis Brown Ltd and Julia O'Faoláin Marines for 'Lovers of the Lake' from *Selected Stories of Seán O'Faoláin* © 1978 by Seán O'Faoláin; MacMillan Publishers for 'The Hosting of the Sidhe' and 'Lake Isle of Innisfree' from *Collected Poems of W B Yeats* © 1934 by W B Yeats; Copyright Management Inc. for *Kilkelly* by Peter Jones © 1993 Some Sweet Music; Harper Collins Publishers for *Ireland: An Illustrated History* by John Ranelagh; Alfred A. Knopf, Inc. and Andre Deutsch Ltd. for *The Price of My Soul* by Bernadette Devlin © 1969; John Murray (Publishers) Ltd. for *A Place Apart* by Dervla Murphy; Faber and Faber Ltd. for *The Collected Poems of Louis MacNeice*.

Editor: Barry Parr
Series Editor: Anna Claridge
Illustrations Editor: Caroline Robertson
Design: David Hurst
Map Design: Jim Pire

Front cover photos by Anthony Cassidy
Photography courtesy of: **Anthony Cassidy** 4, 5, 9, 11, 16, 38, 46, 47, 50, 55, 58, 59, 62, 66, 67, 71, 75 (top and bottom), 79, 81, 84, 85, 98, 103, 113, 120, 121, 128, 138, 142, 143 (top and bottom), 150, 154, 155, 159, 165, 176, 178, 190, 191, 204, 208, 210, 211, 223, 227, 235, 242, 272; **John Murray** 3, 18–19, 22, 23, 30, 39, 72, 90, 93, 106, 116–117, 130, 146–147, 154, 169, 173, 187, 193, 197, 230, 239, 250, 251, 260–261, 264; **Jacqueline O'Brien** 87, 88, 89, 255; **The Board of the National Library of Ireland** 26, 27, 33, 195, 245; **Hulton Deutsch Collection Limited** 73, 94, 149, 221; **Trinity College Library** 77; **The Mansell Collection** 167; **The National Gallery of Ireland** 218; **Dover Publications** 17, 42, 108, 156, 162, 214

Production House: Twin Age Limited, Hong Kong
Printed in China

For Suzanne

Contents

Literary Excerpts

Special Topics

Maps

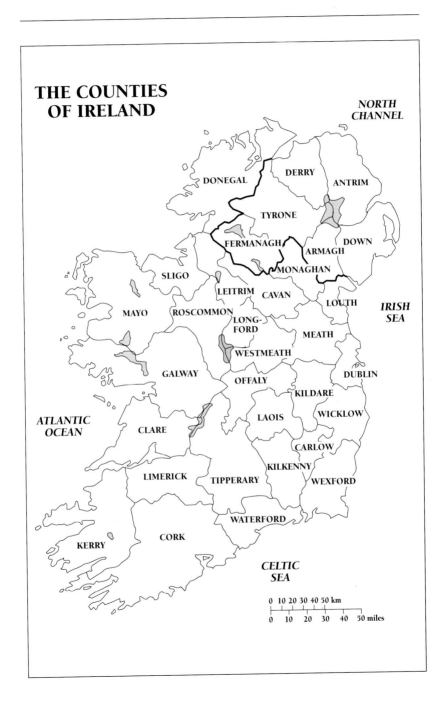

THE COUNTIES
OF IRELAND

NORTH
CHANNEL

DONEGAL

DERRY

ANTRIM

TYRONE

DOWN

FERMANAGH

ARMAGH

MONAGHAN

SLIGO

LEITRIM

CAVAN

LOUTH

IRISH
SEA

MAYO

ROSCOMMON

LONG-
FORD

MEATH

WESTMEATH

GALWAY

OFFALY

DUBLIN

KILDARE

ATLANTIC
OCEAN

LAOIS

WICKLOW

CLARE

CARLOW

KILKENNY

LIMERICK

TIPPERARY

WEXFORD

WATERFORD

KERRY

CORK

CELTIC
SEA

0 10 20 30 40 50 km

0   10   20   30   40   50 miles

Acknowledgements

A debt of gratitude is owed to the many people who have helped in many ways to bring this book to completion. Thanks first of all go to Barry Parr, for his patient and always thoughtful editing. Thanks also to Mary Catherine Lamb for meticulous proofreading and to David Hurst for imaginative design work. Thanks to Magnus Bartlett for the opportunity.

Thanks to Mary Orr for tea and sympathy, and to Laurie Fullerton, Judy Jewell, Bill McRae and Stuart Warren for their encouragement. Thanks to Jennifer Snarski, Elizabeth Rhudy and Pauli Galin for their hard work and contributions. Thanks to Mary Byrne Kline for her many useful suggestions, and to Linda Taylor for her comments and additions on Northern Ireland.

Go raith maith agat to Michael Herlihy and family of Dingle and to John and Finuala Murray of Dublin for generous hospitality; to Cormac McDonagh, Turlough Downes and Conor Brennan for the Gaelic levity; and to Eileen and Joe Scott for the scones and for many warm evenings of spirited inspiration.

Thanks to Aer Lingus, Mr. Paul Murphy in particular, for generous support, and to the Irish Tourist Board (Bord Fáilte) and the Northern Ireland Tourist Board for their assistance. Thanks to the Multnomah County Library of Portland, Oregon.

Lastly (but not leastly), heartfelt thanks to Suzanne Scott for constant support, patience and boundless encouragement.

❧

Anthony Cassidy would like to thank Eugene Lennon (Cork), the Jankinson Family (Kerry and Dublin), Dave and Catrina (Dublin), Loed, Carola and Max (Holland), Cathy Baker (Holland), Monica Longo at Aer Lingus (Amsterdam), and Ann Scholten (Holland). And to the people of Ireland: A big *thank you* for your warmth and hospitality.

❧

John Murray would like to thank Finuala, for her patience during endless hours spent waiting for the light to change.

❧

The publishers would especially like to thank Hugh Hunter and Desmond Guinness for their interest and support.

Tom O'Connor, Co. Kerry

Introduction

"If beauty is heartbreak, no place on earth can compare".

—Nik Cohn

When finally, after the droning hours across the furrowed water, the white thread of breakers shows through the morning haze and the famous green fields heave into view, even the visitor with no tangible roots in Ireland—with no emigrant ancestors to trace, no family waiting, no business here at all, really, save curiosity —could be forgiven for imagining the arrival as a homecoming of sorts.

Ireland, the old irony goes, is the home one must always leave. The fact that more Irish live outside Ireland than in it proves the sad truth of it. "I showed my own appreciation of my native land in the usual Irish way", G.B. Shaw admitted crustily, "by getting out of it as soon as I possibly could". But for many others—those neither born nor bred here but drawn nevertheless by some filament of memory perhaps—Ireland seems to be the home to which they are always returning.

One has to wonder what contradictory forces are at work on this small island, which drives its own children out yet seems so inviting to strangers. What is it that brings the Americans, in their shamrock-green cardigans, to knock about a musty churchyard in County Down searching for their great-great-granny's tombstone? What ticklish impulse draws an Australian around the globe, to show up hopefully at the door of century-removed strangers who happen to share the same surname? What makes the sensible Germans, in their thousands, bid *auf Wiedersehen* to their Teutonically engineered auto-bahns to rattle along with the sheep down a potholed *boreen* in Kerry?

In the uncertain hurly-burly and uprootedness of modern times, there's something irresistibly comforting about Ireland.

From a distance, it's only too easy to sentimentalize it into a welcoming ancestral homeland, an island holdover from gentler times, suffused in the warm amber light of nostalgia. But no country, least of all Ireland, is so simple as that.

Life on this island, stingy in its natural resources and long excluded from the main currents of progress, has forged a steady self-reliance. But genera-tions of rough poverty and the indignity of foreign domination have also bred a hazy ambivalence in the Irish and insecurity beneath their pride.

"It is not a place of easy joys", wrote Nik Cohn, who grew up alongside Lough Swilly in Donegal. "Its present is hard-scrabble, most of its history bitter.

On every road there is a remembrance of pain—burned abbeys and gutted cottages, fields abandoned, broken graves. But the loveliness is imperishable".

Scarcely 300 miles from top to bottom, Ireland can be crossed from one stony coast to the other in one short day. The island's entire population is smaller than London's. Yet, in the imagination's often distorted geography, Ireland sprawls to mythic proportions, and its influence extends well beyond its own humble boundaries. In science and music, in the arts and, of course, in literature, Ireland has immeasurably enriched the world. But in their diaspora over the last two centuries—whether by choice or from grim necessity—it's the Irish people themselves who have been the country's most enduring export.

In America, the Irish have contributed a dozen presidents and have had such a profound effect on the national psyche that some 40 million people now claim Irish ancestry, a figure far out of proportion with the facts. It's one measure of the sentimental allure Ireland possesses: what other land, of any size, exerts such a pull on the wistful heart?

For the guidebook writer, any country can be a brier patch of clichés on which it's easy to get snagged. This feels especially true of Ireland, where, as the Irish filmmaker Neil Jordan has said, "You feel every inch of the landscape has been written about. It can be burdensome". But beneath all the romantic clichés about Ireland and the Irish, of course, there resides a foundation of truth, and much of it *is* unabashedly romantic: the tang of turf smoke in the air; the children's shy eyes and quick smiles; sunlight spilling through pewter clouds onto a new-mown meadow in Wexford or Clare's old, bony hills; a fiddle's dark, sinuous twining through the murmur of a blue-smoked pub.

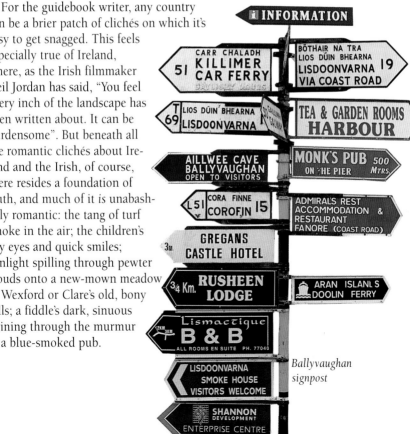

Ballyvaughan signpost

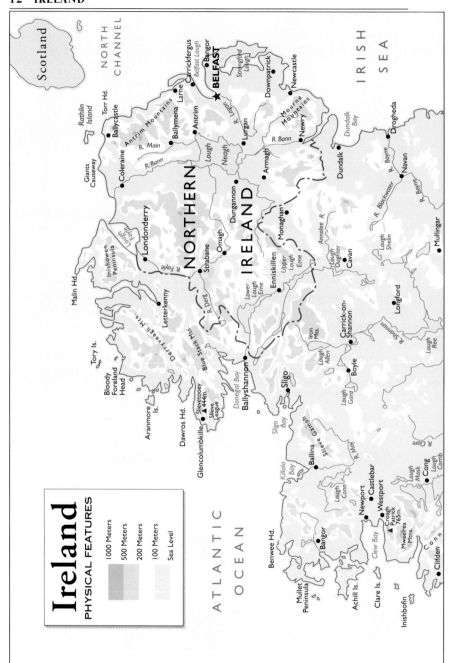

Ireland
PHYSICAL FEATURES

1000 Meters
500 Meters
200 Meters
100 Meters
Sea Level

Scotland

NORTH CHANNEL

IRISH SEA

ATLANTIC OCEAN

NORTHERN IRELAND

Rathlin Island
Torr Hd.
Ballycastle
Giants Causeway
Coleraine
Antrim Mountains
R. Main
R. Bann
Ballymena
Antrim
Larne
Carrickfergus
BELFAST
Bangor
Belfast Lough
Strangford Lough
Downpatrick
Newcastle
Mourne Mountains
Lurgan
R. Lagan
R. Bann
Lough Neagh
Armagh
Newry
Dundalk Bay
Dundalk
Drogheda
R. Boyne
Navan
R. Boyne
Malin Hd.
Inishowen Peninsula
Lough Foyle
Londonderry
R. Foyle
Strabane
R. Derg
Omagh
Dungannon
Monaghan
Annalee R.
Lough Oughter
Cavan
Lough Sheelin
Mullingar
Letterkenny
Derryveagh Mts.
Enniskillen
Upper Lough Erne
Lower Lough Erne
Longford
R. Shannon
Lough Ree
Tory Is.
Bloody Foreland Head
Aranmore Is.
Dawros Hd.
Blue Stack Mts.
Glencolumbkille
Slievetooey 444m.
Slieve League
Donegal Bay
Ballyshannon
Iron Mts.
Lough Allen
Carrick-on-Shannon
Boyle
Lough Gara
Sligo
Sligo Bay
Killala Bay
Slieve Gamph
R. Moy
R. Clare
Benwee Hd.
Mullet Peninsula
Ballina
Lough Conn
Newport
Castlebar
Westport
Croagh Patrick 765m.
Mweelrea Mts.
Lough Mask
Cong
Lough Corrib
Bangor
Clew Bay
Achill Is.
Clare Is.
Inishbofin
Clifden
R. Conn

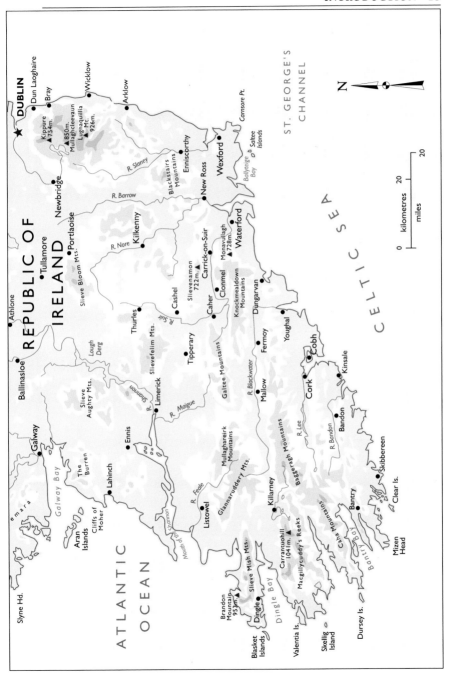

The Land

Mention Ireland to ten people and in their imaginations they'll likely conjure as many different landscapes: the electric-green valleys of *The Quiet Man*, perhaps, or crashing seacoasts, heathery bogland, blue-granite mountains, undulating pastureland, glinting loughs and peat-stained rivers.

For such a small island (just 84,426 square kilometres/32,597 square miles), the diversity of terrain is genuinely surprising. After millennia of habitation, there were glens in Kerry so remote that they didn't get electricity until the 1970s, and such inhospitable mountains in Donegal that Irish climbers use them to prepare for Everest. There's the fractured limestone pavement of the Burren and the Aran Islands, which look like patches of moonscape, and yet for contrast there are miles of pastoral countryside so gentle it could've been painted by Constable.

At the turn of the century, William Bulfin free-wheeled around Ireland and made this observation:

> *The more you see of Ireland the more cautious you become about making any definite statement as to which part of it is the most beautiful. You may think Northern Connacht excels until you have been in Donegal. You may think Donegal supremely beautiful until you have seen the twilight fading out of some of the valleys in the Midlands. You may think the hush of a moonlit night in Westmeath the acme of romantic loveliness until you have seen the sunrise gilding the Munster side of the Shannon. You may look down upon the Golden Vale and think that here at last is the gem of gems of rural beauty, until you have stood on the Dublin mountains and watched the morning mists rolling seaward out of the Vale of Shanganagh.*

Ireland's greatest length is 486 kilometres (302 miles); it's 275 kilometres (171 miles) at its broadest. Overall, the island's topography is something like a shallow dish, with a low-lying central plain rimmed by mountains. "The men of Ireland are mortal and temporal, but her hills are eternal", G.B. Shaw wrote. And they have mellifluous names to match their physical beauty: the Comeraghs, the Mournes, the Slieve Blooms, the Blackstairs, the Ballyhouras, the Knockmealdowns.

The whole landmass is tilted higher in the west, where the island's tallest mountain, County Kerry's Carrantuohill, rises to 1,041 metres (3,414 feet) and much of the coast falls into the sea in abrupt cliffs. In the west, too, the sea has worked the hardest, biting out deep, fjordlike bays and splitting off hundreds of islands from the mainland.

In contrast to the often niggardly land, Ireland's waterways and surrounding seas are among the most productive anywhere. The unpolluted waters yield up abundant catches of trout, salmon, cod, mackerel, plaice, herring and shellfish. Thousands of lakes punctuate the land, and hundreds of rivers drain the interior. The Shannon, the longest river in the British Isles, rises in County Cavan and flows south and west through central Ireland to its broad mouth between Kerry and Clare.

Until Neolithic farmers began to whittle away at them 5,000 years ago, forests covered every corner of the island. The relentless felling eventually left Ireland the least-wooded country in Europe, with just 5 percent of its area under forest. By the middle of the 1700s, a Gaelic poet lamented, "Ah! what shall we do for timber? The last of the woods is down". Extensive tracts have now been planted with sombre, blue-green conifers, though these crop forests somehow seem more melancholy and sterile than denuded hillsides.

At the same time that the early Irish started cutting down the trees, the climate was gradually growing cooler and wetter. Without the sheltering woodlands, rain began to leach the soil of its nutrients, leaving it too acidic to support anything but peat mosses. In its cycle of growth, decay and regeneration, layer upon layer of dead moss blanketed the lowlands—to a depth of ten metres (34 feet) in places; the spreading bog drove out first the other plant life and then the people, who could no longer work the land. In modern times, turf cutters in the vast Mayo bogs have in places revealed the intact ancient strata below: stone walls, huts and grave sites, even the plowed furrows of abandoned fields under a heavy cloak of black peat.

Peat bogs today cover one-sixth of Ireland. Peat, or turf, is the island's principal natural fuel resource, burned for heat in homes as well as in massive electricity-generating stations. The supply is expected to last another century.

Ireland's plant and animal life generally resembles that of much of the rest of northwestern Europe, with some notable anomalies. It's true that there are no snakes in Ireland, but not because St. Patrick banished them nor, as James Connolly suggested years ago, because they've all gone into American politics. They simply never made it across the land bridge that joined Ireland with the continent up to about 10,000 years ago. The Gulf Stream, which so moderates the climate, also helps account for such startling oddities as palm trees, fuchsias, arbutus and other plants that really have no business growing this far north.

The island of Ireland is, of course, politically divided. The 26 counties of the independent Republic of Ireland, or Éire (population 3.6 million), occupy a bit more than four-fifths of the total land area, while the balance is made up by the six counties of Northern Ireland, also called Ulster (population 1.6 million), currently part of the United Kingdom.

Centuries before it was sorted into the present 32 counties, the island was carved into four principal kingdoms, the "four green fields" of Irish balladry: **Connacht** or Connaught (comprised of Counties Mayo, Galway, Roscommon, Sligo and Leitrim), **Munster** (Kerry, Waterford, Cork, Clare, Limerick and Tipperary), **Leinster** (Meath, Westmeath, Laois, Kildare, Dublin, Wicklow, Wexford, Offaly, Carlow, Kilkenny, Louth and Longford), and **Ulster** (Down, Antrim, Armagh, Fermanagh, Tyrone and Derry in Northern Ireland; and Counties Donegal, Monaghan and Cavan, which are in the Republic).

While these provincial divisions are no longer politically important (with the obvious exception of Ulster), they're still very much a part of Irish cultural geography. An old Irish saying draws these distinctions:

> *The Leinsterman affable,*
> *The Munsterman boastful,*
> *The Connachtman sweet-mouthed,*
> *And the Ulsterman proud.*

History

Open any account of Irish history at random and it seems a history written in tears—a long, unhappy litany of battles and retribution, tragedies and lamentation. Of calamity and woe, surely, Ireland has endured more than enough to write the sorrowful tales of a dozen nations. There has been joy, too, though in a smaller measure, and always there was enough determination to see the people through the worst of their adversities. The fact that Ireland exists at all—even a divided Ireland—is the proof of it.

Ireland's is a history of conquests, yet even in their darkest days the Irish could not quite be conquered in spirit. The burden and the pride of this are kept alive in the hearts of Irishmen and Irishwomen, in whom there resides a formidably tenacious memory. In Ireland, centuries-old grievances are brooded upon and kept as fresh and painful as this morning's headlines; the triumphs, though these are fewer, are celebrated just as vigorously.

The key to understanding Ireland and the Irish lies in the frenzied tumult of the past. One needn't travel far to find it. "Everywhere you walk in Ireland", wrote Katharine Scherman in her engaging *Flowering of Ireland,* "you are conscious of overlapping layers of human history, visibly crumbling one into another". The tangible reminders are everywhere, so abundant in places that they're taken for granted: that pile of rubble you stub a toe upon may once have been a bustling monastery; the rough limestone plinth the cattle scratch their haunches against might have been erected over a dead chieftain 2,500 years ago. And the slogans painted just last night on the walls of Belfast or Derry are history, too, the latest artifacts of a long, passionate, cross-grained story that is still playing out.

(following pages) Dunluce Castle, Co. Antrim

THE FIRST IRISH

When Ireland's sheath of Pleistocene glaciers receded some 12,000 years ago, there came a slow advance of fauna and flora from northwestern Europe. Among the last to arrive, before the rising sea inundated the land bridges connecting Ireland to the continent, were Ireland's first human inhabitants. These were Mesolithic hunter-gatherers who probably walked across dry land circa 8000 BC. A few crude stone tools, rubbish heaps and campfire charcoal are about all the traces they left behind.

Around 6800 BC, after Ireland had become an island, another group of people came, this time by crossing the narrow North Channel from Scotland in hide-covered coracles. These tribes were attracted perhaps by the precious flint deposits of the Antrim coast. The Ireland they discovered was a densely forested place, teeming with fish, fowl and game. For 3,000 years they populated the northern two-thirds of the island. They stayed near the coasts and inland waterways, unable or unwilling to penetrate the thick woods.

Their long isolation ended about 3700 BC, when the first waves of a more advanced, Neolithic people came to these shores. The newcomers, arriving perhaps via France, the Low Countries and Cornwall, may have been tribes displaced from as far away as the Mediterranean or even the Middle East. Accomplished spinners, weavers, potters and toolmakers, they settled Ireland's first communities. With polished stone blades, they plowed the rich virgin soil to plant barley and wheat and began felling the woodlands for their livestock, striking the first blow in the relentless deforestation of the island.

These early Irish are also the people who constructed hundreds of megalithic tombs—dolmens, court graves and passage graves—between about 3000 and 2000 BC. The court-grave style consists of an open courtyard from which several burial cells radiate, covered by an elongated cairn. The later passage-grave style, usually built on a hilltop, is a rounded cairn pierced by a passage leading to a central burial chamber. These monumental tombs suggest a society with both a sophisticated organization and a belief in an afterlife; the dead, or their cremated remains, were often interred with weapons, tools and other utilitarian items.

Copper technology reached Ireland around 2000 BC, and bronze followed about two centuries later. Soon the island boasted superlative smiths whose axes, swords and other implements were exported to Britain and the continent. The Bronze Age Irish also excelled at goldsmithing, and their jewellery was prized as far afield as the eastern Mediterranean. Europe in this era, historians are finding, was far less static than had previously been thought, and Ireland, though on the geographic fringes of the continent, was hardly isolated, but rather was an important link in a trading circuit that apparently stretched from Scandinavia to Egypt.

THE FORGING OF CELTIC IRELAND

From about 2100 to 1300 BC Ireland absorbed another significant influx of migrants, known as the Beaker Folk for the elegant pottery they introduced. These people may have been the Tuatha Dé Danaan, a race that, after its conquest by the Celts, passed into legend as one of supernatural beings—the fairies and "little people" of Irish folklore.

The Celts (pronounced "kelts") were the immigrants who would most profoundly mold the Irish nation. A branch of the Indo-European racial family, in the third millennium BC these seminomadic shepherds had begun to spread from their original homeland on the steppes of western Russia into India, Europe and the Middle East. By the third century BC, they were the dominant power in Europe and spread from Yugoslavia to Portugal, Germany to Italy.

These vigorous, innovative people invented the scythe, barrel, bucket and trousers (to facilitate the riding of horses). Though quite advanced culturally, the Celts were considered barbarians by the Romans because they disdained written language. Their three-tiered society was composed of farmers, serfs and a warrior aristocracy whose greatest passion was armed combat, though they also valued poetry and eloquence as highly as prowess on the battlefield. This duality would later strongly inform the Irish character as well.

Around 600 BC, two Celtic branches spread to the British Isles—the Brythoni in Britain and the Gaels in Ireland—bringing with them iron implements and oats, a grain well suited to the wet climate. By the second century BC, Gaelic influence on Ireland was unmistakable.

The Gaels developed a complex body of customary law, called Brehon Law, which was orally passed with extreme accuracy from generation to generation by professional jurists called *brehons*. Their legal system and social organization would persist overtly into the 17th century, while the underlying ethos contributes to the definition of Irish culture to this day. These tribal people were ruled by elected, rather than hereditary, chieftains, they practiced slavery, and they reckoned their wealth and status in the currency of cattle. Cattle raiding and highly ritualized warfare were endemic.

With their iron tools, the Celts accelerated the building of raths and cashels, circular earthen or stone enclosures erected to keep livestock in and enemies out. Some 30,000–40,000 of these rings remain throughout the countryside; superstition against plowing over or otherwise disturbing the "fairy rings" explains why so many have survived. These people were probably also responsible for constructing the magnificent stone forts such as Dun Aengus on Inishmore.

Mingling their fierceness and Iron Age technology with the Bronze Age Irish, the Celts moulded the Irish character for the next thousand years. "The result", in Katharine Scherman's words, "was an exciting blend of tenacity and temperament, self-discipline and anarchy, poetry and casuistry, which the Christian religion would transform into a clear flame of genius".

While Celtic culture was planted in Ireland, it was doomed on the continent. Fearsome warriors though they were, the Celts' independent spirit proved to be their downfall. Unable or unwilling to consolidate a unified defense, their scattered resistance was systematically overcome by the Roman legions. This Celtic trait—a reluctance to organize, even against a common enemy—would later cost the Irish their country.

Julius Caesar's conquest of Gaul in 51 BC ended the Celtic reign in Europe. Though the Romans held sway in Britain for four centuries, no Roman army ever crossed the Irish Sea, and so Celtic culture flourished here in its last outpost. The conquest of Ireland would be left to an altogether different authority from Rome—the Church.

Severed heads—potent symbols in Celtic mythology—incorporated into the doorway of 12th-century Clonfert Cathedral, Co. Galway

CHRISTIANITY

By the fourth century AD, the Gaels had divided the island into five (and sometimes more) principal kingdoms—Leinster in the east, Munster in the southwest, Connacht in the northwest, Ulster in the north, and the roughly central kingdom of Meath—with about 150 other petty kingdoms, called *tuaths*, forming various alliances with them.

When Christianity arrived in Ireland, it didn't generally encounter the hostile reception that it often met elsewhere. Early missionaries were canny enough to tailor their gospel to suit the pagan Irish, frequently co-opting local mythology to illustrate Christian doctrine. The *tuath* structure expedited the spread of the new religion, for when a chieftain converted, his clan was obliged to follow. Proselytizers began their mission here as early as the third century, but credit for the wholesale conversion of the natives goes to St. Patrick, who probably arrived in the year 432, and his successors.

Far from Rome, the church in Ireland adapted to local custom rather than rigidly imposing a dogmatic foreign system. Ireland lacked the roads and political cohesion necessary for a hierarchical church structure; instead a monastic system developed which saw scattered monasteries bloom as vigorous centres of scholarship. The island's reputation spread as a place of tolerant sanctuary for the devout, and while the barbarian hordes washed over Europe, ushering in the Dark Ages, Ireland flourished as a haven for the arts, literature and scholarship, attracting thousands of pilgrims and students. By the seventh century, Ireland was sending its own missionaries and scholars back to the continent to found monasteries and to reteach the Europeans the knowledge that had been lost. In 870, one French commentator complained, "Almost all Ireland, disregarding the sea, is migrating to our shores with a flock of philosophers".

High cross, Monasterboice, Co. Louth

In addition to the new faith, the missionaries to Ireland had introduced Latin, and with it, literacy. The Irish, who had long possessed an affinity for oral literature, had developed a cumbersome and limiting script called *ogham*, which usually consisted of lines cut along the corners of a stone grave marker. The learned class readily abandoned *ogham* in favour of Latin script and took up writing with enthusiasm. Scribes laboured untold hours by taper light, copying precious manuscripts and compiling scrupulously detailed annals of Irish history and current events. A number of these have survived and not only offer priceless insight into earlier times but stand among the finest artistic achievements of medieval Europe. It was during this fruitful period of the seventh to ninth centuries, Ireland's Golden Age, that the glorious illustrated texts such as the renowned *Book of Kells* were produced.

Another legacy of Irish Christianity are the magnificent stone crosses, among the few medieval treasures not pilfered by the Vikings. Many of these crosses, such as Monasterboice's tenth-century Muiredach's Cross in County Louth, were profusely carved with biblical scenes to illustrate for unlettered converts the key events of the Old and New Testaments.

"Deliver Us, O Lord"

In 795, sleek, high-prowed longboats appeared out of the north and pillaged Lambay Island off Ireland's east coast. The Vikings had arrived. The first raiding vessels were followed by thousands more, a "countless sea-vomiting of ships and fleets" in the phrase of one ninth-century Irish chronicler. The Gaels, again with no central authority or unified resistance, were overrun by the ferocious Norsemen. "From the fury of the Northmen, O Lord, deliver us", went a medieval prayer.

Time and again, the monasteries were plundered and the countryside ransacked. The singular round towers which still punctuate the landscape like exclamation points were a final refuge against the marauders; the occupants pulled the entry ladder behind them into the single doorway high above the ground, and they and their treasures were as secure as they could hope to be. One anonymous Irish scribe, taking temporary comfort from the storm-battered seas, jotted in the margin of his text:

> *Fierce is the wind tonight,*
> *It ploughs up the white hair of the sea*
> *I have no fear that the Viking hosts*
> *Will come over the water to me.*

Saint Patrick, Apostle of Ireland

The son of a Christian official in a Roman–British settlement on Britain's west coast, Magonus Succatus Patricius—Patrick—was born probably around AD 390, during the twilight of Roman influence there. As Rome's power waned, these outskirts of its empire were harassed by marauding bands from across the Irish Sea. At the age of 16, Patrick was captured in one of these raids and sold into slavery in Ireland. He lived for six years near Slemish Mountain (now in County Antrim), tending the flocks of his master, a pagan king named Miliucc.

Though he had been raised a Christian, it was during his servitude that Patrick was seized by religious zeal. One night in a vision, the angel Victoricus appeared to Patrick, revealing that the time for his escape was nigh. Making his way south, Patrick found a ship and sailed to Brittany. Christianity was already well rooted in Gaul (France) at that time, and Patrick spent at least eight years studying at the Monastery of Auxerre, where he would be confirmed as a bishop before returning to Britain to rejoin his family.

It was in Britain that Victoricus again appeared to Patrick, and in the vision he bore letters from the Irish beseeching the "holy youth" to return to Ireland. In AD 431, the first official episcopal mission to Ireland ended in failure, and the following year Pope Celestine I commissioned Patrick to the task of converting the pagan Irish.

Patrick took up his mission with a resolute fervour. While travelling around Ireland with his retinue for the next three decades, he is credited with converting 120,000 souls and with founding some 300 churches (including his head church at Armagh). He died in 461, and was buried at Downpatrick, near the place where he had converted his first pagan years before. In 1900, a granite slab inscribed "Patric" was set in the churchyard of the lovely Down Cathedral to mark the site where the saint is believed to lie. In spring, it's covered with daffodils left by pilgrims. (Nearby, in the town's 18th-century gaol, the St. Patrick Heritage Centre tells the story of Pat with a video and other displays.)

A tantalizing glimpse into the life and mind of Patrick comes from his own hand, in two surviving documents known as the *Confessio* and *Letter to Coroticus*, written in a rustic, frontier Latin. But much of what we know today (or think we know) about him derives from the work of two early biographers who lived two centuries after their subject. Later hagiographers enlarged the body of legends surrounding Patrick, attributing countless miracles to the saint: healing the sick and lame, restoring sight to the blind, occasionally raising the dead.

The best known of Patrician legends, however, reported by the 12th-century biographer Jocelyn, is one that never could have happened—Patrick's banishing of the snakes from Ireland. The creatures had never lived in Ireland, so whatever Patrick cast out, they were not snakes—at least in the reptilian sense.

For two centuries the sackings continued, but eventually the Vikings began to settle down and marry Irish girls. By the tenth and 11th centuries, they had established Ireland's first real towns, at Dublin, Waterford, Limerick, Wexford, Wicklow and Cork. In 1014, BrianBorú, the first "high-king" (whose authority was recognized throughout the island) rode out from his palace at Kincora and defeated a host of Vikings from Dublin. His victory ended the Norsemen's reign, but Brian also met his death that day.

THE NORMANS

As traumatic as the Viking invasions had been, a more enduring shock was soon to come. Its effects profoundly shaped the course of Irish history, and its legacy is deeply felt to this day.

Strife among Ireland's petty kings vying for primacy was continual. When Dermot MacMurrough (see page 232), king of the province of Leinster, sought military assistance from England in 1169, he got more than anyone had bar-

Strongbow

gained for. With their superior military technology, the Anglo–Norman mercenaries who came to his aid easily overcame MacMurrough's rivals and captured Dublin. Their leader, the earl of Pembroke (known as Strongbow), wed MacMurrough's daughter and himself became king of Leinster on MacMurrough's death. The English had arrived, and Ireland would struggle for the next eight centuries to be rid of them.

Allying themselves with local chieftains and conquering others, the Anglo–Normans rapidly expanded their control; within 80 years they possessed three-quarters of the island. These newcomers too were quick to adopt the native language, manners and surnames, becoming, as has often been written, *hibernicis ipsis hiberniores*— "more Irish than the Irish themselves"—and setting the pattern for later arrivals. Attempts by successive English monarchs to stem the assimilation were ineffectual, and even the stern 1366 edicts of the parliament at Kilkenny, forbidding "the English born in Ireland" from wearing Irish clothes and hairstyles and from speaking Irish, went largely unheeded. "Lord, how quickly doth that country alter one's nature!" Edmund Spenser would write two centuries later.

The Irishized Anglo–Norman barons owed nominal allegiance to England, but, remote from English rule, they pursued their own interests in what were in effect their own kingdoms. Crown control, by the early 1500s, was confined within fortified boundaries around Dublin known as the Pale.

In an attempt to reign in the anarchy, Henry VIII in 1534 decreed that all Irish lands be surrendered to the Crown, whereupon they would immediately be regranted as formal fiefdoms. But it remained for Henry's daughter, Elizabeth I, to thoroughly enforce the mandate, and this she did with a vengeance. Many complied with this largely symbolic act, but the native Irish lords and many of the Old English (as the naturalized colonists were known) bridled at this meddling by the foreign monarch. Their rebellions were ruthlessly quashed. Sir John Davies, solicitor-general for Ireland, expressed the prevailing sentiment of the time: "A barbarous country must first be broken by war before it will be capable of good government".

The End of the Gaelic Order

For England, the dilemma of Ireland was that she was too far away to be easily governed, yet too close to be ignored. When Henry VIII broke with Rome in 1535 and made England Protestant, the conflict between the two countries took on a religious dimension. The Protestant Reformation which had swept Britain barely brushed Ireland, which made the English all the more uneasy with their Catholic neighbour. Elizabeth feared that her Catholic enemies might use Ireland as a back door through which to further their struggles against England. And not without justification: in 1580, for example, a force of 600 Spaniards and Italians, commissioned by the pope to help liberate the island, invaded the Dingle Peninsula. (They surrendered to a superior English army and were promptly executed.) Over the next two centuries, other aid would be dispatched from the continent, but always too little, too late.

As England tightened her grip, the latter half of the 16th century became a period of insurrection in Ireland, culminating in the rebellion of two Ulster noblemen, Hugh O'Neill and Hugh O'Donnell. O'Neill had been reared in England and vested as earl of Tyrone by Elizabeth. More than once he had helped suppress rebellious Old English on the queen's

Dermot MacMurrough

behalf. But he was still Irish, and he bristled at the ever-increasing strictures placed on him in his hereditary Irish kingdom.

In 1598, O'Neill defeated an English army at a site called the Yellow Ford, a few miles north of Armagh. The dramatic victory inspired other risings, and England's hold was shaken. Irish optimism was short-lived, however. O'Neill, O'Donnell and their Spanish allies were routed in December 1601 at the Battle of Kinsale in County Cork (see page 133). O'Neill gained the queen's pardon, but he and other lords of Ulster would within a few years go into exile on the continent, forfeiting their lands to the Crown and leaving their Irish subjects to founder without native leadership. The defeat at Kinsale and the subsequent "Flight of the Earls" (see page 245) sounded the death knell for Gaelic Ireland.

The Plantation of Ulster

Beginning in 1610, the lands of the vanquished earls O'Neill and O'Donnell—Donegal, Derry, Armagh and Tyrone—as well as Cavan and Fermanagh, were systematically divided and parcelled out to veterans, private companies and to English and Scottish settlers. Only a small portion of the lands—almost invariably the poorest plots—were set aside for the native Irish. This region of northeastern Ireland, comprising most of the ancient province of Ulster, would become Northern Ireland three centuries later. The usurpation of the Catholic natives by Protestant newcomers here sowed the seeds of acrimony that still bear fruit in department-store bombings and other acts of sectarian violence.

"Plantations" intended to uproot the truculent Irish and replace them with loyal Protestant subjects had been attempted in the 1550s and 1570s, but each had faltered for lack of support. But these Ulster plantations, well funded and well organized, were carried out on a much larger scale. Within a dozen years the settlers numbered about 13,000; in their fortified homesteads—islands in a hostile sea of dispossessed Irish—they flourished. Most prosperous of all were the industrious Scottish Presbyterians, who settled in eastern Ulster.

The success of the Ulster models led to other plantations in the other three provinces. Bitter was the mood of the native Irish as they saw their lands wrenched away by foreigners. Catholic Bishop David Rothe of Kilkenny noted in 1617: "They have been deprived of weapons, but are in a temper to fight with nails and heels, and to tear their oppressors with their teeth".

The great fear of the Protestant minority was realized when Irish resentment brimmed over in September 1641 and rebellions against the plantations erupted in Ulster and spread rapidly throughout Ireland. The risings were marked by widespread reports of atrocities against the Protestants; reprisals against the Catholic Irish were said to have been equally brutal and undiscriminating. When the carnage ebbed, several thousand settlers were dead and many others were driven out of Ireland.

Soon the rebels held most of Ireland. The foremost Gaelic and Old English families attempted to set aside their differences and unite themselves in common defense. They raised an army and declared Kilkenny Town the capital of an independent Ireland, but by 1648 their shaky confederation dissolved in factional squabbling.

CROMWELL

Before the decade was out, the Protestant dead of 1641 were mercilessly avenged. Oliver Cromwell and his 12,000-strong Puritan army, having helped relieve King Charles I of his head in the English Civil War, turned to Ireland to extirpate every hint of rebellion there. This they accomplished with an iron fist. With appalling cruelty and chilling efficiency, they sacked Drogheda in September 1649, slaughtering soldier, priest and civilian alike, and repeated the barbarity at Wexford.

"I am persuaded", Cromwell explained, "that this is the righteous judgement of God upon those barbarous wretches who have imbrued their hands in so much blood". In October, the English Parliament declared a national Thanksgiving Day in celebration of the carnage.

By 1653 every corner of Ireland was subjugated, and the English Parliament confiscated all Irish lands. Irish landowning families were banished west of the River Shannon—offered the choice between "Hell or Connacht"—while the more desirable domains east of the Shannon were divided among Cromwell's soldiers and others loyal to the English cause. Cromwell also deported thousands of Irish to the English colonies in Virginia and the Caribbean to toil in slavery. "The curse of Cromwell" was complete, and what came to be known as the Protestant Ascendancy—the domination of the Irish-speaking, Catholic peasantry by a Protestant British ruling class—was born.

KING JAMES AND KING BILLY

Following the restoration of the English monarchy in the 1660s, some of the Irish landowners regained their land, but overall Irish ownership of the country had fallen from about 60 percent before Cromwell to about 20 percent after the "transplantation". By 1714, the Irish would own a mere seven percent of Irish land.

When James II, a staunch Roman Catholic, was crowned king of England in 1685, Irish hopes for liberation were rekindled. James placed Catholics in high office, and in his reign the Irish Parliament, now dominated by Catholics, revoked Cromwell's land settlements (though this was never carried out). James's actions alarmed Protestants in England, inflaming already potent anti-Catholic sentiment, and in 1688 the king was obliged to flee to France. With the support of Louis XIV, James landed at Kinsale to claim the last corner of his realm still loyal to him.

James's son-in-law, William of Orange, a Dutch Protestant, assumed the English throne as King William III in 1689. With an army of 36,000, he landed at Carrickfergus then roundly beat James's forces at the Battle of the Boyne in July 1690—an event celebrated in Ulster to this day with considerable pomp. James himself slunk off to France, never to return. For more than a year the Irish continued to resist, with some French support, but in October 1691 the last holdouts capitulated at Limerick.

Old Ireland was in ruins. Egan O'Rahilly, a Gaelic poet of the era, wrote these despairing lines:

> *The Shannon and the Liffey and the tuneful Lee,*
> *The Boyne and the Blackwater a sad music sing,*
> *The waters of the west run red to the sea—*
> *No matter what be trumps their knave will beat our king.*

The Penal Laws

William's promises of religious tolerance for the vanquished were short-lived, as pressure from Protestant constituents compelled him to abrogate the favourable terms of surrender. What replaced them was a series of vicious anti-Catholic measures, known collectively as the Penal Laws, which ushered in the bitterest century of English oppression yet in Ireland.

Under the statutes, enacted from 1702 to 1715, much of the land remaining in Catholic hands was confiscated. Catholics were effectively barred from buying land, or from holding a lease of longer than 31 years. They were forbidden to vote, hold public office, possess arms, attend university, practise law, perform military service or even to own a horse valued over 5 pounds. All clergymen above the level of parish priest were banished, on pain of imprisonment or execution.

Corcomroe Abbey, the Burren, Co. Clare

Edmund Burke characterized the Penal Laws as "a machine of wise and elaborate contrivance, as well fitted for the impoverishment and degradation of a people, and the debasement in them of human nature itself, as ever proceeded from the perverted ingenuity of man". The lord chancellor under King George succinctly described their effect when he said, "The law does not suppose any such person to exist as an Irish Roman Catholic". To drive a further cynical wedge between the two religions, any son who converted from Catholicism had the right to turf out his family and lay claim to their holdings for himself. Few did.

As vindictive as they were, the Penal Laws nevertheless were far from impermeable. If enforced to the letter they might well have fulfilled their purpose of exterminating Irish Catholicism. But the faith survived—furtively, or under the winking eye of local authority. Mass continued to be held, albeit in remote, secret places, and Catholics managed to cobble an education in outdoor "hedge schools". Toward the end of the 1700s, as the settlers felt less threatened by the subdued natives, application of the laws began to relax.

SEEDS OF DISCONTENT

In the late 18th century, a number of secret societies—with names like the Whiteboys and the Defenders—were organized among Irish countrymen with the purpose of protecting tenant farmers against landlord abuses. They meted out a raw justice—burning barns, slaughtering livestock, lynching tax collectors—in response to rent racking, evictions and other maltreatment.

While repression fostered solidarity among the downtrodden Irish peasantry, discord among the conquerors weakened their grip on the country. England's patronizing attitude toward Ireland in general helped to polarize even loyal Protestant settlers, many of whom began to identify themselves more as "Irishmen" than as English or Scots merely living in Ireland.

Protectionist laws passed in England crippled the Irish wool industry and other trades. And the Irish Parliament and the Anglican Church of Ireland— nearly as hostile toward Scots Presbyterians and other "dissenters" as to Catholics—alienated that important segment of Ireland's populace. Faced with obstacles to commerce and suffering many of the indignities imposed by the Penal Laws, many Presbyterians emigrated to America; those who stayed grew ever more resentful of the British administration, making them the unlikely potential allies of Irish Catholics.

In such an environment, it's not surprising that the revolutions in America and France dramatically galvanized the current of Irish politics. For the first time, a viable notion of Irish nationalism—transcending to some degree the old battle line of Protestant versus Catholic—began to emerge. Amid this spirit of independence, and with growing restlessness among the Protestant Irish, the lawyer Henry Grattan in 1782 secured considerable autonomy for the Parliament in Dublin. In 1793, Catholic landowners gained voting rights.

In 1791, a young Protestant lawyer named Theobald Wolfe Tone founded the Society of United Irishmen, which rapidly gained broad support among both Protestants and Catholics. The Society's aims—to "abolish all unnatural religious distinctions, . . . to unite all Irishmen against the unjust influence of Great Britain", and to establish a republic modelled on France's—found no success through legal political channels. In December 1796, Tone sailed into Bantry Bay with a French fleet, but foul weather foiled the invasion (see page 137). Over the next two years, confused nationalist rebellions broke out in Wexford and Ulster, but, lacking central planning, they were largely futile. When French troops finally returned, at Killala Bay in Mayo (see page 213), the momentum had dissipated. The French were defeated and Wolfe Tone arrested. Sentenced to death, he cheated the executioner and took his own life while in prison.

UNION AND EMANCIPATION

Following the unsettling events of 1798, debate on both sides of the Irish Sea intensified over the question of formally joining Ireland and England. Supporters hoped a stricter economic and political alliance would make the island more governable. Ironically, old Protestant families in Ireland generally opposed the proposal, having already tasted English hegemony. Many Irish Catholics on the other hand welcomed the prospect, hoping for fairer treatment than they had gotten thus far from the self-interested Protestant minority which ruled the island.

On 1 January 1801, Ireland and England were joined in a United Kingdom and Ireland's Parliament was dissolved. It was not long, however, before the two Irish factions largely reversed their sentiments: Protestants—Presbyterians especially—began to fix their hopes of maintaining their ascendancy

Theobald Wolfe Tone

through the preservation of the Union, while Catholics took up the cause of Irish sovereignty with renewed vigour.

The engineer of the Act of Union, English prime minister William Pitt, had promised a repeal of the hated Penal Laws, but this was overruled by King George III and Catholics remained Ireland's lumpen underclass. They found a champion in the Kerry-born Catholic lawyer Daniel O'Connell (see page 149). A brilliant strategist and passionate orator, O'Connell overwhelmingly defeated the government candidate in the 1828 elections, though the Penal Laws still barred Catholics from public office. Fearing a massive uprising among O'Connell's millions of Irish supporters, the government passed the Catholic Emancipation Act in 1829, which allowed "the Liberator" to take his seat at Westminster and also swept away many of the most pernicious anti-Catholic statutes.

The long night of the Penal Laws at last was over, but an even more devastating calamity loomed—the great Famine of the 1840s. See "Years of Hunger".

HOME RULE

In 1867, the government crushed the uprisings of two secret organizations, the Fenian Brotherhood and the Irish Republican Brotherhood, which effectively ended armed revolt in Ireland for the next 50 years. The alternative route to "Home Rule"—legislative independence from Britain—lay in legal political efforts. In the 1870s and 1880s, the canniest leader in the struggle for land reform and Home Rule emerged from an unlikely quarter. Charles Stewart Parnell, a charismatic Protestant landowner, vigorously championed tenants' land rights in Parliament and so earned the support of Catholic farmers. Parnell managed to achieve considerable reforms, including procuring loans that allowed tenant farmers to buy land. But he failed to secure Home Rule, due mainly to the stiff resistance from northern Protestants, who feared that Home Rule would mean Catholic domination. A scandalous affair with a colleague's wife, Kitty O'Shea, sabotaged Parnell's political career, and he died a broken man in 1891.

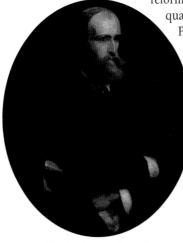

Charles Stewart Parnell

Years of Hunger: 1845–1849

From 1800 to 1841, the Irish population exploded, from about four and a half million to over eight million. Such growth would have been impossible but for the proliferation of an extremely cheap food crop introduced from South America in the 16th century. It thrived in poor soil where otherwise only weeds would deign to grow, and even a tiny plot could sustain a family for most of the year. Nutritious, simple to cultivate, and superbly predisposed to growing conditions in Ireland, the potato before long was grown in every county of the island. By the 1840s, the poorest one-third of the population subsisted on a diet consisting almost exclusively of potatoes and water, sometimes augmented with buttermilk. In densely populated County Mayo, fully nine-tenths of the people relied entirely on this tenuous diet.

Such a precarious existence was easily disrupted, with terrible results not difficult to foresee. Potato crops had failed locally dozens of times over the preceding century and a quarter, ushering in hunger, disease and death. Dire predictions of worse calamities had been heard for years; as late as 1845 an official enquiry into conditions in Ireland reported a dizzying three-fourths of the workforce unemployed, the most wretched poverty in all Europe, and a population chronically at the precipice of starvation. The report, however, contained "nothing of striking novelty" and was dismissed by the government in London.

Ireland's summer of 1845 was unusually warm and fine, and harvests promised to be of "the most luxuriant character". Then, in September, the *Freeman's Journal* reported alarming news: a "disease in the potato crop".

It attacked ferociously and spread quickly. Potatoes which were apparently sound when harvested were, within a few days, reduced to a stinking, putrescent mass "unfit for the use of man or beast". Fields which produced wholesome potatoes one day yielded only rotting pulp the next. The mysterious affliction was blamed wildly: on recently introduced guano manure, on "mortiferous vapors" rising from the earth, even on static electricity produced in the atmosphere by the smoke of steam locomotives. All remedies levied against it proved futile.

The real culprit—although it would not be diagnosed for many years—was a fungus, *Phytophthora infestans*, which had just weeks earlier appeared in England, France and Holland. In those countries, where even the poorest could afford substitute foods, the loss of the potato crop posed no serious threat. But in Ireland, where the survival of millions depended utterly on the tuber, the prospects were exceedingly grim.

The ominous tidings were initially received in London with skepticism. British Prime Minister Robert Peel delayed relief action because of his belief in the

continues

"tendency to exaggeration and inaccuracy in Irish reports". By November, however, the worst fears were confirmed: starvation on a mass scale loomed.

To his credit, Peel ordered the importation of corn from America, intended not so much to feed the masses but as a market lever to be released at low cost in order to keep down other food prices. He also set in motion works projects to employ the destitute and relaxed the restrictive duties on grain imports. Generous private donations from America and England helped some, but these and additional official efforts proved pathetically inadequate.

By spring of 1846, many had grown desperate from hunger. The *Freeman's Journal* reported in April:

> *There have been attacks on flour mills in Clonmel by people whose bones protruded through the skin which covered them—staring through hollow eyes as if they had just risen from their shrouds, crying out that they could no longer endure the extremity of their distress and that they must take that food which they could not procure.*

That summer, the harvest again looked healthy, but the spores of blight lay waiting, and the crop failed completely. It was said that scarcely a single potato in the land escaped the rot. To make matters worse, many landlords, foreseeing a season of unpaid rents, began wholesale evictions of their penniless tenants. The government's aid policy contributed to the uprooting: in order to qualify for food at the workhouses, many of the poor were forced to abandon their homes and last few possessions.

From "Funeral at Skibbereen", by H. Smith

With famine followed typhus; an epidemic soon spread across Ireland. Everywhere corpses lay where the people had died, by roadsides, in their hovels, in the streets of the towns. For many, there were not coffins to hold them, nor strength in the survivors to bury them. Whole families were found huddled in their miserable cabins, three or four generations sometimes, all dead of hunger and disease.

Under mounting pressure, the government in 1847 passed the Soup Kitchen Act, whereby free rations were distributed to the destitute. That summer, nearly half the country was receiving some form of assistance. The harvest that year was a partial success, and on that slender hope the government immediately began dismantling the relief programs, throwing the helpless Irish back to charity funded solely by Irish sources and to the cold-blooded "operation of natural causes". England washed its hands of responsibility in the famine. But for Ireland, more was yet to come. The blight would ravage the crop again in 1848 and 1849.

Perhaps the most bitterly recalled fact of those terrible years is that, aside from potatoes, during even the worst of the crisis there was no absolute shortage of food in Ireland. With an obdurate resolve bordering on religious fervour, the British government refused to interfere with the sacred workings of the "ordinary course of trade". And so ships sailed from Irish ports daily, groaning under their loads of bacon, butter, oats, flour, eggs, cattle and sheep.

For the Irish, there were but two routes of escape: death and emigration. Historians estimate that upwards of one million died during the famine years, while another one and a half million emigrated, three-fourths of them to America, others to England and Canada. Thousands more died on the Atlantic passage, victims of disease on the overcrowded "coffin ships".

Emigration continued steadily throughout the 19th century, and by 1914 nearly five-and-a-half million had departed. The country has never fully recovered from this massive hemorrhage: the population today is about what it was two centuries ago, and in places a sense of keen loss is still palpable. Jan Morris, in *Ireland: Your Only Place*, muses:

> In the west there are empty moors, wild and lonely, which were once farmlands; in the heartland villages sometimes seem to be enduring a perpetual holiday, so empty are their wide streets, so quiet even in the middle of the day. I feel in such a place not only the sorrow of the village, but the homesickness of its children far away.

The mantle of leadership passed to Arthur Griffith, who founded the nationalistic Sinn Féin ("Ourselves Alone") party in 1905. The turn of the century also brought with it a dynamic resurgence of Ireland's Gaelic culture: the Irish language was reintroduced to schools. W.B. Yeats, Douglas Hyde and others helped to reawaken Ireland's appreciation for its native literature. And the Irish began to find in themselves a new sense of pride and confidence.

In 1914, a Home Rule bill was finally passed, but the militant Protestant Orange Order succeeded in amending the bill, leaving six counties of Ulster with the option to remain with Great Britain. Furthermore, implementation of the bill would be postponed by World War I.

THE EASTER RISING

On Easter Monday, 24 April 1916, armed citizen-soldiers of the Irish Volunteers and the revived Irish Republican Brotherhood took control of Dublin's General Post Office and other key positions in the city. Because of confused orders and counter-orders, fewer than 1,200 men—nearly all of them in Dublin —took part in what had been planned as a nationwide uprising.

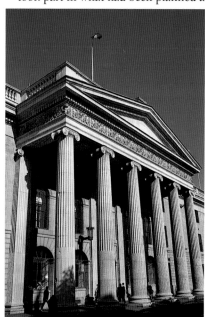

General Post Office, Dublin

From the Post Office steps, the Brotherhood's leader Patrick Pearse read aloud the Proclamation of the Republic of Ireland, which began:

Irishmen and Irishwomen: In the name of God and of the dead generations from which she receives her old tradition of nationhood, Ireland, through us, summons her children to her flag and strikes for her freedom.

They held the Post Office as their headquarters for five days, surrendering on Saturday with Dublin smoking and shattered around them. The 15 signatories to the proclamation had signed their own death warrants: they were tried by court-martial and executed by firing squad within two weeks (see page 83).

Leinster House, Dublin, where the Dáil (House of Representatives) and Seanad (Senate) convene

Their deaths made martyrs of the leaders and transformed public condemnation into veneration. Their Easter Rising had been one of the briefest—but ultimately, the most effective—of all Irish insurrections.

CIVIL WAR AND INDEPENDENCE

Instead of fading away as an historical footnote, the 1916 Rising galvanized the nationalist movement by setting public opinion squarely against the British. In the general election of 1918, the Irish voted a landslide slate of 73 Sinn Féin candidates to the British Parliament. The members (those not in English prisons) declined to take their seats at Westminster, but instead convened in Dublin as the Dáil Éireann ("Assembly of Ireland"), headed by Eamon de Valera, the most prominent survivor of the Easter Rising. The Dáil in January 1919 proclaimed Ireland an independent republic and asserted itself as its legitimate government.

Britain refused to recognize the Irish parliament and promptly gaoled de Valera and other leaders. The two countries were at war. It was at this time that the Irish Volunteers were reconstituted as the Irish Republican Army (IRA), and under the capable leadership of Michael Collins, the greatly outnumbered rebels carried out an effective hit-and-run campaign against British authority. To maintain control, Britain enlisted ex-servicemen, called the Black and Tans for their mixed army and police uniforms; they quickly came to be hated by the Irish for their viciousness and excessive force.

In 1920, after two years of bitter, bloody fighting, Britain proposed a compromise—the Government of Ireland Act. It divided Ireland into two separate countries, allowing each some domestic powers but keeping both under the British umbrella. Northern Ireland—comprised of the six counties (Fermanagh, Derry, Tyrone, Down, Antrim and Armagh) of Ulster which could safely maintain an unassailable Protestant majority—accepted the proposal and cleaved to the United Kingdom.

In the southern 26 counties, however, there were profound divisions on the issue. Eventually the Dáil decided to parley and in 1921 sent a delegation headed by Michael Collins and Arthur Griffith to negotiate with Lloyd George in London. Their resultant Anglo-Irish Treaty gave dominion status in the British Commonwealth and an unprecedented amount of freedom to southern Ireland, the "Irish Free State".

Collins considered this just a stepping stone toward a united, independent Ireland, but he foresaw the conflict to come. "Think, what have I got for Ireland?" he wrote to a friend the day he signed the treaty. "Something she has wanted these past seven hundred years. Will anyone be satisfied at the bargain? Will anyone? I tell you this: early this morning I signed my death warrant".

"A Landlord's Garden in County Wicklow"

Everyone is used in Ireland to the tragedy that is bound up with the lives of farmers and fishing people; but in this garden one seemed to feel the tragedy of the landlord class also, and of the innumerable old families that are quickly dwindling away. These owners of the land are not much pitied at the present day, or much deserving of pity; and yet one cannot quite forget that they are the descendants of what was at one time, in the eighteenth century, a high-spirited and highly cultivated aristocracy. The broken green-houses and mouse-eaten libraries that were designed and collected by men who voted with Grattan, are perhaps as mournful in the end as the four mud walls that are so often left in Wicklow as the only remnants of a farmhouse.

—J.M. Synge, 1907

A narrow Dáil majority ratified the treaty in 1922, but de Valera and a faction of the IRA rejected it, and Ireland drifted into a civil war between pro- and anti-Treaty forces. Before it ended the following year, an Irish bullet would kill Collins, and nearly 4,000 more died in the fighting.

The pro-Treaty faction eventually prevailed and the Irish Free State set to work building a nation. In 1937, Prime Minister de Valera's government drafted a new constitution which changed the name of the Free State to Ireland, or Éire in the Irish language, loosened ties with Britain and asserted its claim to the six counties of Ulster. Finally, on 18 April 1949, the Republic of Ireland severed its last bonds with the Commonwealth, free at last.

NORTHERN IRELAND

One of the many ironies of Northern Ireland is that this British enclave was the corner of Gaelic Ireland that most vehemently resisted the waves of British colonization over the centuries. Now it is with equally fierce resolve that the two-thirds Protestant majority opposes attempts to bring the province into the Catholic Republic of Ireland.

Unlike most other groups of settlers in Ireland, the northern Protestants never assimilated into the cultural mainstream, but instead have always virulently guarded a distinct identity. In spite of—or because of—their insecurity within a predominantly Catholic island, they also maintained a rigid grip on the region's political and economic power, when necessary through intimidation, violence and flagrant gerrymandering of voting districts.

Taking a lesson from the American civil-rights movement, Ulster Catholics began to agitate peacefully for an end to discrimination in housing, employment and political representation in the late 1960s. They were brutally resisted by a biased police force and by Protestant paramilitary groups. The dormant IRA, aroused to renewed militancy, stepped in to defend northern Catholics and at the same time launched a bloody guerrilla campaign of bombings and shootings across the North and in England.

Since this ongoing round of "Troubles" began, more than 20,000 people have been injured or killed. In 1969, British army troops were sent in to restore order; in 1972 Britain suspended the ineffectual Northern Ireland Parliament at Stormont and instituted direct rule over the province.

In 1985, the Anglo-Irish Agreement established a framework for cooperation between North and South. The agreement gives Dublin a voice in Northern Ireland affairs in exchange for the Republic's recognition that Northern Ireland shall remain a part of the United Kingdom so long as a majority desires it. Unfortunately, instead of increasing rapprochement the agreement inflamed sectarian violence, which had for some years been on the decline.

Northern Unionists felt betrayed by the Anglo-Irish Agreement, and they have largely boycotted parliamentary activities conducted under its aegis. Many northern Catholics, too, felt that they had been abandoned as the Republic appeared to be relaxing its claim to the North.

Today, Northern Ireland remains polarized. "The 'voice of sanity' is getting hoarse", as Seamus Heaney has written. The many people of peace and good will on both sides of the issue lend hope for some sort of eventual reconciliation. But there are also more than enough violent extremists and deep-rooted intransigence to keep the wound festering indefinitely.

In December 1993, however, British Prime Minister John Major and Irish Prime Minister Albert Reynolds met and produced a "framework for peace", which was welcomed cautiously in most quarters as a positive step forward. The complexly worded document reaffirmed the principles set out in the Anglo-Irish Agreement, and went a bit further. In it the Irish government agreed to reassess its constitutional claims to the northern counties and to reconsider "any elements in the democratic life and organisation of the Irish state" that Unionists might perceive as a "real and substantial threat to their way of life and ethos". This suggested that Ireland might re-examine the influence of the Catholic Church in temporal and political affairs—anathema to many northern Protestants—if that would contribute to an eventual accord. In addition, the IRA was offered a seat at the bargaining table in return for a renunciation of violence.

Though it was confusing and contradictory, many felt at the time that the seven-page joint declaration offered the best chance for a peaceful solution proposed so far. (Most encouraging is the simple fact that most nationalist parties on both sides did not reject the declaration outright.) Despite the flaws, its message was clear: a united Ireland is possible—but only with the consent of Northern Ireland's Protestant population.

In September 1994, the IRA initiated a "complete cessation of military operations". The move at once elicited great hopes for peace, as well as scepticism, since past IRA cease-fires, in 1972 and 1975, dissolved into cycles of renewed violence. This time, however, conditions seem ripe for real progress. While the announcement stopped just short of promising a permanent end to violence, if the unilateral ceasefire holds for three months it is expected that Sinn Féin would be invited to join in exploratory peace talks on Northern Ireland's future.

The Irish Language

Given the Irish reputation for eloquence and the permanent impression they've made on English literature, people often are surprised to learn that English has not always been the island's primary language. For a thousand years the Irish spoke and wrote in the language that the Celts had brought with them.

Irish-Speaking Areas
(Gaeltachts)

Called Gaelic or, more properly, Irish, this was the language of the scholars, saints and kings that gained dominion over the entire island from the sixth to ninth centuries. Scots Gaelic, Welsh and Breton are related tongues also introduced by the Celtic tribes, as were the now-extinct Manx and Cornish. In the Middle Ages, Irish was the only vernacular in Western Europe to usurp Latin as a medium for education and writing. As late as 1600, English barely made a ripple outside the stronghold of the Pale. But as England's power grew, the native Irish came to recognize English—the speech of government, commerce and education—as the language of opportunity. Even the eminent 19th-century patriot Daniel O'Connell, himself fluent in Irish, rejected it on practical grounds in favor of English. He is said to have delivered a speech in Irish only twice, when he thought police spies were present.

In the mid-1800s, more than half of the population—over four million people—spoke Irish, but within 50 years scarcely 21,000 monoglots remained. The Famine and subsequent emigration hastened this wholesale linguistic erosion, for it was the Irish-speaking peasants who did most of the dying and moving away. Even the Roman Catholic Church adopted English as the medium for saving souls.

In 19th-century Ireland (as later in India and Africa), one of colonialism's cherishable ironies was that the very debate on independence from England should be conducted in English. England and Ireland were, in G.B. Shaw's memorable phrase, "two nations divided by a common language". It was in part a reaction against this state of affairs, and a desire for "the de-anglicization" of Ireland, that led to the formation of the Gaelic League (Conradh na Gaeilge) in 1893 by Douglas Hyde and others. "The moment Ireland broke with her Gaelic past", wrote Hyde, "she fell away hopelessly from all intellectual and artistic effort. She lost her musical instruments, she lost her music, she lost her games, she lost her language and popular literature, and with the language she lost her intellectuality".

The Gaelic League, enjoying enormous influence between 1893 and 1916, secured legal status for the Irish language and promoted Irish music, dance, theatre, literature and other arts. By resurrecting pride in the country's Celtic heritage, the league helped to galvanize support for independence, founded on a broad-based sense of cultural—as opposed to political—nationalism. In the 1937 Constitution, Irish gained protection as "the national language", while English was recognized as the "second official language".

Today, however, despite the government's decades of concentrated effort—in the form of mandatory primary- and secondary-school education in Irish, for example, and development grants to the Gaeltachts (Irish-speaking areas)

—the number of people who use Irish on a regular basis continues to shrink with every census. What had once been a sea of Irish speakers has evaporated, leaving behind just a few beleaguered linguistic tidepools, so to speak, most of them scattered along the far west of the island.

In the seven Gaeltachts, an estimated 70,000 tongues still wag in the melodic native speech, and it's worth seeking out these relatively remote places. The greatest concentration of Irish speakers—some 23,000—remains in Donegal, spread along the county's western coast. The second largest is the Galway Gaeltacht, with 20,000 native speakers in southern Connemara and the Aran Islands. The other western Gaeltachts are in Mayo, Kerry and Cork, while tiny Irish enclaves survive at An Rinn (Ring) on the Waterford coast and in County Meath.

Some Irish words have made it into the English lexicon, such as shanty, from *sean tigh* ("old house"), galore, from *go leór* ("enough"), smithereens, from *smidiríns* ("small fragments"). It's little surprise that the word "whiskey" derives from the Irish *uisce beatha* (literally "water of life").

For some words and phrases in Irish, see the Irish Vocabulary Appendix, page 288.

Traditional Music

> "We are the music makers,
> We are the dreamers of dreams".
> —Arthur O'Shaughnessy

No other art form gives voice to a country and the soul of its people like music. Its sensation is pure and immediate: a good melody, after all, needs no translation, requires no explanation or footnote. The folk of Ireland have produced an unsurpassed wealth and variety of music—far, far more than the stereotype of quartets clad in fishermen's sweaters.

The ancient Celts attributed supernatural effects to music; to them it was as much conjury as art, and the stories of Finn MacCool and other myth cycles are woven through with magical harps and horns. The Irish divided music into one of three categories, according to its properties: music that draws forth weeping from the listener; music that induces merriment; and music that throws the listener into a bewitched slumber.

Ireland was widely known as a land of music makers long before O'Shaughnessy noted it in the 1800s. In the seventh century, when the queen of France wanted choristers for her new abbey of Nivelle, it was not to Italy or Germany or England that she sent, but to Ireland. Even the 12th-century chronicler Gerald of Wales, while generally contemptuous of the Irish, had to begrudge a bit of praise for their musical arts: "They seem to me", he wrote, "to be incomparably more skilled in these than any other people that I have seen"

And George Frideric Handel, having heard "Eileen Aroon" in Dublin, declared that he'd sooner have composed that beguiling air than all his oratories combined.

Irish traditional music is built upon modes, ancient musical forms that don't fit neatly with the modern notions of major and minor scales. Some speculate that early Irish music was the basis for Gregorian chants, or vice versa. Thomas Moore, Ireland's 19th-century "national poet", who popularized (some would say bowdlerized) a number of traditional airs, certainly sensed the music's modal nature, even if he didn't quite understand the wherefore of it: "Even in their liveliest strains", he observed, "we find some melancholy note intrude—some minor third or flat seventh—which throws its shade as it passes, and makes even mirth interesting".

Considering its vigorous blossoming of popularity over the last couple of

Tipperary fiddler

decades, it's hard to believe that just a generation or so back traditional Irish music looked to be in danger of dying of neglect. The older players and singers were inevitably thinning out, not appreciated as they once were. And the young musicians who might have been carrying on the tradition would have been mortified to be seen with anything so square as a pennywhistle or accordion.

But it would have taken much more than the brief vagaries of favour to snuff out one of Europe's oldest and richest musical heritages. Today, far from any risk of disappearing, the music is kept very much alive by formidably skilful players (and equally discerning listeners) not only in Ireland but in places as distant as Hong Kong and Berlin.

Formerly, distinct regional playing styles distinguished musicians of one part of Ireland from another. A knowledgeable listener could place the county or even the town from which a fiddler hailed, for example, based on his manner of bowing, the style in which he ornamented his notes, and his repertoire. Though regional subtleties persist, much of Irish music playing has undergone a certain homogenization due to the influence of recordings and to the much greater mobility of people compared with even just a few decades ago.

The vast mainstay of Irish music consists of thousands of tunes for dancing —reels, jigs and hornpipes. The **reel** is a steady four-to-the-bar piece that

Young buskers, Grafton Street, Dublin

skips along brisk as a bee. The **jig** is usually played more slowly, galloping in 6/8 time or, less commonly, in the older 9/8 signature of the **slip jig**. The dotted rhythm and slower tempo of the **hornpipe** make it sound something like a reel with a limp. Other dance cadences, mainly **polkas and waltzes**, crop up as well, though less frequently.

But the gem of the Irish repertoire is the **slow air**. In most cases, a slow air, as played by an instrumentalist, was originally a song, of varying antiquity, stripped of its lyrics to reveal the gorgeous melody. While many airs do appear in the brighter major keys (or their modal equivalents), most spool out in a minor mood, tinted by sadness and full of dark turnings.

Noisy, crowded and smoky, pubs aren't always the best venues in which to appreciate Irish music seriously. Then again, for atmosphere, a really good pub is hard to beat, and alternatives, in any case, are few. The more or less informal gathering of musicians and singers, which materializes in a corner of the pub, is called a session—*seisiún* in Irish. Part of the adventure of the session is tracking it down, for the elusive best ones, in out-of-the-way pubs, seem to be advertised more by rumour than by newspaper notices.

Ireland's reputation for ballad singing hardly needs an introduction, except to say that it's very much alive—in pubs, at festivals, on records and on the streets. An older tradition, however, that's making a comeback after nearly dying out is *sean-nós* **singing**—a mesmerizing solo sung in the Irish language. If you're fortunate enough to come across this strange, plaintive art form, it'll likely be out in the west or northwest of Ireland—Galway, Mayo or Donegal. See page 189 for a fuller description.

INSTRUMENTS

Cultures the world over have developed some species of **bagpipe**, but in the Irish version, called union or *uilleann* or simply Irish pipes, the technology has reached its zenith. Of all the instruments common to Irish music, the pipes are the most expressive—most closely resembling the human voice—and the most difficult to master. Irish pipes differ considerably from the better-known piercing highland pipes of Scotland. They're first of all much quieter, span a wider tonal range and are capable of extreme subtlety. The breath of the Irish pipes comes from a bellows pumped with the player's elbow, as opposed to air from the mouth as in the Scottish pipes. (An old chestnut is that the Irish introduced the highland pipes to Scotland as a practical joke—which everyone but the Scots has figured out.) Finally, what sets Irish pipes apart from all others is the addition of up to three "regulators", keyed pipes which can add chords or harmonic drones.

If the *uilleann* pipes are the king of Irish music, then the **fiddle** must be their feminine counterpart. Many people wonder what the difference is between a fiddle and violin. The instruments are one and the same; it's the music and the playing style that distinguish one from the other.

The **flute** used in Irish music is almost invariably of wood, a model which predates the metal orchestral variety and produces a fuller, mellower timbre. Its woodwind cousin is the **pennywhistle** (also called a tin whistle)—one of the simplest instruments to learn but also one fully capable of supporting virtuoso performances. Other popular instruments are the **accordion** and four-stringed **tenor banjo**.

The **harp** (or *clarseach*), still one of Ireland's proudest cultural symbols, was for centuries the premier instrument in the country's musical pantheon before being supplanted by the pipes and fiddle. The population held the harp in such great esteem, and harpers wielded such power in Irish society, that the English found themselves obliged to suppress both. (See "Turlough O'Carolan", page 218.) Queen Elizabeth considered their effect so seditious that, in 1603, she ordered her magistrates "to hang all harpers wherever found". Lately, the harp is experiencing a strong renaissance. Because of its quietness, it's rarely played at sessions but can be heard in solo or small-ensemble settings.

The pulse of Irish music comes from the *bodhrán* (pronounced bow-RON). In skilled hands, this deceptively simple goatskin drum, played with a short double-headed stick called a tipper or beater, can produce surprisingly complex rhythms. By striking different areas of the head and by altering the skin's tension with hand pressure, the player can change the tone from bass to a taut falsetto, make it flutter like bird wings or rumble like hooves.

Facts for the Traveller

Getting There

BY AIR

From the United States, Ireland's national carrier **Aer Lingus** flies frequently to Shannon and Dublin airports from New York and Boston. By arrangement with TWA and American airlines, Aer Lingus also offers a "through fare" to travellers originating in other U.S. cities; TWA and American flights connect in New York and Boston with Aer Lingus flights bound for Ireland. For Aer Lingus reservations and information, call 212-557-1110 in New York only, 800-223-6537 in the rest of the U.S., 416-362-6565 in Canada.

Delta Airlines (tel. 800-241-4141 in the U.S.) flies direct from Atlanta to Shannon and Dublin. Charter flights from North America also connect Chicago, New York, Detroit and Toronto with Shannon, Cork, Dublin, Knock and Belfast airports; a good travel agent should be able to help with these arrangements.

From Great Britain, a number of airlines operate regular service to Irish destinations, including Aer Lingus (tel. 081-569-5555 in U.K.), British Airways (tel. 081-897-4000), British Midland (tel. 071-589-5599), Dan Air (tel. 071-378-6464) and Ryanair (tel. 071-435-7101). Aer Lingus offers the most options, flying from 11 British cities to Dublin and Shannon as well as to regional airports in Derry, Sligo, Knock, Galway, Kerry, Cork and Waterford.

Aer Lingus flies to Ireland from Amsterdam, Copenhagen, Dusseldorf, Frankfurt, Rome, Milan, Paris and Zurich. Air France, Air Portugal, Sabena, Swiss Air, SAS, Lufthansa and Iberia also offer regular flights from the Continent.

Northern Ireland is well connected by air from cities throughout Scotland and England. From North America, there are frequent scheduled and charter flights to Belfast from New York, Boston and Toronto. Aer Lingus connects Dublin with Derry.

From Australia, the best option is to fly to London, then continue on any of the air or surface connections described in this chapter.

By Sea

Traditionally, ferries have been the main mode of transport from Britain to the isle. While it takes three times longer than a flight, you have the option of taking a car. (Car rental in Ireland is expensive; depending on the length of stay, it may be more cost-effective to rent a car in Britain and take it across on the ferry.)

Sealink (tel. 0233-647047 in Britain) runs daily, year-round ferries from Holyhead, Wales, to Dún Laoghaire ($3^{1}/_2$ hours), and from Fishguard, Wales, to Rosslare daily year-round ($4^{1}/_2$ hours). B & I Line (tel. 071-491-8682 in London, 01-724711 in Dublin) operates ferries from Holyhead to Dublin and from Pembroke, Wales, to Rosslare. Swansea Cork Ferries runs seasonally between those two cities (10 hours).

Belfast is linked to Liverpool by Belfast Car Ferries (tel. 051-922-6234 in Liverpool; 9 hours), and Larne is joined with the Scottish ports of Cairnryan (P & O European Ferries, tel. 05812-276 in Scotland; 2 hours) and Stranraer (Sealink, $2^{1}/_4$ hours).

Irish Ferries (tel. 01-610511 in Dublin) connects Le Havre, France, with Cork and Rosslare (each route takes about 21 hours) and Cherbourg with Rosslare (about 18 hours). Brittany Ferries (tel. 021-277801 in Cork) operates a seasonal ferry from Roscoff, Brittany, to Cork.

The glory days of the trans-Atlantic steamers are history, but Cunard's *QEII* occasionally calls at Cobh en route from New York to Southampton.

By Land

Combined train-ferry tickets from Britain to Ireland can be booked at British Rail stations and through travel agents. Less expensive and less comfortable are bus-ferry packages. National Express buses (tel. 071-730-0202) depart from London's Victoria Bus Station to Dublin; the trip takes about 12 hours. Slattery's buses travel to various destinations in Ireland from their own London terminal (tel. 071-724-1741).

Visas

British citizens do not need a passport to enter the Republic or Northern Ireland. American, Canadian and Australian nationals must have a passport, but no visa is required for either the Republic or Northern Ireland for stays of up to three months. Citizens of European Community member nations must have a passport to enter Northern Ireland or the Republic, though neither state requires a visa.

Getting Around

BY AIR

Ireland is so small that internal air travel is generally worthwhile only for the very harried traveller with no time for scenery. Aer Lingus (tel. 01-844-4777 in Dublin) and Ryanair (tel. 01-677-4422 in Dublin) connect Dublin with Derry, Sligo, Knock, Galway, Shannon, Cork and Waterford. Aer Arann (tel. 091-55480 in Galway) links Galway City and Connemara Airport (near Inverin) with the Aran Islands.

BY TRAIN

In the Republic, state-owned Córas Iompair Éireann (CIE) operates Irish Rail, the national train network. Main lines radiate out from Dublin to Rosslare, Waterford, Cork, Limerick, Tralee, Galway, Westport, Ballina, Sligo, Belfast, Derry and intermediate towns, though large areas of the country are not served at all. Train travel in Ireland is generally faster, but also considerably more expensive, than bus travel. Eight- and 15-day Rambler Passes (available for rail only, bus only or combined bus-rail) can make it an attractive option, however. Details are available in the U.S. from CIE (tel. 800-243-8687); passes can be purchased at train and bus stations throughout Ireland.

BY BUS

Bus Éireann in the Republic and Ulsterbus in Northern Ireland reach nearly every corner of the island. Some areas not covered by them (such as northern Donegal) and busy routes (such as Sligo-Dublin, Galway-Dublin, etc.) may be served by private companies. The bus systems are generally adequate and reliable; the main drawback is the sometimes frustrating slowness of travel (with the exception of express routes).

A variety of bus and bus-train passes are offered (see "By Train"), including passes for the Irish Republic only, for Northern Ireland only, and all-Ireland passes. A bus timetable, available at bus stations, can be essential, especially in the off-season, when a bus may service out-of-the-way areas just once or twice weekly.

By Car

The shortcomings of public transport—combined with enticingly uncrowded roads through beautiful countryside—should conspire to make driving an excellent alternative. Unfortunately, renting a car in Ireland can be rather costly. In the Republic, a Ford Fiesta with tax and insurance costs roughly US$40–50 per day in summer, less on a per-week basis and in the off-season. A roomier midsize costs approximately US$350–400 per week, while a week's minivan rental in summer can set you back close to US$1,000. Prices are somewhat lower in the North.

Gasoline in the Republic runs approximately US$5 per imperial gallon; it's about 40 percent cheaper in the North. Sharing the costs among two or three congenial companions, of course, can make car travel affordable and very attractive to the budget-minded.

The well-known international rental agencies operate in main cities and popular tourist areas, while local firms pick up the slack there and elsewhere. Budget Rent-A-Car (tel. 800-472-3325 in U.S., 01-370919 at Dublin Airport, 061-61688 at Shannon Airport) has competitive rates.

On both sides of the border, driving is done on the left-hand side of the road. Caution is called for: even relatively major roads can be quite narrow and potholed, herds of complacent livestock can appear when least expected, and many Irish motorists seem to take to the roads fueled by an unshakable conviction in their own immortality.

Road distances are usually signposted in kilometres, often with mile equivalents; in the Republic, however, old black-on-white road signs showing distances in miles only are not uncommon.

Crossing the border between Northern Ireland and the Republic must be done at official crossing points, which are clearly signposted and marked on highway maps. There are about two dozen of these, located on all major and some minor routes across the border. Most border posts stay open 24 hours, though some close overnight. Crossing is a simple affair, requiring a driver's license or other piece of identification.

By Bike

Travelling Ireland by bike can be a most rewarding and spectacular way to go—providing the weather cooperates. The pace is just right for the island's modest size, roads are generally traffic-free, and distances are manageable. On a dry day, there's nothing quite like freewheeling along the countless miles of scenic byways, meeting the people and soaking up the sights, sounds and smells of

Bolus Head, Co. Kerry

the countryside. It's another story in rain or wind, however, which can sabotage the most buoyant spirits. Just about any time of year the weather can change from glorious to awful and back again over the course of an hour, so the best approach is to pray for sun but be prepared for the worst with foul-weather gear.

Other hazards include poorly paved roads in some areas and narrow or nonexistent shoulders. Wearing a helmet is always a good idea. Like cars, bicyclists ride to the left.

Rental bicycles available at shops and at many youth hostels are generally fine for a day's jaunt, but serious cycle tourers will probably want to bring their own bikes and gear.

General Information

CLIMATE

"There is such a plentiful supply of rain", Giraldus Cambrensis complained in the 12th century, ". . . an ever-present overhanging of clouds and fog that you will scarcely see even in summer consecutive days of really fine weather". Well, maybe. But a 20th-century chronicler, Heinrich Böll, saw Irish weather in a different light: "The rain here is absolute, magnificent, and frightening. To call this rain bad weather is as inappropriate as to call scorching sunshine fine weather".

"Wet and mild" sums up the Irish climate. Although the island lies at the same latitude as Canada's icy Labrador Peninsula, the warm Gulf Stream curling across the Atlantic softens temperature extremes here. Irish weather throughout the year is notoriously capricious, and it's not uncommon to get a taste of all four seasons in a single day. Grey skies are frequent, often accompanied by a gentle drizzle—weather the Irish call "soft".

But few days pass that don't see at least a little sun. Regardless of the season, it's advisable to bring sweaters and other warm clothes; an umbrella or waterproof parka is worth its weight in dry clothes.

Summers are cool and the sun sets late in the evening; July and August are the warmest months, May and June generally the sunniest. Winters are usually mild and damp, coldest in January and February. In Dublin, the average summer temperature is 16–21° C (61–70° F); winter averages 4–7° C (39–45° F). Across the island, Galway City's temperature averages 4–9° C (39–49° F) in January and 13–20° C (55–68° F) in July.

Because of westerly winds from the Atlantic, the west coast is the wetter side, averaging 203 centimetres (80 inches) of rain per year. On the east coast and in the central plain, rainfall averages 76 centimetres (30 inches) and 101 centimetres (40 inches) respectively. Snow is a rarity and seldom stays long on the ground when it does fall.

CURRENCY

As in travelling anywhere abroad, the current exchange rate will play a large role in determining what value you get for your money in Ireland. A strong dollar, for example, means relatively reasonable transport, accommodations and so on; but when the dollar is weak against the pound, Ireland's already high prices can really pinch the budget.

Currency in Northern Ireland is the pound sterling, as in Great Britain, while the Republic uses the Irish pound, or *punt*. Both currencies are divided into 100 pence. Irish pounds won't be accepted in the North, though in the South individuals and businesses will generally take payment in pounds sterling at face value, as it's usually worth a bit more than its *punt* equivalent.

The exchange rates against the U.S. dollar constantly seesaw up and down, but as a rough rule of thumb, the rate generally falls into the range of US$1 = 1.50–1.75 Irish pounds; the pound sterling is usually valued at 5–10 percent higher than the *punt*.

Banks in larger towns nearly always offer better exchange rates than hotels, airports, shops, tourist offices, etc. Rates and service fees for changing money can vary considerably from bank to bank, so it's worth shopping around a bit. Banks in the Republic are generally open Monday to Friday 10 am–12:30 pm and 1:30–3 pm; until 5 pm on Thursdays. In the North, hours are Monday to Friday 10 am–12:30 pm and 1:30–3:30 pm; most Belfast banks stay open through the lunch hour.

Shopping

Most shops and businesses open Monday through Saturday from 9 or 9:30 am until 5 or 5:30 pm. Most shops close on Sunday and may also close up early one day during the week.

Travellers' cheques and major credit cards are widely accepted; bed-and-breakfasts and small or out-of-the-way shops, however, may prefer cash or may not be equipped to accept cards.

Tourists are entitled to a refund of the value-added tax (VAT) on goods they've purchased in and are taking out of Ireland. In the Republic, the VAT on various goods ranges from 10 to 23 percent; in the North it's 17 percent. When making your purchase, ask the shop for the requisite refund forms. Many shops which regularly deal with tourists will pack and ship your purchases home for you, in which case the VAT will not be charged to the price.

When exiting the Republic, refunds are made right at Dublin or Shannon airports (minus a service charge). In Northern Ireland, the process is more cumbersome: the VAT relief form must be stamped by customs, then you mail it to back to the store where you purchased the items for the refund.

Caveat emptor rules at airport duty-free shops, where jewellery, watches, clothing, perfumes, tobacco, alcoholic beverages, crystal and china are the main goods sold. There are some bargains to be had, but some items may actually cost less at a retail shop, so it's smart to know going prices beforehand.

Miscellaneous

Electrical current is 220 volts AC in the Republic, 240 volts AC in Northern Ireland. Outlets everywhere are of the large, British three-pin style; most hotels and many bed-and-breakfasts have special sockets for electric razors. Electrical devices from the U.S. require an adapter to accommodate the higher voltage and different outlet configuration.

Tipping is not widespread in Ireland. Taxi drivers often expect a tip of about 10 percent, hotel porters about 50 pence per bag. A service charge of 10–15 percent may be added to meal bills at hotels and restaurants; otherwise, tip at your discretion. Tipping is not usual in pubs, though a tip to a server who waits on your table in a lounge or hotel bar won't go amiss.

Post offices in the Republic and Northern Ireland are found in every town and the smallest villages. Hours in the Republic are weekdays 9 am–5 pm Dublin's main post office is open Saturday mornings. Post offices in the North are open weekdays 9 am–5:30 pm, and to 12:30 pm on Saturdays.

Food and Drink

Until recently, "Irish cuisine" has been a dubious pairing of words inclined to bring an oxymoronic arch to the gourmet's eyebrow. How much of that

John Quinn takes a pint, Co. Mayo

skepticism is deserved—and how much is just left over from the scorn so glee-fully heaped upon bland British cooking—is a question best left to the buds of the taster.

It's true that, on the whole, boiling or frying have been the predictable fates of most anything edible in the Irish diet. The Irish board tends toward simple but hearty fare, albeit high in meat and dairy fats and with hapless vegetables cooked into abject submission. Salads can come as a disappointment, too; often they're just a bit of tomato or cucumber and a few sad wee flaps of let-tuce that can leave real greens lovers crying.

But there is a new culinary sophistication abroad in the land, as Irish cooks are exploring more healthful and varied cuisine and adapting some of the best that other cooking traditions have to offer.

Meat is central to the Irish meal. Beef, pork and mutton are home-grown and all of superior quality. Vegetarian cooking appears now and again, but it's still a rarity, especially outside the cities. The palette of vegetables available in markets and on menus is usually limited to carrots, cabbage, turnips and cauliflower, with peas making an occasional showing. Potatoes still are a mainstay in the Irish diet, whether baked, boiled, fried or served up as "chips" (French fries).

Leen's Bar, Killorglin, Co. Kerry

From Irish pastures come excellent dairy products—butter, milk, cream and delicious cheeses. Baked goods are tasty, too, especially the ubiquitous Irish soda bread, round loaves of coarse-ground whole-wheat flour that perfectly complement almost any meal.

An appreciation for seafood is steadily growing in Ireland, and there is much to appreciate: fresh mackerel, cod, plaice, sole, scallops, mussels, lobsters and the famous oysters and Atlantic salmon, though much of the harvest from the rich Irish seas is destined for export to the Continent.

In Ireland, eating out and eating well are not necessarily the same thing. The past few years have seen a profusion of fine restaurants serving delicious and imaginative meals. These places tend to be rather upscale, and the best chefs often work in exclusive country houses and luxury hotels. At the same time, American, or American-style, fast-food chains are proliferating, and all the usual culprits are in evidence in the cities. Ireland, too, has its share of fish-and-chips shops, which often are the only places open for a late-night bite. Finding really satisfying choices in between can often be frustrating. An adequate, filling supper can be had for roughly £8–10 per person (excluding drinks), but for something more gastronomically memorable, expect to pay £15 or more.

Hotels and bed-and-breakfasts reliably serve filling and good-value breakfasts, usually including hot or cold cereal, juice, tea and coffee, eggs, tomatoes, a variety of sausages, bacon (not the dripping ribbons of fat that pass for bacon in America, but smoky, thick-cut, meaty slices) and piles of toast or scones.

For lunch, a pub can be a delightful, affordable alternative to restaurants. For a few pounds, many a pub serves simple sandwiches, thick soups, bread-and-cheese plates, smoked salmon and the like, while some prepare more elaborate dishes such as pasta, casseroles, quiche, etc.

The pub, of course, is also the place for drinking, but it offers much more than that. After the church and the family, the pub must be the most central and enduring institution in Irish life. There's hardly a hamlet in the land that doesn't have at least one pub, and even a small village might have several. Each has its own personality, depending on the publican and his clientele, but for the most part Irish pubs are convivial, welcoming places, with an ambience that bars across the Atlantic just can't match.

The TV is intruding, inevitably, into this civilized domain ("the death of the Irish pub", grumbled one patron in a Kinsale pub). Mercifully, the sound at least is often kept off. Many pubs are venues for live music—jazz, or ballads or traditional sessions—usually free for the listening and of quite high calibre.

But conversation is the real currency of entertainment here, minted anew each day and evening. For an outsider, even a teetotaller, the pub can offer one of the best opportunities for meeting and talking with the locals or simply for people-watching. It's common to see whole families in on a weekend evening, the kids snacking on lemonades and crisps (potato chips) while their parents catch up on the news with friends.

For those who don't drink, usually tea and sometimes coffee are available, as well as sodas. For those who do, there is some of the best beer and best whiskey in the world. To the aficionado, a well-poured pint of stout in a good Irish pub is one of life's keenest pleasures. Guinness stout, brewed in Dublin, is the best-known brand, and exported around the world; but slightly sweeter, smoother Murphy's and Beamish's, both brewed in Cork City, have their devotees as well. For half a pint, ask for "a glass". Guinness also produces a lager, called Harp, which is quite good and a little heavier than most American or German lagers (which are also available bottled or on tap in many pubs). Smithwick's is a bitter ale that's quite popular, and for a change of taste there's hard cider, which packs a wallop.

Power's, Paddy's and Jameson's are whiskeys distilled in the Republic, while Bushmills comes from County Antrim in Northern Ireland. These are all smooth, mellow and delicious, but not inexpensive. The portions are more generous than in the American bars, although, as Oliver Gogarty rightly observed, "There is no such thing as a large whiskey".

In the Republic, pubs have summertime hours of 10:30 am–11:30 pm Monday to Saturday, closing a half-hour earlier in winter. Sunday hours are 12:30–2 pm, 4–11 pm year-round. In the North, hours are Monday through Saturday 11:30 am–11 pm, Sundays 12:30–2:30 and 7–10 pm.

The Poetry of Irish Places

During the first Ordnance Survey of the British Isles, begun in 1834, Ireland was mapped and Irish place-names were cobbled into English. Many of these transliterations are quite recognizable: Fanore from Fan Oir, for instance, or Donegal from Dun na nGall. Other changes, such as Colman to Arthurstown, are more difficult to fathom.

Except in the Gaeltachts, where the Irish name may be given alone, most towns and other sites throughout the country are signposted with the anglicized name, often accompanied by the original Irish name. Irish signposts are rarely seen in Northern Ireland.

To confuse matters, sometimes buses appear with their destination marked with just the Irish name, such as Baile Átha Cliath (the "Town at the Ford of the Hurdles", an ancient but still-used name for Dublin) or Corcaigh (Cork City), apparently at the whim of the driver.

Still, whether the name is in Irish or bowdlerized by the English, there is poetry in the least of them, and the plum-round vowels fit so pleasingly in the mouth and fall so softly on the ear that they bear recitation just for the pleasure of it: Connemara, Ballyvaughan, Lissadell, Inishowen, Mooncoin, Cashel, Slievenamon.

Many place-names, such as Lismore, meaning "Large Fort", or Glendalough, "Valley of Two Lakes", contain clues about their history or setting, and it takes only a rudimentary vocabulary to begin teasing out their meaning. Common descriptive words include:

agh, augh—field	inis, inish—island
áth, átha—ford	kil, kill, cil—church
ar, ard—height	knock, cnoc—hill
as, eas, ess—waterfall	lis, lios, liss—fort
aw, atha, abhainn—river	lough—lake
baile, bal, balli, bally—town	ma, magh, may, moy—plain
beag, beg—small	mór, more—large
caher, cahir, cathair, carraig,	owen—river
carrick—rock	rath—fort
cashel, caiseal, caislean—castle	ross—headland, peninsula
dun—fort	sliabh, slieve—mountain
glen—valley	tra—beach

Dublin

> Strumpet city in the sunset
> Suckling the bastard brats of Scot, of
> Englishry, of Huguenot
> Brave sons breaking from the womb,
> wild sons fleeing from their Mother
> Willful city of savage dreamers,
> So old, so rich with memories!
>
> —Denis Johnston, The Old Lady Says "No!"

Were Dublin someday destroyed, James Joyce boasted, the city could be remade from the details caught in the pages of his books. Braggadocio, perhaps. The artist left Dublin while yet a young man, though he would spend the rest of his life gazing back at it. If Joyce could not live in Dublin, neither could he forget it. Through the fixed picture of memory and the alchemy of his craft, he transmuted perishable cobble and brick and frail humankind into a kind of immortality.

As much as her architects, politicians, labourers and tradesmen have shaped the capital city, her writers too have created something enduring, if not exactly tangible, out of the fabric of Dublin. Generations of poets and playwrights have drifted the streets, haunted the pubs and drawing rooms and breathed inspiration from "dear, dirty Dublin".

But Joyce was not alone among them whom the city chafed like a too-tight jacket. Oliver Gogarty noted the long, ironical list: Swift, Goldsmith, Burke, Wilde, Yeats, Shaw. "All these men lived in Dublin, but most of them died elsewhere". Wrote Joyce:

> This lovely land that always sent
> Her writers into banishment.

The capital city it may be, with its face turned outward to Europe, but many see it simply as Ireland's largest village—a typical settlement grown up at a ford on a river, full of the same characters, and vices, and prejudices, and small epiphanies of most any provincial town, teetering in the balance between comfortable and claustrophobic. "There was no doubt about it", said one of Joyce's *Dubliners*—articulating not just the author's but the Irish dilemma in general—"if you wanted to succeed you had to go away".

If for centuries Dublin has been the country's economic centre of gravity, the lodestone of its cultural aspirations, through successive eras it was also

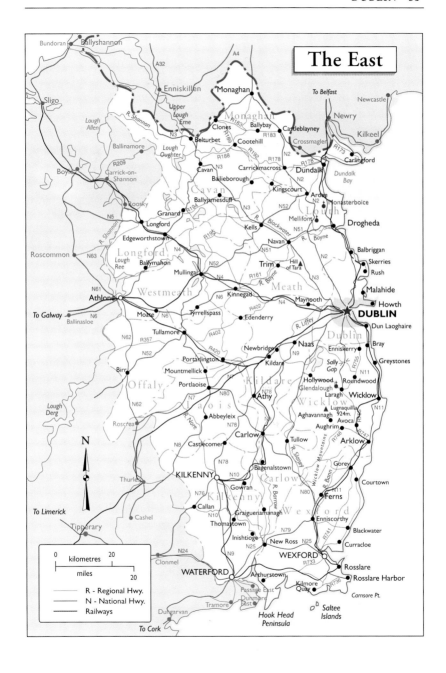

The East

On Grafton Street, Dublin

the focus of foreign domination, through the Viking, Norman and British eras. It's no wonder a feeling of irreconcilable ambivalence pervades the city's character and its people.

Dublin's an ancient city, yet still in its salad days of independence, eager to expunge the vestiges of colonialism and assert a fresh identity. Caught between those imperatives, Dublin seems ever to be ignoring its past or rushing to demolish it. Glass-sheathed modern structures muscle out the venerable Georgian and Victorian edifices. Everywhere there are decrepit treasures that forlornly testify to the wages of neglect. But there is regeneration too, and a new appreciation for the rich inheritance from the past. This thousand-year-old city has recognized its own priceless value almost too late, but at last seems to have found an equilibrium.

By day, Dublin pulses with the brash hurly-burly of a million people going about their business: shawled and wizened old women in the market, nuns and priests, shopgirls breaking for a smoke, wan students shuffling between classes, barking newspaper vendors, peach-cheeked children, leatherbound punks, suited executives, young mothers wheeling shiny prams. They're Dubliners all of them, famous for their buoyant self-assurance, for the sardonic equanimity with which they alternately defend and deride their city, and especially for their barbed, irreverent wit, which pricks every pretentious bubble it touches.

Come nightfall and it's a different city again. In the late hours, when the pubs have closed and the echoes of their patrons faded, Dublin is at its most magical. On O'Connell Street, Joyce leans upon his slender cane. Stray pages from the *Times* eddy on the empty sidewalks. The upstretched arms of Jim Larkin exhort none but the incongruous gulls wheeling overhead. All's silent but for the occasional shambling footsteps of late-nighters and snatches of song from tipplers lurching homeward after a hooly. *Gardai* patrol the darkened

Moore Street Market, Dublin

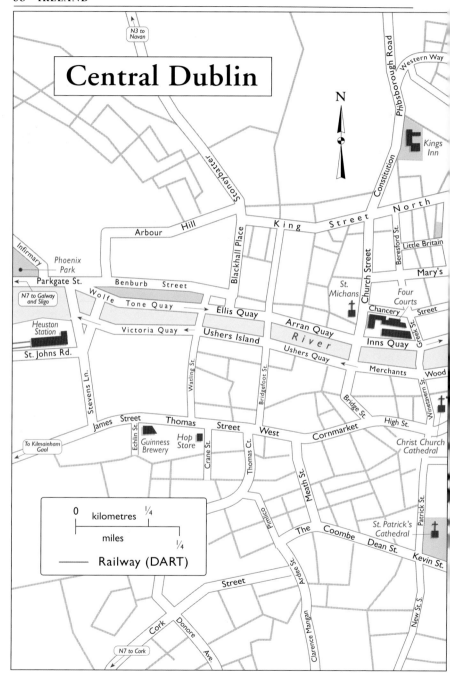

Central Dublin

N3 to Navan

Phibsborough Road

Western Way

Kings Inn

N

Stoneybatter

Constitution

North

Beresford St.

Little Britain

Arbour Hill

King Street

Blackhall Place

Church Street

Mary's

Infirmary

Phoenix Park

St. Michans

Four Courts

Parkgate St.

Benburb Street

Chancery

Greek St.

Street

N7 to Galway and Sligo

Wolfe Tone Quay

Ellis Quay

Arran Quay

Heuston Station

Victoria Quay

Ushers Island

River

Inns Quay

St. Johns Rd.

Ushers Quay

Merchants

Wood

Stevens Ln.

Watling St.

Bridgefoot St.

Bridge St.

High St.

Wintavern St.

James Street

Thomas Street

West

Cornmarket

Christ Church Cathedral

To Kilmainham Gaol

Echlin St.

Guinness Brewery

Hop Store

Crane St.

Thomas Ct.

Meath St.

Patrick St.

Pimlico

The Coombe

St. Patrick's Cathedral

Dean St.

Kevin St.

Clarence Mangan

Ardee St.

New St. S.

| 0 | kilometres | ¼ |

| | miles | ¼ |

Railway (DART)

Street

Cork

Donore Ave.

N7 to Cork

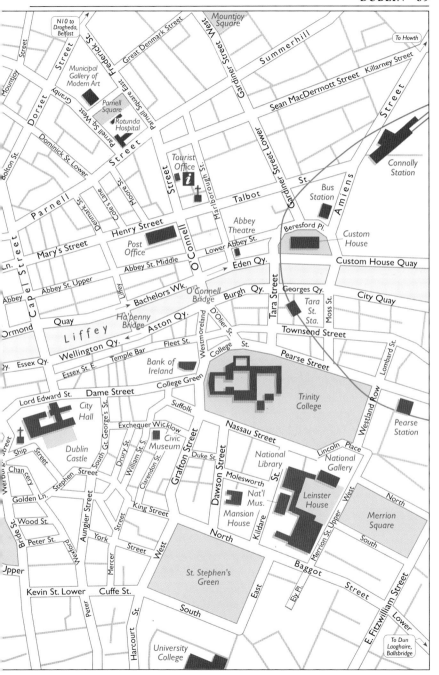

side streets in pairs. Under shop eaves, couples embrace then hurry on, collars raised against the wind. And on the Liffey, starlight and lamplight fall and shatter against its surface, onyx-black now at midnight, curling languidly to the sea.

"Take heart of grace from your city's hidden splendour", urged Seán O'Casey. "Our city's in th' grip o' God".

The Liffey is Dublin's shorthand demarcation of class consciousness: to the north is workingman's Dublin, the city of Joyce's *Dubliners* and O'Casey's tenement dwellers, the once-fashionable quarter abandoned by the 19th-century gentry after the Act of Union dimmed the city's prospects for greatness. They fled south to the polished, conservative, middle-class side of the river.

But Dublin is full of contradictions that quickly confound such oversimplifications. On either side you'll find a share both of bankers and beggars, dispirited public housing and still-gracious Georgian homes, with their doors painted in crayon-box colors under delicate fanlights.

North of the Liffey

When Sackville Street was laid out in the 18th century, planners envisioned it as the city's most elegant residential thoroughfare. Renamed **O'Connell Street** in 1924, in honour of Daniel O'Connell, the wide boulevard's former glory has been somewhat obscured by the choke of traffic fumes and the neon glare of pernicious fast-food joints.

The majestic **O'Connell Monument**, erected in 1854 at the foot of the street, anchors the statue-lined central mall. The statue of "the Liberator" stands over the four winged figures of Courage, Eloquence, Fidelity and Patriotism. A cuckoo in the nest of O'Connell Street's more staid monuments (which include William Smith O'Brien, Charles Stewart Parnell and labour organizer James Larkin) is Anna Livia, the incarnation of the River Liffey, reclining "in the nip" amid cascading fountains. Dubliners were quick to nickname her "the floozy in the Jacuzzi".

On Easter Monday, 24 April 1916, the Irish Republican Brotherhood and the Irish Volunteers took over the **General Post Office** on Sackville Street, making it their headquarters during the doomed but ultimately successful Easter Rising (see page 38). Shells from an English gunboat on the Liffey inflicted heavy damage on the Post Office (and bullet scars can still be seen). In the lobby, the rebels are commemorated with an heroic statue of Cuchulain, the indomitable warrior of Irish legend.

Around the corner is bustling Henry Street, Dublin's busiest shopping district, with several department stores and countless small shops. Branching off is the **Moore Street Market**, a genuine slice of boisterous urban Irish commerce that seems hardly different from a scene novelist Gerald Griffin described in 1830:

> *The street . . . was covered with small wooden tables, extending nearly the whole length, on which were exposed for sale pig's pettitoes, ears, knees, tongues of beef, iron and brass nails, huge cakes of coarse griddle bread, heads of cabbage, scissors and smoothing irons, locks, onions, sickles, gingerbread, St. Patrick's brogues, and other articles of humble luxury as well as use. Booths were hung with shawls and handkerchiefs, striped heavy woollen waistcoats, and beads of glass and horn.*

The perpetually busy **Tourist Information Office** at 14 Upper O'Connell Street is helpful, but for a really well-informed guide to the city's happenings, pick up the weekly *In Dublin* magazine at any newsstand.

At the top of the street, the statue of Parnell points toward the **Rotunda Maternity Hospital**, Europe's first, built in the 1750s and still in use. Behind it are the Gate Theatre and the small but excellent **Hugh Lane Municipal Gallery of Modern Art**. The gallery looks out on the red brick town houses of **Parnell Square**, the former heart of fashionable Dublin. This area is more notable now for its literary connections than for any other attractions, which makes it a fitting site for the **Dublin Writers Museum**. This recently opened museum, in a thoughtfully refinished 1760s town house, features rare editions, original manuscripts, portraits, etc., relating to Ireland's three Nobel winners —Yeats, Beckett, Shaw—and others.

The peripatetic Joyce family moved around Dublin more than 15 times, as James's alcoholic father had a marked aversion to paying rent. From 1893 to 1898, young James attended the Jesuit Belvedere College in Great Denmark Street, where he briefly contemplated a vocation to the priesthood.

Walk up Great Denmark and Gardiner streets to once-elegant **Mountjoy Square**, the city's first Georgian square, to see what 150 years of neglect can do. This was the decaying "Hilljoy Square" of Seán O'Casey's *Shadow of a Gunman*. The last of 13 children, O'Casey was born not far from here, at 85 Upper Dorset Street (now a bank), in 1880, the year Dublin was officially declared the unhealthiest city in the world. It was also in this neighbourhood, at 422 North Circular Road, that he wrote his potent, comical tragedies, *The Plough and the Stars*, *The Silver Tassie* and *Juno and the Paycock*.

Brendan Behan grew up at 14 Russell Street, near the Royal Canal. The Joyce family lived close by for a time at 17 North Richmond Street. In 1914, the street and its residents appeared in *Dubliners*: "North Richmond Street was

Ha'penny Bridge, Dublin

a quiet street . . . the houses, conscious of decent lives within them, gazed at one another with brown imperturbable faces".

Back at the river on Inns Quay, west of the city centre, is the **Four Courts**, which houses Ireland's main courts. It's an inspired masterpiece of neoclassical design from the 18th-century architect James Gandon. The foyer, under the jade-green dome, is open to the public, as are some court sessions.

Around the corner, in Church Street, is a Dublin oddity that has had a strange appeal to curious tourists for generations. Seventeenth-century **St. Michan's Church** itself is fairly ordinary, apart from its organ, played by Handel in 1742, and the

Seán O'Casey

charming woodcarving of a cornucopia of musical instruments above the loft. The rather more lurid attraction lies beneath the church in the crypt, where the dry air and some quality in the limestone foundations have preserved— for centuries—the several vellum-skinned corpses on display.

Phoenix Park is an agreeably forested, grassy pleasure garden farther west, about three kilometres (two miles) from O'Connell Street. In 1617 it was walled in as a deer park by the first duke of Ormonde, and deer can still be seen browsing among the groves. The park takes its name from a natural spring rising here, which the Irish called *fionn uisce* ("bright water") and the English misunderstood as "phoenix". Within the seven square kilometres (1,760 acres) are playing fields, small lakes, Áras an Uachtaráin (the president of Ireland's official residence), the American ambassador's residence, a race-course and the Dublin Zoo. A 19th-century ditty about Phoenix Park and its zoo runs like this:

> *I brought me mot up to the Zoo*
> *For to show her the lion and the kangaroo;*
> *There were he-males and she-males of each shade and hue*
> *Inside the Zoological Gardens.*

South-Central Dublin

A remark attributed to Brendan Behan lamented that the British, while improving Irish morals, did not do as much for their architecture. The long, handsome façade of the **Custom House**—best viewed from the south-side quays across the river—is a striking argument to the contrary. Completed in 1791, it's another of the neoclassical masterpieces designed by the superlative Georgian architect James Gandon. Not open to the public.

At the corner of Westmoreland and College Green, the magnificent **Bank of Ireland** (originally the Parliament House), with its imposing porticoes of Ionic and Corinthian pillars, clearly demonstrates the grand notions the capital city had for itself in the 18th century. The original 1729 design was by Edward Lovett Pearce, with later additions made by Gandon. Here in 1782, in the House of Commons, Henry Grattan declared, "Ireland is now a nation". For the next 18 years "Grattan's parliament" did enjoy legislative independence from Great Britain. But in 1800, with the Act of Union, the well-bribed Irish Parliament compliantly voted itself out of existence. For better or for worse, Ireland and England were wed. Two years later the building was sold to the Bank of Ireland, which occupies it still. Guided tours are given during business hours.

Across the speeding traffic of College Green is the 1759 western façade, the "surly front", of **Trinity College**. Statues of Edmund Burke and Oliver Goldsmith, two of Trinity's many notable alumni, flank the entrance. Queen Elizabeth founded the 1.6-square-kilometre (40-acre) campus in 1592, on the site of a monastery sacked by her father, Henry VIII. Among the roster of illustrious graduates from Ireland's oldest and leading university are Jonathan Swift, William Congreve, Theobald Wolfe Tone, Oscar Wilde, J.M. Synge and Samuel Beckett, to name a few. Until 1793, it was an exclusively Protestant domain; even then, Catholic students who attended were threatened with excommunication by their archbishop.

Trinity's library is Ireland's greatest storehouse of books and papers, but the treasures of the Long Room are of the most interest. Here are the so-called Brian Ború harp (pictured on Irish coinage and the emblem of Guinness), the artfully illuminated *Book of Durrow, Book of Armagh, Book of Dimma* and the most famous of the medieval Gospels, the priceless, eighth-century *Book of Kells.* The endless inventiveness of its initial capitals, the elaborately intertwining human and zoomorphic figures and the overall harmony of the text and illustrations are simply a marvel. One vellum page is turned each day. "Here you may see the face of Majesty divinely drawn", wrote the 12th-century historian

The Custom House (top) and Trinity College, Dublin

Giraldus Cambrensis. "You will make out intricacies, so delicate and subtle, so exact and compact, so full of knots and links, with colours so fresh and vivid, that you might say that all this is the work of an angel, not of a man".

Grafton Street, one of Dublin's smartest shopping streets, connects the college with St. Stephen's Green. When Leopold Bloom of *Ulysses* walked it on 16 June 1904, "Grafton Street gay with housed awnings lured his senses". He stopped in for a Gorgonzola sandwich at Davy Byrne's "nice quiet bar", around the corner in Duke Street, then ambled on into literary history.

For a few coppers Grafton's buskers will turn a reel for you. The lean, gnomish poet who sets up on the street might recite "She Moved through the Fair", or another poem from a creel full of Irish verse, with such a passionate intensity you'd think the lines had just come to him still burning from the poet's pen.

Grafton Street's *de rigueur* spot for people-watching is old-fashioned **Bewley's** coffee house, a Dublin institution since the 1840s. (Bewley's has two other branches nearby, in Westmoreland Street and South Great George's Street.)

Near the south end of Grafton Street Molly Malone wheels her barrow still. The life-sized bronze depicts the beloved heroine of "Cockles and Mussels", the most widely travelled of all Irish ballads. Tradition says that Molly sold her baskets of shellfish nearby in Fishamble Street, where there was a medieval fish market, but

> *She died of a fever*
> *And no one could save her,*
> *And that was the end of sweet Molly Malone,*
> *But her ghost wheels her barrow*
> *Through streets broad and narrow,*
> *Crying cockles and mussels, alive, alive oh!*

An industrious researcher, who recently claimed to have found her death certificate in 18th-century parish records, archly hinted that her mortal fever was really a euphemism for venereal disease, suggesting that cockles and mussels were not all Molly was peddling on Dublin's streets. It's as likely, though, that typhoid did the old girl in, contracted from eating tainted seafood from polluted Dublin Bay. Molly's ample cleavage—bared by a scandalously swooping décolletage—invites passersby to toss in a coin and make a wish.

Running parallel to Grafton are Dawson Street, with a number of fine bookshops, and Clarendon Street, where the **Powerscourt Town House Centre** is located. This sumptuous 1771 mansion has been transformed into an opulent shopping mall with restaurants and boutiques arranged around the glass-roofed courtyard.

"The Arrest of Christ", from the Book of Kells

Portrait of James Joyce by J.E. Blanche

Up until 1663, St. Stephen's Green was an open common where the lord mayor grazed his livestock, Dubliners cut their firewood and public executions were held. Now it's a welcoming public park, with flower gardens, grassy swards, summer concerts and ornamental ponds that are home to demure swans and murmuring coots. Just south of St. Stephen's is the original building of University College, the Catholic alternative to Trinity and alma mater for Patrick Pearse, Eamon de Valera and James Joyce. On the north side of the green—known as the Beaux Walk for the dandies who used to stroll here—is the statue raised in memory of the patriot Wolfe Tone, backed by granite slabs; it wasn't long before some wag rechristened it "Tonehenge". Across the street is the venerable and luxurious Shelbourne Hotel.

The novelist George Moore lived for a time at 4 Ely Place, off Baggot Street east of St. Stephen's Green; surgeon, writer, and wit Oliver St. John Gogarty lived at No. 25. Moore's house and the garden across the street turned up *Hail and Farewell*, his reminiscences on life in Dublin. Moore ired his neighbours by painting his door bright green instead of white like all the others; as litigation loomed, he would rattle his walking stick along the wrought-iron fences as he walked home late at night, waking all the dogs. The neighbours retaliated by hiring an organ grinder to play outside his window as he sat down to write.

A short walk up Kildare Street leads to the massive twin rotundas housing the entrances of the **National Library** and **National Museum**. The preponderance of Ireland's finest treasures are here in this museum, siphoned from around the country (to the impoverishment of regional museum collections). Dazzling hoards of Bronze Age gold and silver adornments (torques, bracelets, earrings), a panoply of quotidian artifacts from the Viking era, Ireland's finest ecclesiastical relics such as the Cross of Cong, and more secular masterpieces such as the Ardagh Chalice and the Tara Brooch highlight the superb exhibits.

Also in Kildare Street is **Leinster House**. When the duke of Leinster commissioned the stately Palladian town house in the 1740s, the fashionable core of Dublin lay to the north of the Liffey, and this site was an empty field. "Where I go", the duke accurately predicted, "fashion will follow". Since 1921, the *Dáil Éireann* (House of Representatives) and the *Seanad Éireann* (Senate) have met here. Public galleries of both houses are open during legislative sessions.

George Bernard Shaw spent many an hour in the **National Gallery** next door, dreaming of becoming a painter. He credited the experience as a large part of his education, and in gratitude he bequeathed the gallery a third of his estate. His statue now greets visitors in the forecourt. In addition to 17th-century French, Italian, Spanish and Dutch paintings, the museum's strongest suit is its collection of 17th- to 20th-century works by Irish artists.

The red brick Georgian houses around **Merrion Square** have been lived in over the decades by quite a succession of distinguished residents. Plaques mark the homes of Sir William and Lady Wilde and their son Oscar at No. 1, Daniel O'Connell at No. 58, W.B. Yeats at No. 82, Sheridan Le Fanu at No. 70 and George Russell (Æ) at No. 84. For more well-preserved Georgiana, stroll southward a few short blocks to Fitzwilliam Square.

A short walk southeast along Baggot Street leads to the **Grand Canal**, constructed in 1772 to link Dublin with Midland towns and the River Shannon. Until the advent of the railway 80 years later, thousands of passengers travelled the waterway annually, and freight barges relied on it until just a generation ago. Real Dubliners—or Jackeens—are said to be those born between the enclosing parentheses of the Grand Canal and the Royal Canal, its north-side counterpart.

Monaghan-born poet and journalist Patrick Kavanagh, author of *The Great Hunger* and *Tarry Flynn,* loved the leafy environs of the Grand Canal. After his death in 1967, friends erected a stone bench near the canal locks at Baggot Street Bridge, in fulfillment of his wishes:

> *O commemorate me where there is water,*
> *Canal water preferably, so stilly*
> *Greeny at the heart of summer . . .*
> *O commemorate me with no hero-courageous*
> *Tomb—just a canal-bank seat for the passer-by.*

Kavanagh was a regular at McDaid's pub in Harry Street (off Grafton Street), as was Brendan Behan, who could often be found there with his typewriter and a pint glass. In 1942, at an IRA commemoration at Glasnevin Cemetery in north Dublin, Behan snatched a revolver and fired in the direction of some Special Branch police; he was sentenced to 14 years—one for every yard he missed them by, his father, Stephen, remarked dryly. Sent to Mountjoy Gaol, where he spent six years, Behan came away with material for his play *The Quare Fellow,* first performed in 1954. When the 41-year-old writer died in 1964, Dublin waked him with one of the largest funerals Ireland has ever seen.

Continue on Baggot Street over the Grand Canal and you're in the crisply starched Victorian suburb of **Ballsbridge**, home of the Royal Dublin Society Showgrounds, where the Dublin Horse Show attracts the best of the equestrian set each August.

Follow the canal west about one kilometre (half a mile) and turn up Charlemont Street. **An Béal Bocht** is an unpretentious little pub, with music nightly and a more or less permanent engagement of its namesake, Flann O'Brien's deliriously mordant play, whose name translates as *The Poor Mouth.*

Temple Bar and Points West

The **Temple Bar** district lies west of the Bank of Ireland, between the river and Dame and Lord Edward streets. This self-consciously hip warren of cobblestone streets—full of galleries, theatres, boutiques, pubs and intimate restaurants—is being assiduously marketed as Dublin's answer to the Left Bank. The lively quarter was the backdrop for some scenes in *The Commitments* and *Far and Away.* From Aston Quay, the lacy steel arch across the Liffey is the **Ha'penny Bridge**, so named for the toll pedestrians were formerly charged to cross it.

Dublin Castle, dating from King John's first Dublin court around 1204, continued as the epicentre of British rule until being handed over to the Irish provisional government in 1922. In 1591, Red Hugh O'Donnell escaped from the still-extant Record Tower, where he'd been imprisoned on Queen Elizabeth's orders (see page 245). Bram Stoker, the author of *Dracula,* moiled as a clerk here for ten years in the 19th century. The castle is used today for presidential inaugurations and other state ceremonies. The guided tour is worth taking for a look at the sumptuously appointed State Apartments, former residence of the English viceroys.

A short walk along Lord Edward Street is Protestant **Christ Church Cathedral**. Dublin's Norman conqueror Strongbow demolished the 11th-century Viking wooden church on this site and began construction of this massive stone edifice, which took some 70 years to complete. Strongbow's tomb, marked with the black-stone effigy of a knight, lies in the south aisle.

The area between Christ Church and the Liffey was the location of the original Viking settlement of Dyfflin (from the Irish Dubh Linn, meaning "Dark Pool"). Excavations during the 1960s and '70s revealed thousand-year-old quays, houses, streets and an abundance of minutiae illustrating daily Dublin life in the ninth to 11th centuries. (Many of the artifacts are displayed at the National Museum.)

Georgian doorway, Dublin

Before the archaeological work could be completed, however, Dublin City Corporation destroyed the site by putting up its two enormous office buildings at Wood Quay, despite loud protests.

To the south along Nicholas and Patrick streets is august **St. Patrick's Cathedral**, Ireland's largest church, founded in 1191 and now the national cathedral of the Church of Ireland. The interior, with its soaring nave enveloping a great volume of luminous air, is awe-inspiring. Dublin's foremost citizen, Jonathan Swift, was born within the sound of its bells at Werburgh and Ship streets in 1667. Swift had hoped for an English bishopric but instead served the last 32 years of his life as dean of St. Patrick's from 1713 to 1745. The desk at which he wrote his brilliant satire, *Gulliver's Travels,* is preserved here, along with other memorabilia. Swift is interred within the church, in repose now "where savage indignation can no longer rend his heart".

The choirs of both St. Patrick's and Christ Church blended their voices on 13 April 1742 to perform a new work by the visiting composer George Frideric Handel. Handel had come to Dublin for a respite from the savaging London critics, and he brought with him a massive 256-page score, an oratorio for orchestra and choir. The venue for its première was Neal's Music Hall (now a steelworks) in Fishamble Street, just a shout away from the cathedrals. In order to accommodate a larger audience, the notice for the event requested "that the ladies come without their hoops, and the men without their swords". From the harpsichord, Handel himself conducted, and he found the audience's warm reception to the first performance of his *Messiah* a refreshing turnabout.

The old residential area west of St. Pat's is known as **The Liberties**, because it lay outside the medieval city's jurisdiction. In the late 17th century, Huguenots fleeing religious persecution in France found asylum here and established a flourishing local textile industry. Dublin's oldest watering hole, the **Brazen Head**, is here in Bridge Street. In the 1790s, this was a favorite locale for the furtive meetings of the United Irishmen Wolfe Tone and Lord Edward Fitz-Gerald, and later for Robert Emmet, leader of the hopeless 1803 insurrection. The present inn was chartered in 1688, but a tavern of some sort has stood at this site since probably the 12th century.

A walk west along Thomas and James streets takes you to the enormous **Guinness Brewery**. It is not open to the public, but the adjacent Guinness Hop Store exhibition centre in Crane Street is. The story goes that, in 1759, a young brewer named Arthur Guinness accidentally scorched a batch of barley; he gave away the resulting dark beer for free, thinking it worthless. The next day his customers were back, asking for more, and a steadfast following was born. In the 19th century, Dublin could boast 55 breweries; Guinness,

Europe's largest brewer, is the very last of them. Guinness stout—black as bogwater, with a blond head like spindrift and creamy as custard—is something of an acquired taste, but a taste worth acquiring, as many will attest. Try it for free at the Hop Store.

Farther west—but still within reasonable walking distance of the city—is **Kilmainham Hospital**, a splendid neo-classical building founded in 1680 by James Butler, duke of Ormonde, as a home for pensioner soldiers. Extensively restored and reopened in 1985, it now houses the National Centre for Culture and the Arts and hosts travelling exhibits, concerts and other performances.

Cheerless **Kilmainham Gaol** was erected in 1796, just in time to hold rebels captured in the Rising of 1798 and subsequent generations of recalcitrant Irishmen. The crumbling prison is now open as a grim but fascinating and strangely moving museum. The roll call of inmates reads like a who's who of Irish independence: bold Robert Emmet, Charles Stewart Parnell, Countess Markievicz, Michael Collins and the leaders of the 1916 Easter Rising. Its last prisoner, Eamon de Valera, later became prime minister and president of Ireland.

Between 3 and 12 May 1916, James Connolly, Patrick Pearse, Thomas Clarke and 12 others involved in the Easter Rising were led out into the stone-breakers yard and executed by firing squad. Connolly, severely wounded during the fighting, had to be brought from hospital and strapped in a chair for his execution. Seventy-five others had their death sentences commuted to prison terms. The Irish public had almost universally condemned the Easter rebellion, but the leaders' brave deaths made martyrs of them and galvanized Irish sentiment into revulsion against the harshness of British rule. Yeats wrote soon afterward:

> *We know their dream; enough*
> *To know they dreamed and are dead;*
> *And what if excess of love*
> *Bewildered them till they died?*
>
> *I write it out in a verse—*
> *MacDonagh and MacBride*
> *And Connolly and Pearse*
> *Now and in time to be,*
> *Wherever green is worn,*
> *Are changed, changed utterly:*
> *A terrible beauty is born.*

Entertainment

Again, the best source of information on music, art, theatre and other happenings is *In Dublin* magazine, published weekly.

In 1904 Lady Gregory and W.B. Yeats opened the **Abbey Theatre**, Lower Abbey Street, as an outlet for contemporary indigenous drama. The Abbey's boards have seen the première performances of such works as *The Playboy of the Western World* and *The Plough and the Stars*—both of which provoked riots from their offended audiences. The old Abbey burned down in 1951; the new building, opened in 1966, also houses the **Peacock Theatre**, which concentrates on more experimental works.

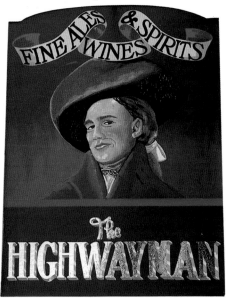

The **Gate Theatre**, in Parnell Square, was established in 1928 as an international counter-weight to the more Irish-focused Abbey. Dublin's last two 19th-century playhouses, the **Gaiety**, South King Street, and the **Olympia**, in Dame Street, offer a mixed bill of musicals, comedy, drama, opera, concerts and revues. If you're after Irish plays, don't overlook the bare-bones but earnest **Players Theatre** in Trinity College, which often puts on afternoons of Beckett, Yeats, Synge and other warhorses.

The **Project Arts Theatre**, 39 East Essex Street, and the **New Eblana Theatre**, in the basement of Busarus (central bus station), are good venues for contemporary and avant-garde plays.

Central Dublin has over a dozen cinemas, the majority of them clustered on O'Connell and Abbey streets. Disappointingly, they serve up mostly reheated American pabulum, the latest multimillion-dollar mediocrities, though there's the occasional Irish production and the odd import from Europe now and then.

As everywhere else in Ireland, the public house is the centre of social life in Dublin. A dedicated study of Dublin's pubs would take most of a lifetime and probably a liver transplant to carry out successfully. At last count there were over 800, some of them modern, fluorescent-light-and-plastic variety, some cozy and determinedly old-fashioned, and all manner in between.

Ryan's, west of the city centre near Heuston Station, is a wonderfully traditional old place with snugs (private booths) and lots of polished brass and mahogany, hardly changed since its last remodelling—in 1896. Slattery's in Capel Street is nothing fancy, but there's usually some music on the upper floor and all-caution-to-the-wind set dancing downstairs. Hughes's, in Chancery Street behind the Four Courts, is a fine old establishment with a comfortable snug hosting traditional sessions nightly and regular set dancing. Just across the Liffey, the

Dubliners in St. Stephen's Green

Merchant in Bridge Street is also popular for set dancing.

Characterful old **Mulligan's**, in Poolbeg Street since 1782, claims the subjective but nonetheless prestigious honour of pulling the tastiest pint of Guinness in the city. **O'Donoghue's** in Merrion Row has a reputation for ballad sessions of a high calibre. Victorian-era **Doheny and Nesbitt's**, Lower Baggot Street, is the haunt of Ireland's fourth estate, the ladies and gentlemen of the press; likewise **Doyle's**, in Fleet Street. One of the most opulent old watering holes is **Long Hall**, 51 South Great George's Street, with traditional music and acres of mirrors. Pilgrims on the trail of Leopold Bloom frequently stop in at literary-minded **Burton's** (the Bailey of *Ulysses*), Duke Street, where the door of Molly and Leopold's No. 7 Eccles Street home is enshrined, and **Davy Byrne's** across the street, which sells some 500 Gorgonzola sandwiches to hungry Joyceans every Bloomsday, the 16th of June.

The **Rock Garden** in Temple Bar and the **Pink Elephant**, South Frederick Street, are two nightclubs currently in vogue. **Whelan's**, at 25 Wexford Street, is good for blues, roots rock and even a hint of trad.

Saving Irish Country Houses

The Irish Georgian Society was formed in 1958 to work for the preservation of Ireland's architectural heritage, with particular reference to the Georgian period. Its efforts in rescue and repair work have helped save many beautiful and historic buildings that were abandoned to the mercy of wind and weather.

Among the prominent successes of the Irish Georgian Society are Tailor's Hall and St. Catherine's Church in Dublin, the Damer House in County Tipperary and Doneraile Court and Riverstown House in County Cork. When the latter was restored by the society and opened to the public in 1966, it became the third house in the Republic to open its doors to visitors on a regular basis. Rescue operations have also been carried out on the O'Callaghan Mausoleum in Shanrahan graveyard, County Tipperary, which houses a grandiose monument carved by David Sheehan in 1742. Numerous follies, gateways, columns, temples, funereal monuments and chapels around Ireland have also benefited from society efforts.

The society's foremost achievement has been the saving of Castletown, a magnificent Palladian house in County Kildare, which for 16 years served as the society's headquarters, and to which members enjoy free access. Castletown was the first great house open to the public in the Dublin area. The Historic Irish Tourist Houses and Gardens Association (HITHA), recently renamed Irish Heritage Properties, was born there, as was the Festival of Music in Great Irish Houses, which takes place in June each year. The house is now owned and run by an independent body, the Castletown Foundation.

Funds are raised by chapters in the United Kingdom and the United States, as well as in Ireland. The Samuel H. Kress Foundation has been a most generous contributor. The society works with Aer Lingus on a scheme for U.S. museum members to visit Ireland to see the art and architecture of the Georgian era, and a per capita donation is incorporated into the cost of the tour. The Scalamandre fabric and wallpaper company of New York and the Kindel furniture company of Michigan have both developed an Irish Georgian line; and a percentage of their sales will help further the society's restoration work in Ireland.

The society has always believed that State involvement in the saving of the Irish heritage will only come about through tourism. For more information about society activities and membership, write: The Irish Georgian Society, 42 Merrion Square, Dublin 2, Ireland.

—Desmond Guinness

(above) Ashford Castle, built in 1870 by Sir Arthur Guinness, stands at the head of the Lough Corrib. (below) Powerscourt suffered a disastrous fire in 1974 and is now a ruin.

The walls of the saloon at Russborough are covered in wine-red cut Genovese velvet.
Inlaid wood floors are seldom found in Ireland.

(above) The long gallery at Castletown. Three vast Venetian chandeliers were bought for the room; the colours in the glass are echoed in the ceiling.

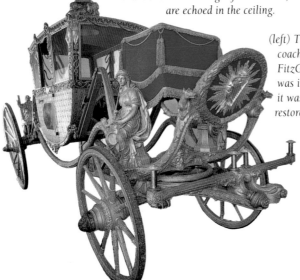

(left) The Lord Chancellor's coach, made for 'Black Jack' FitzGibbon in 1790, was itself black until it was recently restored.

County Wicklow

As a young man, John Millington Synge dumbfounded his strict Protestant family by announcing that he had "relinquished the Kingdom of God" and intended instead to seek the kingdom of Ireland. Synge turned his back on suburban Dublin, where he had grown up, and set about discovering the wildest parts of the country he could find. He started with County Wicklow. As he described in "Prelude":

> *Still south I went and west and south again,*
> *Through Wicklow from the morning till the night,*
> *And far from cities, and the sights of men,*
> *Lived with the sunshine, and the moon's delight.*

Wicklow remains a much-loved refuge for city-weary Dubliners, who can leave behind the jostling crowds of O'Connell Street and in 30 minutes be quite alone in what seems another country. The adjacent capital poses a striking contrast to Wicklow, whose lonesome glens, brooding conifer forests, crashing rivers and heathery moors wouldn't be out of place among the hinterlands of Kerry or Mayo.

On Luggala Estate, Wicklow Mountains

The county has its tamer side, too, with Victorian seaside resorts, patrician estates such as Russborough House and Powerscourt, and broad swaths of softly folded farmland. The Irish like to call it "the garden of Ireland".

But it's the Wicklow Mountains that really define the county. They're high by Irish standards, reaching their apex atop 926-metre (3,037 foot)-high Lugnaquillia, and in winter they get an occasional dusting of snow. The rounded peaks and intervening valleys make Wicklow superb walking country, served by a network of hostels and trails. The 130-kilometre (81-mile) Wicklow Way—running from south Dublin, along the eastern side of the Wicklow Mountains, to Clonegall in County Carlow, can be joined at various points along its route for hikes short or long.

The mountainy landscape, too, has always been full of hiding places, which for centuries sheltered some of Ireland's most tenacious rebels. Two families especially, the O'Byrnes and the O'Tooles, and guerrilla fighters such as Michael Dwyer, made themselves thorns in Dublin's side from Norman times right up to the early 19th century.

Northern Wicklow

One of the county's most familiar landmarks, the 503-metre (1,650-foot)-high cone of **Great Sugarloaf Mountain**, can be seen along much of eastern Wicklow, and even from Dublin, standing out proudly against the horizon. The mountain owes its distinctive profile to a cap of erosion-resistant granite, which prevented Ice Age glaciers from grinding it into a hillock. In summer the mountain is especially lovely, when yellow gorse and purple heather carpet the slopes.

Below Sugarloaf are the seaside towns of **Bray** and **Greystones**, popular with Dubliners for the safe swimming, strolls along the esplanade, and amusement arcades. The slightly worn-at-the-edges resort ambience of Bray was the setting for Neil Jordan's underrated film, *The Miracle*, made a couple of years before his 1992 *succès fou*, *The Crying Game*.

West of Bray are the pretty village of Enniskerry, in the valley of the River Glencullen, and the adjacent 56-square-kilometer (14,000-acre) estate and gardens of **Powerscourt**. In 1974, restoration of the opulent Georgian mansion at the heart of the estate had just been completed when the house was gutted by fire; the original furnishings, paintings, and priceless heirlooms were all lost. Today, Powerscourt House is just a shell, like some startlingly elaborate *trompe l'œil*. But the magnificent grounds are quite worth visiting. From the circular Triton Pool, with its spouting Neptune fountain, a broad walkway climbs through the formal gardens up a series of statue-flanked terraces to the house. The panorama from the upper terrace, looking out across the luxuriant valley to Sugarloaf Mountain, is as handsome a prospect as one could desire. A signposted, four-kilometre (2.5-mile) trail leads through the grounds to Powerscourt Waterfall, where the River Dargle cascades 90 metres (295 feet) into a boulder-strewn glen—the highest waterfall in Ireland and Great Britain.

To the south the Wicklow Mountains begin to build up. They're nearly uninhabited and remarkably empty here, though the area is within sight of the country's densest population centre. Here and there the black scars of turf-cutting stand out against the green bracken and white tufts of blooming bog cotton. Tracts of land here are leased out for their turf, and on weekends many Dubliners come down to dig and dry their season's "bogwood" around the desolate crossroads called the **Sally Gap**. Nearby the River Liffey—at first just an unprepossessing trickle of bogwater—begins its 130-kilometre (80-mile) wending to Dublin.

Through the gap runs the so-called **Military Road**. After the Rising of 1798, the English—frustrated at their inability to subdue the rebellious Wicklowmen—cut this road through the wilderness and built barracks along its route in order to finally control the region. Samuel Beckett described the road he remembered from his youth: "It leads to nothing any more. A few ruined forts, a few ruined dwellings. The sea is not far, just visible beyond the valleys dipping eastward, pale plinth as pale as the pale wall of the sky".

Actually, it leads to, and through, quite a lot of tremendous scenery. Stretching from the south Dublin suburb of Rathfarnum to Aghavannagh, the Military Road is still the only north-south artery through these mountains. From the forbidding country of the Sally Gap, the highway contours along the eastern side of **Glenmacnass**, a wide gorge with a waterfall spilling into one end, and continues on to the turnoff for Glendalough.

Glendalough

Glendalough, the "Valley of the Two Lakes" cradled in a hollow between steep, forest-cloaked mountains, is one of the loveliest and most important of Ireland's early monastic communities. St. Kevin, a scion of the royal house of Leinster, founded it in AD 520. He discovered here the serenity and solitude he'd been seeking but, according to legend, he was pursued by a beautiful, love-struck girl. Kevin—chaste fellow—fended her off with switches of stinging nettles

St. Kevin's Kitchen, Glendalough, Co. Wicklow

and finally pushed her into the lake to cool her ardour.

But the saint was not left in peace for long. His simple hermitage soon attracted disciples and grew into a monastic city which drew thousands of monks from all over Europe. Throughout the Middle Ages, Glendalough was renowned as one of the brightest centres of learning in Christendom. Like most Irish monasteries, Glendalough was plundered time and again by the Vikings. In 1398, the English came down from Dublin and burned the place, but the monks managed to salvage some of the buildings and remained until the 16th century, when Henry VIII decisively suppressed the Irish monasteries.

The ruins are extensive and quite evocative, and the setting further enhances their transcendent allure; if you've time or inclination to visit just one early Christian site in Ireland, consider Glendalough.

From the helpful visitor centre, you pass through the monastic city's crumbling gateway—the last of its kind—to the principal cluster of buildings east of the Lower Lake. The early ninth-century cathedral, Ireland's largest pre-Romanesque church, is full of inscribed grave slabs. A short walk away through the thicket of ponderous tombstones is the best-known and most enchanting structure at Glendalough—St. Kevin's Kitchen. There's nothing else in the country quite like this solid little barrel-vaulted church, with its round belfry poking up from the western gable. Its steeply pitched stone roof

Mr. Lanigan's School

The school-house, at Glendalough, was situated near the romantic river which flows between the wild scenery of Drumgoff and the seven Churches. It was a low, stone building, indifferently thatched; the whole interior consisting of one oblong room, floored with clay, and lighted by two or three windows, the panes of which were patched with old copy-books, or altogether supplanted by school slates. The walls had once been plastered and whitewashed, but now partook of that appearance of dilapidation which characterized the whole building. . . . Along each wall were placed a row of large stones, the one intended to furnish seats for the boys, the other for the girls, the decorum of Mr. Lanigan's establishment requiring that they should be kept apart. . . . The only chair in the whole establishment was that which was usually occupied by Mr. Lanigan himself, and a table appeared to be a luxury of which they were either ignorant or wholly regardless. . . .

The babble of a hundred voices, like the sound of a bee-hive, filled the house. Now and then, a school-boy, in frieze coat and corduroy trousers, with an ink-bottle dangling at his breast, a copy-book, slate, Voster, and 'reading-book', under one arm, and a sod of turf under the other, dropped in, and took his place upon the next unoccupied stone. A great boy, with a huge slate in his arms, stood in the centre of the apartment, making a list of all those who were guilty of any indecorum in the absence of 'the Masther'. Near the door, was a blazing turf fire, which the

Country school, 1845

sharp autumnal wind already rendered agreeable. In a corner behind the door lay a heap of fuel, formed by the contributions of all the schollars, each being obliged to bring one sod of turf every day, and having the privilege of sitting by the fire while his own sod was burning. Those who failed to pay their tribute of fuel sat cold and shivering the whole day long at the further end of the room, huddling together their bare and frost bitten toes, and casting a longing, envious eye toward the peristyle of well-marbled shins that surrounded the fire.

Full in the influence of a cherishing flame, was placed the hay-bottomed chair that supported the person of Mr. Henry Lanigan, when that great man presided in person in his rural seminary. On his right, lay a close bush of hazel, of astonishing size, the emblem of his authority and the instrument of castigation. Near this was a wooden 'sthroker', that is to say, a large rule of smooth and polished deal, used for 'sthroking' lines in copy-books, and also for 'sthroking' the palms of the refractory pupils. On the other side, lay a lofty heap of copy-books, which were left there by the boys and girls for the purpose of having their copies 'sot' by 'the Masther'.

—Gerald Griffin, The Rivals, 1830

is still intact after a thousand years, likewise the tiny adjacent sacristy. Close by is the 33-metre (108 foot)-high, nearly perfect round tower, which echoes the bell tower of St. Kevin's that together give the site its memorable profile.

Many other buildings and relics are spread about the two lakes; the pleasant walks through the larches and mossy oaks to find them make Glendalough worth a full day's exploration. Despite the frequently disgorging tour buses, there's a powerful serenity to this place.

The road past Glendalough (R756) continues to the west over the Wicklow Mountains to the village of Hollywood. From there, a traveller can loop back up to Dublin, turn south into County Carlow, or descend down onto the fertile green plains of County Kildare.

South to Arklow

Southwest from Glendalough, the Military Road carries on across **Glenmalure**. In this shadowy valley, bordered by sombre plantations of blue-green spruce, the Irish under Fiach MacHugh O'Byrne routed a force of Elizabethan troops in 1580, in a decisive victory that stalled English expansion in the district for a generation.

Synge used the valley as the setting for his play *In the Shadow of the Glen*, which is full of the place-names of Wicklow and the colourful language of

Irish country people. Synge later recollected one source of his inspiration:

> When I was writing In the Shadow of the Glen, I got more aid than any
> learning could have given me from a chink in the floor of the old Wicklow
> house where I was staying that let me hear what was being said by the
> servant girls in the kitchen.

The Military Road ends farther on at **Aghavannagh**, another wild glen
hemmed in by mountains in the heart of splendid tramping country.
Lugnaquillia, the highest mountain outside of County Kerry, overlooks
the head of the valley.

The River Avonbeg, which runs the length of Glenmalure, and the
Avonmore, flowing down from the Glenmacnass valley, merge in the **Vale of
Avoca**, a celebrated beauty spot. Near the confluence, Ireland's "national poet",
Thomas Moore, spent many an hour under a certain tree, composing songs
and poems while contemplating the scene below. In 1807, this "vale in whose
bosom the bright waters meet" inspired one of his best-known works, "The
Meeting of the Waters". Moore's tree is still there, just a stump now and rather
well picked over by souvenir hunters. At Avoca Handweavers, just outside the
village, visitors to Ireland's oldest mill can watch the weavers at work.

The road follows the well-tended farmland along the River Avoca to the
sea at the resort town of **Arklow**. Like the county town, Wicklow, farther
north, Arklow was an important east-coast port for the Vikings in the ninth
and tenth centuries; shipbuilders still ply their trade at the docks. The town's
nautical history is documented in the modest Maritime Museum on St. Mary's
Road. Arklow has an 18-hole golf course and two excellent beaches; other
good white-sand beaches stretch northward.

County Wexford

For those who see in the map of Ireland a dancing terrier or a recumbent lamb,
County Wexford is the stubby tail waggling insouciantly toward Britain. Like
neighbouring Waterford, its coast is warmed by the Gulf Stream, and Wexford
records more hours of sunshine than any other Irish county—for which the
tourism board delights in calling this the "Sunny Southeast".

Wexford and Carlow together formed Uí Chennselaig, a separate kingdom
and dominated for centuries by the MacMurrough clan. At its zenith, the
realm grew so powerful that its king audaciously laid siege to the English

mainland at Bristol in 1068, two years after William the Conqueror had whipped Harold at Hastings. It was the first, and last, such act of hubris. A century later, the wind of conquest would blow from the east, bringing with it Strongbow and his Norman mercenaries. They crossed the Irish Sea at the invitation of King Dermot MacMurrough, to bolster him in his squabble against the O'Conors, thereby opening the Pandora's box of English meddling that would plague the island for the next eight centuries.

The Norman knights who participated in the adventure were rewarded with tracts of fertile land throughout the southeast. In addition to the scores of castles built over the centuries, they also left behind surnames like Devereux and Roche, names still common around Wexford. The archaic dialect spoken by these families, known as "Yola"—from their word for "old"—survived as a local curiosity until the middle of the 19th century. Even today, some Yola words are still heard hereabouts, such as *neape* (turnip) and *stouk* (a truculent woman).

Wexford Town

The Vikings who settled at this spot beside the River Slaney in AD 850 named it Waesfjord, meaning "Muddy Harbour". They would rule for the next 350 years. With its eccentric web of narrow streets leading up from the long harbourside quays, the town's layout still bears the imprint of their 350-year occupation, much like that other Viking metropolis not far away, Waterford.

The town's most famous daughter was born in the Old Rectory in Main Street in 1826. Writing under the pseudonym of Speranza, Jane Francesca Elgee, later Lady Wilde (the mother of Oscar), gained some renown for her fairy stories, essays and Gothic tales, before her reputation was overshadowed by that of her remarkable son. The house, now a women's clothing store, stands at the northeast corner of the Bullring, the public square where the Normans enjoyed the bloody sport of bullbaiting. When Cromwell captured the town in 1649, the Bullring saw a far crueller sport: it became a slaughtering ground where 2,000 citizens of the town were put to death. The statue of an Irish pikeman in this market square commemorates the Rising of 1798.

The West Gate, a short walk away, is the only remnant of the five fortified gates which once guarded the town. Nearby, off Abbey Street, are the spare remains of 12th-century Selskar Abbey, where Henry II passed the season of Lent in 1172 repenting the murder of Thomas à Beckett.

On Crescent Quay, the caped, cutlass-wielding figure of John Barry gazes resolutely out across the harbour. This native son of Wexford, born at nearby Ballysampson in 1745, emigrated to the American colonies and founded the American navy during the Revolutionary War. In 1956, the U.S. repaid the favour with this statue.

At the turn of this century, in *Rambles in Eirinn*, an idiosyncratic memoir describing his bicycle journey around Ireland, William Bulfin described Wexford as "a town that works and prospers, and . . . has the look of a place that enjoys life and minds its business". That Wexfordians still know how to enjoy life is evinced by the spirited cultural scene, and by the fact that the town has around a hundred public houses—about one for every 120 thirsty souls.

Every October, the acclaimed Wexford Opera Festival draws a cosmopolitan, black-tie crowd to the 19th-century Theatre Royal. Since its inauguration in 1951, the program has catered to the musical gourmet, reviving neglected operatic delicacies rarely staged elsewhere, such as Bizet's *Pearl Fishers*. A fringe festival with plays, late-night cabarets and other events has sprouted up alongside the opera to keep up the *frisson*. The Wexford Arts Centre, in the former town hall, puts on a varied program of concerts, dance, drama and art exhibitions year-round.

A good place to help put the dizzying, 9,000-year sweep of Irish history in context is at **Ferrycarrig**, three kilometres (two miles) up the Slaney estuary from Wexford. The outdoor museum of the Irish National Heritage Park re-

creates the dwellings and milieu of life in Ireland from Neolithic ring-forts through the monastic and Viking eras and up to the Norman conquest.

The **Wexford Wildfowl Reserve**, in an area of tidal flats affectionately named the North Slobs, lies northeast of Wexford across the harbour. The reserve is an important wintering ground for Greenland white-fronted geese, Bewick's swans and other migrants. Lookout towers and viewing blinds have been set up. To the northeast at **Curracloe** is one of the county's many excellent east-coast beaches, backed by long stretches of grass-cloaked dunes.

Southern Wexford

As a working port, Wexford Town has been outstripped by busy **Rosslare Harbour** to the south, where ferry traffic for Wales and France comes and goes. A ten-kilometre (six-mile) scimitar of inviting flaxen sand curves along the bay between Rosslare Point and the harbour.

Over a dozen thatched cottages line the long main street shambling down to the harbour of **Kilmore Quay**, a neat fishing village on the county's south coast. The *Guillemot*, a floating maritime museum berthed in the harbour, is the last complete lightship—a sort of floating lighthouse—in the country. Nearby, a fine long beach arcs northwest from Forlorn Point.

From Kilmore Quay a boat can be chartered for the 45-minute ride out to the **Saltee Islands**, one of Ireland's richest bird sanctuaries, about eight kilometres (five miles) due south. Covered with grassy hillocks, wildflowers and bracken, the two islands are entirely uninhabited—except for the estimated three million puffins, cormorants, shearwaters, auks, kittiwakes, razorbills and scores of other species which nest here each spring and early summer. The islands were once the curious princedom of one self-crowned Michael the First, who erected a limestone throne on Great Saltee for himself and his heirs.

The long apostrophe of the **Hook Head Peninsula**, notched with good beaches and saturated with history, forms the eastern shore of Waterford Harbour. The lighthouse at the southern tip is believed to be the oldest extant in Europe; the tower is over 700 years old, but a navigational light has burned here at least twice that long. On the headland at Baginbun, on the peninsula's east side, the invading Welsh and Normans gained a crucial toehold. A small advance guard, sent by Strongbow to consolidate recent Norman gains, landed here in 1169. They hastily threw up a defensive earthwork and sheltered behind it with a herd of cattle. When attacked, they stampeded the cattle, flustering the enemy, and then charged. No quarter was asked or given, and when the Normans captured 70 Waterford men, they first broke their limbs, then hurled them over the cliffs. So an old rhyme runs:

At the creek of Baginbun
Ireland was lost and won.

In August of the following year, Strongbow himself arrived with 200 knights and a thousand soldiers. Referring to Hook Head and to a hamlet across the harbour, the earl vowed to capture Waterford "by Hook or by Crooke".

From the attractive bayside village of **Arthurstown**, near the car ferry crossing to Waterford, the secondary road runs north to **Dunbrody Abbey**. The ruins of this Cistercian monastery, built in the early 13th century, make a sublimely romantic old pile, dappled with ivy but still possessing an ineffable sense of dignity and exaltation.

The **John F. Kennedy Park and Arboretum** near Dunganstown, the birth-place of the president's great-grandfather, spreads over on the southern slopes of Slieve Coillte. Some 4,500 varieties of temperate trees and shrubs from around the world grow among the gardens and forests here. To the north, the medieval streets of **New Ross** rise steeply from the winding River Barrow. From here, highways radiate out to Waterford, Kilkenny, Carlow and northern Wexford.

Enniscorthy and Thereabouts

In the centre of the county, one of Wexford's most appealing towns, **Enniscorthy**, climbs the hills along both banks of the River Slaney. Here the doomed Rising of 1798 came to its lamentable end. In May of 1798, the ranks of the United Irishmen had been infiltrated top to bottom with informers. Just days before their planned general uprising, most of the society's leaders were betrayed and arrested. Rebellions nonetheless broke out spasmodically, mainly in Ulster, where it was an almost exclusively Protestant movement, and in Wexford, where Catholic animosity against the county's Protestant settlers ran high. Led by a priest named John Murphy, the doomed insurrection smouldered longer than elsewhere before it was finally snuffed out, but the lofty ideals of the United Irishmen quickly degenerated into a sectarian bloodbath of Catholics against Protestants.

Father Murphy's peasant army, armed mainly with pitchforks and pikes, captured Enniscorthy in late May, then took Wexford Town. After a rebuff at

New Ross, they retreated to Vinegar Hill, just east of Enniscorthy, where they camped around the windmill whose stump still stands at the summit. On 21 June, the Crown forces under General Lake, supported by artillery, charged the hill and overran the rebels. Many were killed, and Enniscorthy was torched. The Rising, after less than three months, was dead.

The events of that year inspired sheaves of nationalistic ballads, among them "The Rising of the Moon", "Bold Fenian Men", "The Boys of Wexford" and "Boolavogue", which recalls:

*At Vinegar Hill o'er the pleasant Slaney, our heroes vainly stood back to back
And the Yeos of Tullow took Father Murphy, and burnt his body upon the rack.*

Muskets, cannonballs and other relics from the Battle of Vinegar Hill are displayed at the Wexford County Museum, housed in the thoroughly restored Enniscorthy Castle. This monumental 16th-century tower house, built on the foundations of a 13th-century Norman fortress, was leased briefly to the poet Edmund Spenser.

Five kilometres (three miles) north of Enniscorthy the highway divides. The northwest road (N80) continues along the River Slaney through hilly farm country hedged with gorse and over the Blackstairs Mountains into Carlow. The northeast road (N11) follows the River Bann, meeting the coast at Arklow and continuing up to Dublin; en route is the village of **Ferns**. There's not much to it now, apart from the ruined Augustinian abbey and partially restored 13th-century castle to hint at its former glory, but in its heyday Dermot MacMurrough made Ferns the capital of his kingdom of Leinster.

County Kilkenny

For a thousand years, until the arrival of Strongbow in the 12th century, the area that's now County Kilkenny formed the heart of an independent Gaelic kingdom called Ossory. For all their ruthlessness in conquest, the Anglo-Normans were nonetheless enthusiastic supporters of the church, and under their patronage the county saw a flurry of ecclesiastical construction, notably at Kilkenny City, Jerpoint Abbey and Kells.

Visiting the gentle, well-tended valleys of the Nore and the Barrow today, it's easy to see why these foreigners so coveted the rich farmlands of southeastern Ireland. Even as they left their mark here, the country in its turn moulded the newcomers. The Normans were quick to intermarry with the natives and adopt local customs, becoming, in the oft-used description, "more Irish than the Irish"—to the great consternation of the English monarchs.

Oliver Goldsmith, writing 500 years later, described the transition perfectly: "The natives are peculiarly remarkable for the gaiety and levity of their dispositions; the English, transplanted there, in time lose their melancholy and serious air, and become gay and thoughtless, more fond of pleasure and less addicted to reasoning".

And they tended in time, Goldsmith might have added, to ally themselves with the Irish while losing their loyalty to England. Periodic attempts were made to stem the intermingling of the races, culminating in the 1366 edicts of the Irish Parliament at Kilkenny, forbidding "the English born in Ireland" from speaking Irish, wearing Irish clothes and hairstyles, from marrying Irish women and even from playing the national sport of hurling. The edicts applied to the native Irish as well, barring them from living within a walled Anglo town. By that time, however, the Anglo–Normans had been so subtly assimilated that enforcement of the laws was well-nigh impracticable, and they went largely unheeded.

Kilkenny came to the fore again in 1641, when the foremost Gaelic and "old English" families attempted to unite themselves in common defence. This Confederation of Kilkenny declared the town to be the capital of an independent Ireland, minted its own coinage, raised an army and received ambassadors. By 1648, however, the uneasy alliance had dissolved in factional squabbling, and Cromwell ravaged the land, untrammelled by any unified opposition. Kilkenny Town would fall to him in March 1650, after a five-day siege.

Kilkenny City

Theobald Fitzwalter, the progenitor of Kilkenny's ruling family, landed in Ireland with King Henry II's expedition in 1171. Six years later, he was appointed to the high office of chief butler of Ireland. The family eventually adopted "Butler" as its surname, and Theobald's descendants became the earls of Ormonde. In 1391, James Butler acquired Kilkenny Castle and made the town his capital.

Today, delightful Kilkenny is Ireland's most generously preserved medieval town, a fact not lost on the town council and local tourism board. They have tastefully exploited the city's allure to good advantage and positioned

Kilkenny to become one of the country's most popular draws. Neon, for example, has been outlawed from the old districts, and many of the good burghers of Kilkenny have graced their shops with lovely, hand-painted signs.

The Old World feeling is enhanced by the intact original street plan. Atmospheric narrow lanes called "slips" lead left and right off High Street and seem little changed over the centuries. If you follow one of these passages east you'll connect with St. Kieran's Street and find yourself at the **Kyteler's Inn**. This 14th-century residence, the oldest in Kilkenny, now houses a fine restaurant and wine bar, but in 1324 it was the home of Dame Alice Kyteler.

In addition to her exceptionally poor luck with husbands—four in a row died of mysterious causes—this innkeeper and moneylender was accused by the Bishop de Ledrade of practising the black arts of witchcraft. In the stone cellar, the bishop charged, she sacrificed black cocks to the Devil, brewing their entrails in foul potions spiced with the hair and nails of unbaptized children.

With the aid of powerful friends, Alice fled before the death sentence fell, never to be heard from again. Her maidservant Petronilla, however, was less fortunate. The pious bishop, deprived of his prize, took consolation in burning her at the stake in the lady's place.

Economic and political control of medieval Kilkenny came to be monopolized by ten Norman families. One family's Tudor-period home, the meticulously restored **Rothe House**, built in 1594 around interconnecting cobbled courtyards, still stands in Parliament Street. It's the headquarters of the Kilkenny Archaeological Society and houses its collection as well as a genealogical-study centre, but the building is fascinating in its own right for its architectural details, in particular the complex web of hand-hewn roofing timbers, assembled without a nail.

At the top of High Street is the **Tholsel**, Kilkenny's distinctive City Hall, built in 1761 and crowned by a three-tiered clock tower. Around the corner in Rose Inn Street is another fine Tudor survivor, the **Shee Alms House**, established in 1582 by Sir Richard Shee to accommodate "12 poor persons in the city". It now accommodates the Tourist Information Centre.

The old town is bracketed by castle and cathedral—magnificent stone bookends which symbolize the twin spheres of Irish history. In the southeast, **Kilkenny Castle**—said to be the most-visited historic building in Ireland—towers on a hillock above the River Nore. Like all the town's eminent buildings, it was constructed from the locally quarried grey limestone which the polishing hands of passersby transform over time into "marble stones as black as ink", in the words of a well-loved ballad. Thus has Kilkenny come to be called the Marble City.

Strongbow built the original fortress here, which was replaced by a stone castle in 1204. James Butler, the third earl of Ormonde, acquired the place in 1391, making Kilkenny his capital. From 1642 to 1648, the castle was also headquarters of the short-lived Kilkenny Confederation, where the great Gaelic and Anglo-Irish families convened to plot their survival. The castle has been much enlarged and rebuilt over the years, and Butler's descendants continued to live in it until 1935. In the 1960s they handed over the castle and grounds to the people of Kilkenny. Join the insightful castle tour, and afterward take tea or luncheon amidst the gleaming copper pots in the castle scullery.

Opposite the castle, in the former stables and coach house, is the tony **Kilkenny Design Centre**, a complex of artisans' studios and retail shops geared toward the tourist trade.

At the north end of town is the site of the original monastic settlement, founded by St. Canice in the sixth century. Canice's saintly scholars may have put their faith in God, but they nevertheless kept a keen eye on the horizon from their 31-metre (100-foot)-high tower, the sole remnant from pre-Norman times. For a vertiginous, 360-degree view over the rooftops of Kilkenny, follow their footsteps up the wooden stairs which corkscrew to the top, from which you too can scan the Nore Valley for Vikings.

In the 13th century, the grand **St. Canice's Cathedral** was erected in the tower's shadow. Entirely restored and still very much a functioning house of worship, it has remained Protestant since 1650, the year Cromwell stabled his horse within. It's one of Ireland's most beautiful cathedrals, with a number of fine carved tombs inside, including some of the eminent Butler family. In the peaceful churchyard outside, bees hum a requiem over the lichen-stained gravestones.

Close by, in Abbey Street, the so-called **Black Abbey** was founded for the Dominican order in 1225 by Strongbow's successor. In 1348–49, when the Black Death stalked the land, a friar at the abbey recorded the names of the victims, noting that not a family in Kilkenny had lost fewer than two members to the plague. His account grimly concluded with the notation: "I leave parchment to carry out the work if perchance any man survives . . ." His own name then was entered on the rolls, written in a different hand.

In Kilkenny, you're not likely to go hungry or thirsty, or lack for an evening's "crack" (good time). Good restaurants and pubs are plentiful. One of the nicest pubs around is Tynan's Bridge House Bar, close to John's Bridge, which has survived with all its mirrors, brass fittings and other Edwardian appointments intact. For a session of traditional music with your pint, try Peig's or Flannery's, both on John Street, or Caisleán Uí Cuain on High Street.

"Guinness is good for you".

On Parliament Street, cozy John Cleere's pub hosts a Monday-night session and offers plays staged by local actors in the small back-room theatre.

Many consider the end-of-August **Kilkenny Arts Week** to be one of Ireland's most exciting cultural festivals. Classical and traditional music are mainstays, along with readings and art exhibits. The cathedral and castle are main venues.

Hurling is an ancient and quintessentially Irish sport that has been played since at least the first century AD, when it was mentioned in the epic *Cattle Raid of Cooley*. Something like lacrosse and field hockey, hurling moves fast and furious as teams try to slap a small leather ball between the opponents' goalposts using a flared wooden stick called a hurley or *camán*. Kilkenny is justifiably proud of its hurling team, which over the years has captured some two dozen national championships. Check the weekly *Kilkenny People* for match schedules at Nowlan Park.

Around the County

Northeast of Kilkenny on the Dublin road (N78), **Castlecomer** sits in the middle of Ireland's largest coal-mining area, noted for its smokeless hard anthracite. The many Welsh miners brought over to work the seams explains the preponderance of families hereabout named Walsh. The ragtag rebels of 1798 captured the town on 24 June. As they steadied themselves to face the well-drilled royal troops, the English commander, General Asgill, inexplicably withdrew his army, leaving the Irish to roar with derision and self-congratulations, having won the day without firing a shot.

The farmlands of southern County Laois (pronounced "leash") lie to the north. This area was heavily settled by the English in the reign of Queen Mary (mid-16th century), when these lands were wrested from the "wild Irish" and dubbed Queen's County in her honour.

Gowran, 13 kilometres (eight miles) east of Kilkenny, was once the seat of the kings of Ossory. It's best known now for the sport of kings, horse racing, held throughout most of the year. In the ruined Collegiate Church of St. Mary are buried several members of the powerful Butler family. Their monuments include massive tomb chests carved with the effigies of armoured knights and courtly ladies.

The Dublin-Waterford highway (N9) crosses the River Nore at the busy market centre of Thomastown. One of the great ecclesiastical treasures of medieval Ireland, lovingly preserved **Jerpoint Abbey**, lies three kilometres (two miles) to the southwest. This Cistercian establishment, built and amended over the centuries in a melange of styles, was founded in 1158 by Donal MacGiollaPhadruig, king of Ossory. In 1387, the abbot of Jerpoint incurred a heavy fine for accepting Irish monks into his community—a flagrant breach of the rigorous apartheid laws set out by the Kilkenny statutes. What remains of the elegant, partially restored monastery are the chapterhouse (which holds the visitor centre), a crenellated square tower and fragments of cloisters. On the flat-sided columns of the cloisters, don't miss the charming, full-length relief carvings which show off the medieval costumes in startling detail. Inside the church are more wonderful carved figures on the 13th- to 16th-century tombs; particularly fine are the two richly garbed fellows known as the Weepers, flanking a praying angel, the three of them posed with the most inscrutable of smiles.

To the east is **Graiguenamanagh** (pronounced "gregna-mun-NAW", more or less), a pleasant little market town of narrow streets in the sylvan valley of the River Barrow, which forms Kilkenny's border with Carlow and Wexford. Duiske Abbey, perforated by numerous original lancet windows, has been restored to its original 13th-century splendour and continues to be used as the parish church. The stark simplicity of the white-plastered interior belies the great age of its Gothic design, making the church appear quite modern in its clean lines.

At **Inishtioge**, the Kilkenny–New Ross road (R700) crosses one of the comeliest stretches of the Nore, flowing here through a deep-cut valley thick with trees. The square of this pretty village is planted with lime trees and bounded by both Catholic and Protestant churches. It's just a short walk to the riverside, a placid site for picnicking beside the graceful, ten-arched stone bridge.

County Waterford

In the green and hilly county of Waterford, three of the southeast's great rivers —the Nore, the Barrow and the Suir—meet and mingle in Waterford Harbour. Here, too, the three mighty streams of Irish history—Celtic, Viking and Norman—violently converged and forged a new amalgam that would become the modern Irish.

Near the place which the ancient Gaelic *Book of Invasions* called the "sweet confluence of waters", the Vikings founded Vadrefjord around AD 850. This settlement on a superb natural harbour was perfectly sited for the Norsemen's raiding forays to the fertile valleys upriver, and Waterford in those early days grew in significance to rival Dublin. In the 16th and 17th centuries, the town capitalized on its enviable position, developing strong trading links with Europe and even North America.

The opportunistic earl of Pembroke (Strongbow), in alliance with King Dermot MacMurrough of Leinster, besieged Waterford for three days in 1170. After the town succumbed, he wedded MacMurrough's daughter Aoife there and so cemented the Normans' position in Ireland.

The original Gaelic name for the region was Cuan-na-groith, "Haven of the Sun", which reflects southeastern Ireland's relatively balmy climate. The warm waters of the Gulf Stream brush along the Waterford coast, further tempering local conditions, which are exploited at Tramore, Dunmore East and other beach resorts. The western end of Waterford pushes up against the Knockmealdown Mountains, while the Comeraghs and Monavullaghs lie across the middle of the county.

Waterford City

Over the years the name of Waterford has grown nearly synonymous with its most famous export—handmade crystal. Fine glassware was first produced in Waterford in 1783, but heavy English duties killed the industry in the 1850s. Commercial glass-making resumed in 1947, and today the **Waterford Glass Factory**, three kilometres (two miles) southwest of the city centre on the Cork road (N25), ships its splendid wares all over the world. The United States is its biggest customer. Free weekday tours cover each step of production, from mixing the raw ingredients of silica sand, potash and lead to blowing and hand-cutting the pieces; no glass is sold at the factory, however. The tour must be prebooked, either through the Tourist Office or by calling 051-73311.

This busy port city of about 40,000 people is the commercial centre of the southeast. Waterford's riverfront, which can be viewed in a single sweep from Ignatius Rice Bridge, once boasted "the noblest quays in Europe", but some of the riverside warehouses now look a bit down at the heel. Beyond them, however, is a rather lively and genteel town centre.

A number of elegant Georgian relics have survived along O'Connell/Great George's streets and Parnell Street/the Mall. Two of the treasures on the Mall are the Municipal Theatre and Theatre Royal; the latter stages the popular Waterford Light Opera Festival each September. From about 1770 to 1800, the talented local architect John Roberts must hardly have left his drawing board, for most of Waterford's important edifices sprang from his efforts during that period. The aristocratic Chamber of Commerce in Great George's Street, with its beautiful, cantilevered oval staircase and fine plasterwork, is his design. So is the City Hall, on the Mall, which contains an enormous crystal chandelier and other early Waterford creations. Roberts also designed the opulent Holy Trinity Cathedral, along Quay Parade, and the Protestant Christ Church Cathedral, the latter modelled on a design by Christopher Wren. Among the monuments inside Christ Church is the macabre tomb of one James Rice, who died in 1469: the unusual effigy depicts Rice not in the placid aspect of eternal repose, but as a decaying carcass hosting all manner of crawling things.

Intermingled with the 18th-century architecture, something of the town's medieval flavour survives in its narrow lanes, especially Lady Lane, off Upper Barronstrand Street near Holy Trinity Cathedral. Portions of the old city walls and towers remain in Castle Street, Railway Square, Patrick Street and Jenkins Lane.

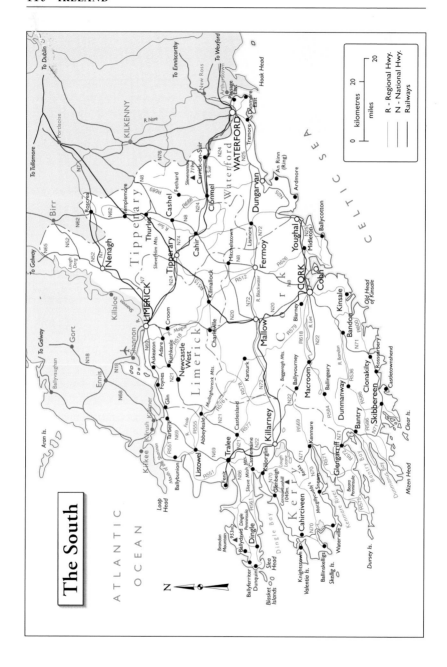

The South

But the showpiece of medieval Waterford is **Reginald's Tower**. Construction of this heavy circular tower at the foot of The Mall near the river is credited to the Viking chief Ragnvald, who strengthened the town in 1003. Strongbow and Aoife took their nuptial vows in the tower, and Prince John, the playboy son of Henry II, caroused here for eight months in 1185.

In 1650, Cromwell tried and failed to capture the tower; his determined general, Henry Ireton, returned later, however, and Waterford capitulated. Reginald's Tower has subsequently housed a mint, a prison and a barracks, and now it's the Civic Museum, containing the city's original charters, maritime memorabilia and other exhibits illustrating Waterford's long history.

Along the Coast

Passage East, a characterful little village on Waterford Harbour, is the ferry port for traffic between Waterford and Wexford. This is where Strongbow landed in 1170, and where King Henry II and 4,000 men arrived a year later to keep him in line.

South of Waterford City are two coastal resorts. Looking out across Waterford Harbour toward the long peninsula of Hook Head, **Dunmore East** serves the well-heeled holiday crowd. Its little harbour nestles among the red sandstone headlands lined with vacation cottages. One 19th-century writer loftily described it as "a fashionable, aristocratic neighborhood which verily looks down on all watering places along the southern coasts". With a long crescent of sand on its own little namesake bay to the west, **Tramore** caters more to the *hoi polloi*. Farther west, between sea cliffs noisy with the cries of kittiwakes and brightened in summer with campions and sea pinks, Annestown and Bunmahon also have good beaches.

Dungarvan, the county's main coastal town, sits in a bowl of low hills beside broad Dungarvan Harbour. It's a popular deep-sea fishing centre. The surrounding area is still known as the Decies, after the Celtic tribe which held sway here from the third century until the coming of the Danes.

Around the bay, **An Rinn** (or Ring or Ringville), is a tiny pocket of about 800 Irish speakers, an anomaly surviving deep within Ireland's Anglicized southeast long after Gaelic has disappeared from the rest of the region. Traditional music and dance still thrive hereabouts as well; Murray's, Mooney's and the Tigh an Cheoil pubs have regular sessions.

The little resort village of **Ardmore** surveys a fine sandy bay southwest of Dungarvan. St. Declan arrived at this place early in the fifth century, introducing the Gospel to Ireland when Patrick was yet a mere strip of a lad. Miracles must have come easier in those days than now, for it's said that the solitary glacial boulder near the shore floated from Rome in the wake of

A Conversation

Walking to Father Keane's to invite him to dinner, I stopped to look at the calves bunched around an empty feeding trough. Seeing me, they came crowding to the gate, all sizes from those born in early Spring to those born a few weeks ago.

"Would you like to buy one?" A heavyset man in gum boots had come up behind. He wore a cap, and a pipe stuck out from his impassive face. Was his question a way of chastising me for being on his property and looking at his chattels? "You can have one for twenty dollars." Thinking it best to answer seriously I explained I was visiting and had no place for a calf. But it was only his way of opening a conversation.

His name was Patrick Cunningham; he was an attractive man with the masculinity that comes from a man's strength being a necessity to existence. I asked him about his farm. He had eighty acres, split into sections, and grew oats and barley for feed, and potatoes for sale and for home use, and sometimes sugar beets. The fresh milk from his cows is picked up morning and evening across the road from a wooden stand raised to the height of the truck for easy transfer. Stands line the road going by the farms with the tall aluminum milk cans looking like silver chimney pots.

A face appeared in the privet beside us, a body followed, and the whole dropped onto the stone wall. Another small white face parted the greenery and remained, staring. Separate arms and legs began to appear from around the pillar on top of the wall. Silently, entire people formed a row on my right and now the man noticed them.

"Get off the wall; get back there, Gerald; into the house, off with you." The horde disappeared at the flash of his hand.

"There are ten of them," he said. "My wife's away for the day and I'm minding them."

We went on talking. No, he said, it would be impossible to get his farm together in one piece. "Another man's acres next to mine may be better than the acreage round his farm and he won't want to sell. And the same goes for me."

We talked about education. He seemed satisfied that his children were getting a good one. He had got one too, he said, except for the tally stick, which was notched for each Irish word spoken and then appropriate beatings were awarded.

"Why," I asked, "was it so important. Why did the English care about the language?"

"Why to take the Irish out of the Irish."

—Debra Love, Annaghkeen, *1970*

Declan's ship, bearing a bell which the saint had left behind. Anyone adroit enough to crawl under the stone will be cured of rheumatic pains.

Rising 29 metres (95 feet) above the teetering headstones in the monastery Declan founded, the gracefully tapering round tower is one of the last and finest erected in Ireland. Two *ogham* stones stand in the chancel of the 12th-century Romanesque cathedral; the notches cut along their corners spell the names of the dead whom they commemorate. But the church's most notable features are the biblical carvings on the exterior of the west gable wall, which was itself incorporated from a building some 500 years older. The weathered scenes depict the Archangel Michael weighing the souls of the dead, King Solomon's judgement between the two mothers, and the Adoration of the Magi.

Around Lismore

West of Ardmore, just after the Waterford–Cork highway (N25) crosses the River Blackwater, a scenic tertiary road branches north, following the river's luxuriant, fertile valley to **Lismore**. The centre of ecclesiastical scholarship founded here by St. Carthach in AD 636 shone like a beacon through the centuries of Europe's Dark Ages. The Vikings looted the place again and again, but it was the Normans who wrought the final destruction of the monastery and abbey in 1173. The 17th-century Protestant cathedral here dates from the 1600s, built upon a 13th-century original sacked by the armies of Elizabeth I.

Lismore Castle, a fabulously crenellated grey neo-Gothic mansion constructed on an older foundation in the 19th century, overhangs the Blackwater. Only the gardens are open to the public.

From Lismore the Vee Road (R688) runs north into the Knockmealdown Mountains to the Vee (see page 120), a stirring viewpoint overlooking the Tipperary plains.

Along a wee boreen

County Tipperary

Apart from its incidental renown as being the place "it's a long way to", popularized in a jaunty First World War song, most visitors to Ireland probably know little of this quiet, agrarian county.

It's reckoned that the ancient mountains around Tipperary—the Galtees and Knockmealdowns in the south, the Silvermines and Slievefelims in the west, the Slieveardaghs in the east—in their youth rivalled the Alps for grandeur. Over the eons, though, they've been worn down to the low, rounded ranges which now spill gently over Tipp's borders from the neighbouring counties. Below them are plains and expanses of rich pasturage, like the fecund Golden Vale, which stretches out in a broad swath across southwestern Tipperary.

The northwestern border is formed in part by the 80-kilometre (50-mile) shoreline of Lough Derg, while the Suir divides Tipperary from Waterford in the southeast. The Vikings made a few forays along these waterways, but otherwise, this large, landlocked county was mostly spared the fury of the Norsemen. This good fortune, along with the fertility of the land hereabouts, helps account for the rich legacy remaining from medieval times and for the county's agricultural prosperity.

Prince John visited in 1185, and then returned as king in 1199, granting Tipperary lands to, among others, William de Burgo and Theobald Fitzwalter. The latter was later appointed to the high office of chief butler to the lord of Ireland; his influential family henceforward adopted the surname of Butler. Norman farmers settled heavily in the south of the county and planted apple orchards as in their native Normandy.

Thanks to the regional power of the Butlers, Tipperary rebuffed all Protestant colonization schemes, until the coming of the implacable Cromwell. In the late 18th century, the Whiteboy movement arose here. Tenant farmers, cloaked in white smocks in order to recognize one another in the dark of night, exacted sharp reprisals against abusive landlords—pulling down fences, slaying livestock, setting outbuildings ablaze. The violence spread for a time throughout much of Ireland, in turn provoking savage countermeasures.

Between 1841 and 1861, Tipperary lost nearly half its population to famine and emigration, and the population continued to wither up until the late 1960s, when agricultural development began to make the county prosperous again.

Nenagh and the North

A one-time Norman settlement, busy **Nenagh** is the chief market town of northern Tipperary's rich agricultural districts. A few characterful old shops and other buildings have been spared the wrecking ball, but the central attraction is the 31-metre (105-foot)-high cylindrical keep of Nenagh Castle. It's the last remnant of a pentagonal castle completed by Theobald Fitzwalter in 1220; the crenellations were a 19th-century addition. The story goes that a bishop of Killaloe, after failing to gather enough American subscriptions for the construction of a new diocesan cathedral, instead used the modest donations to crown this tower with the battlements, which give it the look of an enormous chess piece.

Across the road, the Nenagh District Heritage Centre, in the 19th-century gaol, holds varied exhibits on local history and culture.

Dromineer is a popular water-sports resort northwest of Nenagh on the shore of long Lough Derg. A ruined Ormonde family castle dominates the harbour. In late June, Dromineer celebrates its annual Water Festival with music, dance, boating and other water-sports events. Another centre for boating, as well as for Irish music, **Garrykennedy**, lies across the sheltered little bay to the southwest.

Near the upper end of Lough Derg is **Terryglass**, a likeable village whose 19th-century church keeps a reputed fragment of the True Cross. Atmospheric, old-fashioned Paddy's Pub makes a relaxing spot for a pint.

Roscrea, one of Ireland's oldest towns, has a full complement of historic buildings. The gem among these is the **Damer House**, a once-neglected 1715 Queen Anne–style town house. Like so many of Ireland's fine old beauties over the years, the Damer House was slated for demolition in the 1970s. It would have become a parking lot but for the intervention of the Irish Georgian Society. After years of painstaking restoration, the house is open for tours. The clean lines and uncluttered geometry of the exterior, its rich collection of paintings and period furnishings, and the hand-carved red-pine staircase make the building one of the best remaining examples of its era.

Nearby on Church Street, the western façade of **St. Cronan's Church** is a paradigm of 12th-century Hiberno-Romanesque simplicity. On the high cross just north are interlacing motifs and human figures, including a weathered rendering of the good bishop himself, St. Cronan, who established this site in the seventh century. In 1798, the English lopped some six metres off the top of the round tower across the road after a rebel sniper shot one of their sentinels from it. The modern Church of St. Cronan on Abbey Street incorporates

(following pages) Holy Cross Abbey, Co. Tipperary

the bell tower and wall portions of a Franciscan friary built here in the 15th century.

Travel just a few kilometres west or north from Roscrea and you'll pass into County Offaly; a short drive east takes you into County Laois. Truth be told, these flat inland counties—occupied mostly by farms and featureless bog—aren't the most exciting slice of Ireland. Most travellers slip through in a hurry to the west coast or back to Dublin.

In Offaly, two destinations certainly warrant a detour. Clonmacnois, St. Ciaran's celebrated holy city beside the Shannon, is described on page 219. The town of **Birr**, about midway between Clonmacnois and Roscrea, is a beautifully planned town with broad streets, spacious squares and the unruffled geometry of Georgian homes. The kernel around which this town grew is the opulently Gothic Birr Castle, which is still the home of the earls of Rosse. The castle isn't open to the public, but the enchanting gardens are. The grounds, with an arboretum and large ornamental lake, are lavishly planted with ancient box hedges, rare trees and other flora from around the world. The third earl, a distinguished astronomer, built the (then) world's largest telescope on the estate in 1845; the walls and telescope tube are all that remain.

Along the drive south from Roscrea you pass the 479-metre (1,572 foot)-high **Devil's Bit**. Legend has it that the mountain's prominent cleft was formed when the Devil bit off a piece of the sandstone mountain, which he spat out 30 kilometres (19 miles) south of here to form Cashel's Cathedral Rock. Actually, it was more prosaic glacial action which gouged out the windy gap. The mountain makes a good stop for a picnic or for an easy walk up its flanks to see the circular tower known as Carden's Folly and to take in the fine panorama over the Golden Vale.

The Cistercian **Holy Cross Abbey** southwest of Thurles merits a detour from the main highway. This showpiece of restoration on the banks of the Suir dates back to 1168, when it was built to house a fragment of the True Cross. The romantic ruin stood derelict for years, but now it's in use again as a parish church and is also a major pilgrimage centre.

Cashel

The **Rock of Cashel**, among the most splendid jumbles of ecclesiastical architecture to be found anywhere, is Ireland's Mont St. Michel. The difference here is that the grass-green tide is always in, lapping at the limestone massif thrust up some 30 metres (100 feet) from the surrounding plain. Ramparts encircle the summit, and at the foot of the Rock is the roofless but still impressive Hore Abbey. Eric Newby thought Cashel "the most melancholy ecclesiastical ruins in all Ireland", and indeed it does make a brooding medieval vision against the pearly Tipperary sky.

This was the seat of the Munster kings for seven centuries, where St. Patrick himself is said to have baptized King Aengus in 450. When the saint inadvertently thrust the tip of his crosier through the king's foot (a mighty man, Pat), the stoic novitiate uttered not a peep of protest, thinking the pain a part of the new religion. Patrick also held an early mass at Cashel, and used, it's said, a shamrock's trefoil pattern to illustrate the unity of the Holy Trinity —the Father, Son and Holy Ghost, three leaves unified on one stem. High-King BrianBorú, too, received his crown at Cashel in 977, but in 1101 the kings of Munster—sensing, perhaps, that the prevailing wind was decidedly Christian—ceded the Rock to the church and set themselves up as a dynasty of archbishops.

Except for the magnificent, barrel-vaulted Chapel of Cormac, designed as a miniature cathedral, and the pointed round tower, the structures are roofless and in varying states of ruin. The earl of Kildare, who burned the cathedral, justified his actions to King Henry VII by explaining that he "thought the Archbishop was in it". It was none other than an archbishop of the 18th century who further despoiled the cathedral by stripping its roof in order to sell off the lead. Cormac's Chapel, built of honey-coloured sandstone between 1127 and 1134, is considered by many the finest Hiberno-Romanesque church in Ireland. The lofty high cross also dates from about the same period.

Entrance to the complex is through the Hall of the Vicars Choral, where there is a small collection of stone carvings and other artefacts. The informative guided tours are worthwhile for pointing out the fine carvings, traces of fresco and other architectural details which make this Irish acropolis so rich.

Brú Ború, a modern cultural complex at the foot of the Rock, serves traditional Irish meals in its banquet hall and stages musical and theatre performances.

Cashel town has a few nice shopfronts, particularly Meaney's Pub (also the place to find a traditional session) and others along Main Street. The sumptuous stone and red brick Cashel Palace Hotel, built in 1730, served for 200 years as the residence of the Church of Ireland bishops. A night's stay nowadays is quite dear, but tea and snacks in the Bishop's Buttery will suffice to get you in for a look around at the interior's fine panelling, plasterwork decorations, paintings and other appointments.

Cahir

Filmmaker John Boorman chose the superbly preserved **Cahir Castle** for scenes in his 1981 *Excalibur,* a moody retelling of the Arthurian cycle, and Stanley Kubrick used it in his sprawling epic *Barry Lyndon.* The broad River Suir slips under an arched stone bridge before wrapping itself around the rocky islet from which the fortress rises. This Butler stronghold was considered impregnable, but woe to the prideful: it capitulated in 1599 after a mere three-day siege to Elizabeth's darling, the earl of Essex, and in 1642 submitted within just a few hours to the infamous Lord Inchiquin. When Cromwell arrived eight years later, the defenders negotiated a surrender, thus sparing the castle the tedious Protestant beating which reduced so many another Irish fortress to smoking rubble.

A number of old-fashioned shops line the two main thoroughfares of agreeable Cahir (pronounced "care"). On the square where they intersect, the town house of the last earl of Glengall, who died heirless in 1858, now is the Cahir House Hotel, a congenial place for lunch or a drink. Cahir makes a good base from which to launch walks in the Galtee and Knockmealdown mountains and for salmon and trout fishing in local waters.

The **Vee Road** (R668) lazily curves to the south from Cahir, rising through rhododendrons and woodlands before reaching the eponymous "V", a hairpin

Tipperary cattle fair

turn in the Knockmealdowns below which expansive vistas of the spreading countryside unfold. The fine scenery continues through the Gap on the Waterford border and all the way to Youghal, in County Cork.

Southwest of Cahir, near Ballyporeen (ancestral home of Ronald Reagan), are the **Mitchelstown Caves**. In times of trouble the caverns sheltered rebels on the lam, including the Sugawn Earl of Desmond, who challenged Queen Elizabeth's authority in 1601. Nowadays thousands annually visit the fancifully named Lot's Wife, Demon's Cave, House of Lords and other subterranean formations.

Branching west from the main Limerick-Waterford road (N24) at Bansha, the R663 follows the River Aherlow, threading through the luxuriant **Glen of Aherlow**. Enjoyable walks can be taken all along this scenic route, with the neatly cultivated tracts of farmland spreading below.

The Southeast

Cluain Meala, the Irish name for **Clonmel**, means "Meadows of Honey", an apt description for this salubrious location on the Suir where the fruitful Golden Vale meets the Comeragh Mountains. Even Oliver Cromwell, in 1650, had to grant that "this is indeed a land worth fighting for". Clonmel, the county's

largest town (population 12,500), thrives as a food-processing centre. In 1992 and 1993 it hosted the Fleadh Cheoil na hÉireann, the huge all-Ireland music festival; bibulous celebrants are *still* crawling out of the nooks and crannies to stumble home.

Lawrence Sterne, author of one of the earliest (and longest) novels in English, *Tristram Shandy,* was born here in 1713. In the first part of the 19th century, an Italian immigrant named Carlo Bianconi arrived in Ireland to seek his fortune. With an English vocabulary consisting of the words "one penny" and "buy", he peddled prints of statues and religious images. So industrious was the 16-year-old that eventually he earned enough to start up a carriage-for-hire service in 1815, the Bianconi Long Cars, which plied the 16-kilometre (10-mile) route between Clonmel and Cahir—Ireland's first public transport. The Italian went on to serve twice as mayor of Clonmel. His home, office and stable for his cars and their horsepower is now Hearn's Hotel.

The village of **Fethard**, set below a wooded hill north of Clonmel on the R689, is almost cluttered with historical remains. Portions of the medieval town wall and towers survive, along with three castle keeps and a 14th-century Dominican priory with a fine collection of gravestones. An old railway building houses the Folk Farm and Transport Museum.

The red sandstone flanks of **Slievenamon**, or Sliabh na mBan, rise in grand isolation from the plain to the east. This "Mountain of the Fairy Woman" takes its name from the fairy maidens whom Finn MacCool encountered here. According to legend, Finn organized the love-struck lasses in a race to the summit, promising to wed the victor. But when the breathless girls gained the peak, Grainne, daughter of King Cormac, was sitting there in demure repose, having taken no chances and arrived the night before!

In the confused and abortive 1798 Rising, a local contingent of rebels were routed in a skirmish at the mountain. The defeat is lamented in the defiant martial air, "Slievenamon":

> *Oh bitter pain it is, that thus the day went*
> *Against the Gael in that dreadful fight,*
> *For how the strangers are making game of us,*
> *Our pikes are vain, they say, against their might.*
> *Our major came not, when dawned that day on us,*
> *And we ourselves were in disorder thrown,*
> *Like scattered herds we were without their drover,*
> *On the sunny hill slopes of Slievenamon.*

The Limerick–Waterford highway (N24) from Clonmel follows the Suir east to another town cradled in the river's gentle valley. **Carrick-on-Suir** proudly claims its own favourite sons—world-class cycling hero Sean Kelly and the Clancy brothers, the sweater-clad trio who have done their bit to popularize Irish balladry—and a less fortunate daughter, Anne Boleyn. Henry VIII's luckless second wife was born at Ormonde Castle, a 16th-century Tudor mansion appended to a 13th-century tower house. This was the home of the tenth earl of Ormonde, "Black Tom" Butler, loyal cousin to Queen Elizabeth.

Two elaborately carved high crosses punctuate the graveyard at **Ahenny**, a few kilometres north of Carrick. Dating to the eighth century, these are possibly Ireland's oldest surviving stone crosses, but they've held their detail remarkably well despite their great antiquity. The conical stone caps, a throwback to more ancient times, give them almost phallic overtones.

The Cork-born artist and writer Robert Gibbings found in the twining, ribbonlike ornamentation of such crosses an echo of Irish music: "How like the music of the jigs and reels", he wrote, ". . . are those interlacings and spirals with their continuous yet ever varied and always exciting repetition of the same theme".

County Cork

"It's God's own place", contends an old Irish adage, "and the Divil's own people". With its miles and miles of unspoilt coastline, undulating green farms and pastoral dairyland, sublimely rugged peninsulas and mountains and an energetic, sophisticated main city, Ireland's largest county feels like a country in itself. You'd certainly get that impression, at least, from talking with the inhabitants, who seem quite happy to think of their home as a place apart.

Something about the headstrong "Rebel County" fosters an ardent pride and independence. Residents of Cork City, for example, deem it to be the true cultural, intellectual and social capital of Ireland—not that other town. Local allegiance even extends to the subject of beer: many Corkonians steadfastly prefer their smooth black Murphy's and Beamish's, both brewed within the sound of Shandon's bells, to that other stout from the banks of the Liffey.

The sense of distinctness, too, is underscored by the Cork accent. Some Irish regretfully note that radio and television have levelled the country's regional accents. But apparently this news hasn't yet reached Cork, where people tend to speak with a thick brogue that can baffle even other Irish and makes them sound—to borrow Dylan Thomas's phrase—as if they had the Elgin Marbles in their mouths.

The people of Cork have a reputation, too, for being the most garrulous of all the Irish. "Every Corkman", wrote Seán O'Faoláin, "has the gift of words". It's not surprising then that the place has produced a goodly company of writers: the folklorist Thomas Crofton Croker, novelist and playwright Daniel Corkery, and Michael O'Donovan (better known as Frank O'Connor), as well as O'Faoláin himself, to mention a few.

Cork City

"Cork is the loveliest city in the world", proclaimed Cork native Robert Gibbings. "Anybody who doesn't agree with me either was not born there or is prejudiced". That declaration pretty well sets the tone for the fierce partiality Corkonians feel for their urbane city, and there's enough truth in it to forestall quibbling.

The name of the Republic's second-largest city (population 140,000) is derived from the Irish word *corcaigh,* meaning a marshy place, which is what this site was in the seventh century, when St. Finbarr founded an abbey and school here beside the River Lee. Edmund Spenser, who in the late 16th century was Cork's high sheriff, described the river in *The Faerie Queene* as

> *The spreading Lee, that like an island fayre,*
> *Encloseth Cork with his divided flood.*

That island in the Lee is the heart of Cork, where the city's main business and shopping districts and many of its cultural attractions are concentrated. The river, spanned by more than a dozen "noble bridges", still defines the character of the city. Wherever you turn, there it is; near the quays, its green wet smell wafts up and mingles with the bite of scorched coal from a thousand hearths. Though divided into two main channels now, the Lee formerly braided through in a network of canals, earning Cork the sobriquet of "the Venice of Ireland". Some of central Cork's principal thoroughfares, such as the Grand Parade and St. Patrick's Street, were built upon filled-in channels in the 18th century. Though they haven't felt the tug of a hawser for two centuries, capstans still stand ready on the sidewalks of the Grand Parade. Among the distinguished Georgian houses along the South Mall, you may notice large gateways at street level, with steps leading up to a higher main door. Merchant vessels used to anchor below the warehouses here, and residents still retain the right to dock a boat at their front doors, free of charge.

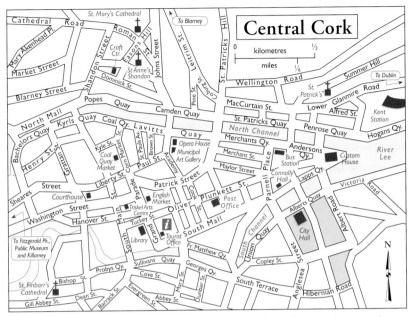

One of Cork's most pleasurable pursuits is simply walking, following the pedestrian's muse, lead where it may. The city is full of small surprises and unexpected turnings: narrow lanes slip invitingly off the bustling main streets, tree-shaded quays follow the river, stately boulevards promenade through the Georgian and Victorian neighbourhoods, and steep back streets climb up into the hills overlooking the city. As you wander the different districts, you may come to agree with Seán O'Faoláin that "Cork may call itself a city, but it is really a big town made up of a lot of little villages".

As good a place as any to start is from Patrick Street Bridge, at one of Cork's best-known landmarks, the statue of Father Theobald Matthew. In the 19th century this "apostle of temperance" managed to transform thousands of upstanding Irishmen into teetotallers (though a good deal of his success was undone by the Famine). Patrick Street, the wide main street, cuts a curve through central Cork. If there were any lingering doubts that Cork is a city that takes its cosmopolitan aspirations seriously, a stroll down St. Patrick's Street will dispel them. The sophisticated boutiques and restaurants, side-walks full of smartly dressed shoppers, and the purposeful flow of activity give it much more of a modern European than a strictly Irish feeling.

And yet, turn right up Corn Market Street from the western end of St. Patrick Street and you're in the **Coal Quay Market**, a motley open-air flea market that's changed little (except its name) from the scene that William Bulfin visited early this century:

You can obtain an infinite variety of things in Paddy's Market—old books, old furniture, new and old clothes, fruit, vegetables, baskets, cradles, crutches, pots and pans and tinware, stockings, sweets, cakes, blackthorns, lace, rosaries, pictures, tubs, and a-hundred-and-one things that you would never think of.

Bulfin also recalled the observation of one exiled Corkonian: "That market is unique. It is the only place that I know of in the world where your handkerchief can be stolen from you as you pass in on one gate, and sold back to you as you pass out on the other". Watch your pocketbook here.

From the Grand Parade, a walkway leads into the more genteel **English Market**, a lively food market under an iron-and-glass roof where the piquant tang of cheeses and fish mingle with the reek of butchered meats and the mellower scents of fresh vegetables and fruits.

A short amble east from Corn Market Street are atmospheric **Paul Street** and Paul's Lane, full of good bookshops and antique dealers, cafés and stylish haberdashers. You may notice buildings hereabouts built with Cork's signature mix of cinnamon-coloured sandstone and silvery limestone, both locally quarried, which have given rise to the term "streaky-bacon architecture".

The eastern end of Paul Street opens onto the red brick former customs house, now the **Crawford Municipal Gallery**. Inside hang works by such Irish notables as the lyrical Paul Henry, and a representative collection by such "Cork school" artists as James Barry and Nathaniel Grogan, as well as works by Cork native Seamus Murphy, perhaps Ireland's most talented sculptor in this century. (Other venues for Murphy's bronze and stone sculptures are University College, Cork, and the Cork Public Museum.) Adjacent to the Crawford is the **Cork Opera House**, which stages ballet, musical comedy and drama, as well as opera.

The Opera House Bridge takes you across the Lee to Cork's hilly north side. Turn left along Camden Quay and then right up John Street to 18th-century **St. Anne's Church, Shandon**. Or simply follow your eyes up the hill to the square-sided, red-and-white bell tower topped by its famous weathervane—a three-metre (11-foot)-long golden salmon swimming high above the rooftops. You can climb the tower and toll out a tune on the celebrated bells, about which Francis Sylvester Mahony (1804–66) wrote the poem for which he's best remembered:

With deep affection,
And recollection,
I often think of
    Those Shandon bells.

Just opposite St. Anne's are the restored buildings of the **Cork Butter Exchange**. Through this market flowed untold quantities of dairy goods and beef from the rich pastures of Munster, which provisioned the British navy and emigrant ships bound for America throughout the 18th and 19th centuries. The buildings now house the tony Shandon Craft Centre and the adjacent theatres, ballet studios and other performance spaces of the Firkin Crane Centre.

From vantage points on these north-side hills, wonderful views of the city spread out below, from the dour warehouses in the east (reminders that Cork is still very much a working port) to the three Gothic spires of 19th-century St. Finbarr's Cathedral, piercing the southwestern skyline.

For a promenade into the city's western reaches, follow tree-shaded Mardyke Parade along the Lee. In Joyce's *A Portrait of the Artist as a Young Man*, Stephen Dedalus passed this way, under "the leaves of the trees along the Mardyke . . . astir and whispering in the sunlight". The riverside walk leads to the grassy haven of Fitzgerald Park and the **Cork Public Museum**, which has exhibits on Cork's rebellious history and some fine pieces from the city's zenith as a silversmithing centre.

Nearby, on the serene campus of **University College Cork**, are Seamus Murphy's life-size bronzes of Corkmen Frank O'Connor and Seán O'Faoláin, two masters of the modern short story. O'Faoláin (1900–89) was at his brilliant best in teasing out the delicate subtleties that drove his characters and in evoking a palpable sense of place and mood. In "Passion", he wondered:

> *Why on earth did I think tonight, after I had left you, of Conny Hourigan, and of that soft, wet night when the lights of Cork down in the valley were weeping through the haze, and everything as still as before dawn; and not a sound but the jolt of an old tram over the worn points, or the drip of the rain on the old tin shed in the backyard?*

As befits the nation's self-proclaimed cultural capital, Cork's vigorous social and intellectual life runs the gamut from earthy to highbrow. Annual events include the International Choral and Folk Dance Festival in spring, the International Film Festival in September and October, and the Jazz Festival on the last weekend in October. The Tourist Office in Grand Parade can provide details. The Triskel Arts Centre, off South Main Street just a short hop away, is one of the city's liveliest venues for film, music, art shows, poetry readings and the like and can advise on goings-on elsewhere around Cork.

There are, of course, an abundance of congenial pubs and hotel bars in which to partake of the local stouts, hear all manner of music and engage in that buoyant and most highly refined of Cork art forms—opinionated conversation. For traditional Irish music, try An Siol Broin in MacCurtain Street, The Phoenix on Union Quay, An Bodhrán in Oliver Plunkett Street or the Gables in Douglas Street. The posh Metropole Hotel in MacCurtain Street, one of the Jazz Festival's principal venues, offers jazz or other music most evenings.

At University College, Cork

Around Cork City

On weekend afternoons, the quiet roads around Cork are the setting for the local sport of road bowls, or bullets. The essence of the game is to roll a .79-kilogram (28-ounce) iron ball, with a vigorous windmill pitch, along several miles of winding road in the least number of throws. Bowlers make quite a science of it, sending a spotter ahead to judge the rake and bend of the road and to recommend the most propitious trajectory.

Eight kilometres (five miles) northwest of Cork is 15th-century **Blarney Castle**, with its famous gab-granting stone, one of the most widely known and popular—if spurious—of Irish tourist attractions. The story goes that Queen Elizabeth called on Cormac MacCarthy, lord of Blarney, to submit to her authority by symbolically surrendering his estate. Again and again MacCarthy promised to comply yet still managed to put her off with one guileful pretext or another. Finally the queen, exasperated, proclaimed, "This is the usual Blarney; what he says he never means!"

Thus a new word entered the language. How a stone set high up in the battlements of Blarney Castle came to be identified as the source of his smooth-flowing palaver is the subject of various legends, but most likely it's the invention of a 19th-century promoter. Thousands of tourists now make a pilgrimage of sorts to Blarney nonetheless. They climb the 120 steps up the tower to await their turn hanging backwards over the parapet in order to plant a kiss on the Blarney Stone and so gain the gift of *plamas*—facile, flattering eloquence.

For an altogether different experience, follow the path from the castle to the mystical Rock Close, an outcrop of weathered stone amidst huge ancient yew and ilex trees. It's thought to have been a place of Druid worship in pre-Christian days.

East to Youghal

Flowing eastward out of Cork, the River Lee soon broadens out into wood-fringed Lake Mahon and wraps around three islands. On Fota Island is **Fota House**, a restored 18th-century hunting lodge, later enlarged in grand style, fronted with Doric columns and elegantly appointed with Regency furnishings and one of the finest collections of Irish landscape paintings. On the landscaped grounds are an excellent arboretum and a wildlife park whose inhabitants include giraffes, kangaroos and penguins.

Just south by bridge on Great Island, which crowds most of Cork Harbour, is the appealing town of **Cobh** (pronounced "cove"), for centuries one of southern Ireland's most important ports. The town and harbour are quite dominated by the flamboyantly detailed St. Colman's Cathedral, built of pale blue Dalkey granite atop the hill; with its soaring spire it's one of the grandest churches in the Republic.

From 1849 until 1922, the town was rechristened Queenstown in honour of the young Victoria, who visited once. Were Vickie to rise from the dead (heaven help us) and return, she might well remember Cobh, as its character is still largely 19th century. It's doubtful that she would receive a very hearty welcome, however, for Victoria is mostly remembered in this country as the "famine queen", who reigned in blithe indifference through some of Ireland's darkest decades. The quays at Cobh witnessed uncounted tearful scenes of parting, as hundreds of thousands of desperate, starved-out Irish sailed away from this port, never to return.

The history of Cobh is bound up as well with two of this century's worst maritime disasters. In 1912, Cobh was the last port for the *Titanic* on her ill-fated maiden voyage. Three years later, when the passenger liner *Lusitania* was torpedoed off the coast of Kinsale, survivors and casualties were brought to Cobh, where many of the dead were buried. On a cheerier note, the first successful trans-Atlantic steamer, the *Sirius*, left from this port in 1838.

Cobh today is mainly a holiday and sailing resort, with brightly painted town houses and forests of pleasure boats bobbing at anchor. The town hosts the International Folk Dance Festival in July and a spirited regatta weekend in mid-August.

The Cork-Waterford highway (N25) speeds traffic eastward. A much nicer detour is the long way around, turning south from Midleton (where the Republic's whiskey-distilling collective is open to visitors) and following Cork Harbour and the sea cliffs and bays of the blustery south coast.

Youghal (pronounced "yawl") was a Viking and later Norman port, set between steep hills and the mouth of the River Blackwater, where Cork and Waterford meet. Youghal prospered in the Middle Ages through sea trade with France, and the town was included in the 168-square-kilometre (42,000-acre) land grant given to Sir Walter Raleigh, who served as mayor in 1588–89. Myrtle Grove, his gabled house at the end of William Street, is still lived in

Sheep's Head Peninsula, Co. Cork

(but is not open to the public). The adjacent St. Mary's Parish Church, begun in the 13th century, is worth a visit. In the impressive interior is the tomb of the countess of Desmond, a spry old gal who died in 1604 after falling out of a cherry tree—at the tender age of 147.

The long Main Street is a colourful slice of Irish life, brightened with pennants and flower baskets hung from shop eaves and busy with people going about their daily business. The street passes right through the round archway of Youghal's best-known landmark—the five-storey **Clock Tower**, crowned with a white cupola and weathervane. The Georgian tower has been used as a prison, and in the 1790s rebels were hanged from the windows as a warning to the restless. Now it has been put to more benign use, housing the Tourist Office, an art gallery and museum. Portions of Youghal's extensive encircling walls, built by the Normans, run east from the tower all the way to St. Mary's Church.

The eight-kilometre (five-mile)-long sandy beach is popular with Irish holidaymakers. Scenes of John Huston's 1956 film version of *Moby Dick*, starring Gregory Peck as Ahab, were shot in Youghal; the Moby Dick pub near the quay displays photos of the filming.

North of Cork City

The Cork-Dublin road (N8) runs northeast through wooded, hilly country to **Fermoy**, a pleasant, orderly 19th-century town on the banks of the Blackwater, noted for its excellent salmon fishing.

The lands to the west of Fermoy are still strongly associated with the Elizabethan poet Edmund Spenser. Spenser came to Ireland in 1580 as the secretary to Lord Grey, Queen Elizabeth's representative. For his service to the Crown, Spenser was granted a 12-square-kilometre (3,000-acre) estate under the Ballyhoura Hills near Doneraile, northeast of Mallow. While living there he wove the sylvan countryside of north Cork into his best-known work, *The Faerie Queene*, one of the longest verse works in the English language. But the contemporary Irish appreciated neither his literary talents nor his politics, which were brutally imperial to the marrow, and in 1598 they showed him just what they thought of him by burning his house down. Spenser lost a child in the blaze, and, it's believed, substantial unpublished portions of *The Faerie Queene*.

This region of Cork was home, too, to Dublin-born novelist Elizabeth Bowen (1899-1973), who inherited her family estate near Kildorrery in 1928.

Bowen's Court, the history she wrote of her family, begins with this portrait of the countryside:

> *Up in the north-east corner of County Cork is a stretch of limestone country —open, airy, not quite flat; it is just perceptibly tilted from north to south, and the fields undulate in a smooth flowing way. Dark knolls and screens of trees, the network of hedges, abrupt stony ridges, slate glints from roofs give the landscape a featured look—but the prevailing impression is emptiness. This is a part of Ireland with no lakes, but the sky's movement of clouds reflects itself everywhere as it might on water, rounding the trees with bloom and giving the grass a sheen.*

Not far away, across the River Awbeg, which Spenser recast as "the Mulla", is the market town of **Mallow**. Now quietly prosperous, Mallow was in the 18th and 19th centuries an elegant spa resort known as the "Bath of Ireland", where the revelry inspired this ditty about its habitués, the licentious "Rakes of Mallow":

> *Beauing, belling, dancing, drinking,*
> *Breaking windows, damning, singing,*
> *Ever raking, never thinking,*
> *Live the rakes of Mallow.*

Some handsome town houses have survived from that era, but the town's architectural showpiece is the stone-and-wood Elizabethan Clock Tower, which looks rather more like something plucked out of a Bavarian burg than what you'd expect in the midst of Irish farmlands. There is horse racing, and Mallow hosts a good folk festival each August. From Mallow, the main highway (N72) continues west along the valley of the Blackwater to Killarney. South of the river rise the Boggeragh Mountains, crisscrossed by a confusing maze of back roads and punctuated by a few scattered villages with such eccentric names as Lyre, Nad and Bweeng.

Kinsale

Tourism has been good to **Kinsale**. Popular with international visitors as well as Irish on holiday, the colourful little town proudly shows off the clean, bright gleam of prosperity, with sparkling fresh paint, upmarket craft shops, blooming flowers and shoals of highly praised restaurants which have earned Kinsale a reputation as something of a gourmet capital. Formerly an important naval port,

Kinsale sits 30 kilometres (19 miles) south of Cork in a sheltering cup of hills on the Bandon estuary, its harbour now full of pleasure yachts and fishing boats.

Among the curios in the Kinsale Museum, housed in the handsome, colonnaded 17th-century town hall, are the town's royal charters and mementos of the *Lusitania*. In May 1915, the passenger ship, en route from New York to Liverpool, was torpedoed and sunk by a German submarine off the Old Head of Kinsale, killing 1,195 people. Germany claimed there were munitions on board, while the United States insisted the ship carried only innocent civilians. Either way, the attack hastened America's entry into World War I. Some of the victims lie buried nearby at 12th-century St. Multose Church.

The well-stocked Tourist Office can outline good walks in the area. The steep streets up Compass Hill lead to quiet perches overlooking the town and the rolling farmland to the south. Two 17th-century forts in the vicinity also make rewarding destinations, especially the well-preserved, star-shaped Charlesfort, two kilometres (one mile) away in Summer Cove.

Just north of town is the site of the disastrous Battle of Kinsale. In 1598, after Hugh O'Neill defeated an English army at the Battle of the Yellow Ford, it looked for a brief sanguine moment as though the tide were turning in Ireland's favor. Catholic Spain sent men, money and arms to help them fight the invaders, but it was too little, too late, and in the wrong place. In September 1601, 4,800 Spaniards landed at Kinsale—not in Ulster, as requested. The English under Mountjoy marched to confront them, while O'Neill and Red Hugh O'Donnell, with a body of 8,000 men, hurried south from Ulster.

On Christmas Eve, the great battle commenced. The Ulstermen, poorly organized and fighting out of their element in the open terrain, were routed, and the Spanish surrendered too soon. The defeat was the beginning of the end for Celtic Ireland. (See "The Flight of the Earls", page 245).

West to Mizen Head

Three main routes from Cork City run to the west coast but, as is so often the case in Irish matters, the roundabout approach is the most revealing path. Even the main southern highway (N71) is full of wiggles and twists, but if you've time enough it's the wayward secondary roads that offer the real treats: forgotten beaches, noisy flocks of seabirds, trim villages and, over the hedges and through the clefts of the hills, blue glimpses of the sea. The seacoast west of Kinsale is so broken up with headlands and cliffs and indented with harbours and hidden coves that there's hardly a mile of straight line in it.

Major Yeates Buys a Horse

Only those who have been through a similar experience can know what manner of afternoon I spent. I am a martyr to colds in the head, and I felt one coming on. I made a laager in front of the dining-room fire, with a tattered leather screen and the dinner table, and gradually, with cigarettes and strong tea, baffled the smell of must and cats, and fervently trusted that the rain might avert a threatened visit from my landlord. I was then but superficially acquainted with Mr. Florence McCarthy Knox and his habits.

At about 4:30, when the room had warmed up, and my cold was yielding to treatment, Mrs. Cadogan entered and informed me that "Mr. Flurry" was in the yard, and would be thankful if I'd go out to him, for he couldn't come in. Many are the privileges of the female sex; had I been a woman I should unhesitatingly have said that I had a cold in my head. Being a man, I huddled on a mackintosh, and went out into the yard.

My landlord was there on horseback, and with him there was a man standing at the head of a stout grey animal. I recognised with despair that I was about to be compelled to buy a horse.

"Good afternoon, Major", said Mr. Knox in his slow, sing-song brogue; "it's rather soon to be paying you a visit, but I thought you might be in a hurry to see the horse I was telling you of".

I could have laughed. As if I were ever in a hurry to see a horse! I thanked him, and suggested that it was rather wet for horse-dealing.

"Oh, it's nothing when you're used to it", replied Mr. Knox. His gloveless hands were red and wet, the rain ran down his nose, and his covert coat was soaked to a sodden brown. I thought that I did not want to become used to it. My relations with horses have been of a purely military character. I have endured the Sandhurst riding-school, I have galloped for an impetuous general, I have been steward at regimental races, but none of these feats have altered my opinion that the horse, as a means of locomotion, is obsolete. Nevertheless, the man who accepts a resident magistracy in the south-west of Ireland voluntarily retires into the prehistoric age; to institute a stable became inevitable.

"You ought to throw a leg over him", said Mr. Knox, "and you're welcome to take him over a fence or two if you like. He's a nice flippant jumper".

Even to my unexacting eye the grey horse did not seem to promise flippancy, nor did I at all desire to find that quality in him. I explained that I wanted something to drive, and not to ride.

"Well, that's a fine raking horse in harness", said Mr. Knox, looking at me with his serious grey eyes, "and you'd drive him with a sop of hay in his mouth. Bring him up here, Michael".

Michael abandoned his efforts to kick the grey horse's forelegs into a becoming position, and led him up to me.

I regarded him from under my umbrella with a quite unreasonable disfavour. He had the dreadful beauty of a horse in a toy-shop, as chubby, as wooden, and as conscientiously dappled, but it was unreasonable to urge this as an objection, and I was incapable of finding any more technical drawback. Yielding to circumstance, I "threw my leg" over the brute, and after pacing gravely round the quadrangle that formed the yard, and jolting to my entrance gate and back, I decided that as he had neither fallen down nor kicked me off, it was worth paying twenty-five pounds for him, if only to get in out of the rain.

—Somerville and Ross,
Some Experiences of an Irish R.M., 1899

ILLUSTRATION BY EDITH SOMERVILLE

The engaging town of **Clonakilty** wears its past well. A number of its handsome older buildings, such as the 19th-century millworks, are enjoying a second life after sympathetic renovation. Clonakilty is also emerging as a locus for traditional music; De Barra's pub is a popular venue, with music nightly through the summer. The focus of the West Cork Regional Museum in Clonakilty is the story of Michael Collins, one of the greatest heroes of the 1916-22 period, who was born not far away at Woodfield.

There are several good beaches in the area; one of the best is the long buttery strand immediately south on the headland of Inchydoney. To the west, the coast becomes increasingly bolder and more rugged.

Between Rosscarbery and Glandore is an enigmatic Bronze Age monument, **Drombeg Stone Circle**. Incorporating one recumbent and 16 man-sized upright stones, this is one of the largest and most accessible of the several score such circles in Cork and Kerry. Their purposes aren't fully understood; some are aligned to point to sunrise or sunset on significant days of the year, while a few, including Drombeg, contained burial remains.

Castletownshend is a prim fishing village consisting of a single street running steeply down to the tiny harbour. Apart from its attractive, forested hillside setting, Castletownshend is notable as the lifelong home of Edith Somerville (1858–1949), one-half of the widely admired writing duo of Somerville and Ross.

Martin Ross was the *nom de plume* of her first cousin, Violet Martin (1862–1915) of County Galway. The two cousins met one another for the first time in 1886, the autumn of their Anglo-Irish gentry class, and they soon began a fruitful literary collaboration under their joint pseudonym. Their first published work was *An Irish Cousin* (1889), followed by an ambitious realistic novel, *The Real Charlotte*, in 1894.

But their greatest acclaim would come from three breezy volumes recounting the contretemps of one Major Sinclair Yeates, an oft-bemused Englishman posted to this corner of Cork in the capacity of resident magistrate. *Some Experiences of an Irish R.M.*, published in 1899, with winsome illustrations by Edith, proved hugely popular and was followed by two sequels.

The cousins possessed a keen collective ear for vernacular and a tinder-dry sense of humour. In their Irish R.M. stories they showed themselves to be sympathetic observers—and gentle lampooners—of all strata of Irish society around the turn of the century.

Somerville continued writing after Violet's premature death, carrying on, she insisted, a psychic collaboration with her late cousin. The two are buried side by side behind St. Barrahane's Church at the bottom of the hill.

Skibbereen, the "capital" of southwestern Cork, is an energetic place, with weekly cattle and produce markets. The international tone of the exhibits at the West Cork Arts Centre reflects the influence of the many "blow-ins", refugees from Britain and Europe who have fallen in love with west Cork and settled down here.

To the southwest of Skibb is the stretch of coast known as **Carbery's Hundred Isles**, described by an early Irish writer as "sea-girt isles, that like to rich and various gems, inlay the unadorned bosom of the deep". From the attractive fishing port of **Baltimore**, regular ferries sail to Sherkin Island, just ten minutes away, and farther out to precipitous **Clear Island**, where Irish is still the people's first language. The little speck beyond Clear Island is **Fastnet Rock**, remembered as the Teardrop of Ireland by the thousands of emigrants sailing by it en route to America. In 1631, Algerian pirates brazenly raided this coast and took away some 200 inhabitants of Baltimore to sell into slavery in North Africa.

Somerville and Ross described **Mizen Head** as a "gaunt spike of a headland that starts up like a boar's tusk above the ragged lip of the Irish coast". The peninsula is a long, splendidly rugged finger of land with tumbling cliffs, wheeling seabirds, some safe beaches and stunning seascapes, especially along the little-travelled north side. Over the years many ships have been wrecked off this coast. By contrast, **Roaringwater Bay**, along the underside of the peninsula, is rather well sheltered—its menacing name notwithstanding—making it a favourite destination for sailing and fishing among its rocky islets. **Schull** hosts a big regatta each August.

Bantry and Beyond

The blending of sea, mountain and sky at **Bantry Bay** has produced what many people feel is one of the world's loveliest landscapes. Two hundred years ago, the bay was the scene of another memorable failure in Ireland's long, spasmodic struggle for independence.

In December 1796, 43 warships carrying nearly 15,000 French troops set sail from Brittany, intent on invading Ireland. With them was Belfast lawyer Theobald Wolfe Tone, a leading light of the revolutionary United Irishmen, whose vision was to remake Ireland on the model of the newborn French republic. A ferocious storm arose in the channel, however, dispersing the fleet; some of the ships were forced to return to France, but the majority made it to Bantry Bay. The near-hurricane gale would not relent, and though the remaining ships were, as Tone remarked, "close enough to toss a biscuit on shore", landing was impossible.

Historians surmise that, had the soldiers been able to land early enough, they might well have overthrown the underprepared British. For six frustrating days the invasion was thwarted before the armada finally weighed anchor in retreat. Yet again for the Irish, defeat was snatched from the jaws of victory.

Meanwhile, a local landowner by the name of Richard White had sounded the alarm. For his loyalty to the Crown he was made the earl of Bantry. His Georgian mansion, **Bantry House**, is surrounded by elegant terraces and gardens and enjoys a gorgeous panorama over the magnificent bay. The second earl, an apparently compulsive but impeccably discerning collector, travelled the Continent in the 1840s buying up Pompeiian mosaics, Aubusson tapestries, Chippendale and Sheraton furniture, paintings and other treasures, all of which he had trundled back to Bantry to sumptuously furnish his humble home.

Ivy-mantled Bantry House is open to the public and also offers refined bed-and-breakfast. In 1982, divers discovered the storm-damaged frigate *La Surveillante*, scuttled in the bay during the abortive French invasion. Models and ship artefacts are the focus of the recently opened Bantry Armada Exhibition Centre, on the Bantry House grounds.

From Bantry, one has several options. To the southwest there's the long, nearly deserted sliver of the Sheep's Head Peninsula to be explored. To the north, a secondary road (R584) veers inland through the rocky Pass of Keimaneigh to **Gougane Barra**, one of the country's most beautiful forest parks and the source of the River Lee. Before he moved on to establish the monastery at Cork, St. Finbarr had a hermitage on the lake-isle in this tranquil glacial cirque. A few kilometres farther east is the village of **Ballingeary**, in the midst of west Cork's inland Gaeltacht.

Northwest of Bantry, the village of **Glengarriff** shelters in a pretty harbourside glen. Just offshore, **Garinish Island** has been painstakingly transformed from a desolate rock into an oasis of luxuriant gardens. Beyond is the wild **Beara Peninsula**, a craggy, rugged, mountainous world unto itself. The signposted Ring of Beara Drive (152 kilometres/95 miles) around the peninsula easily rivals the more famous Ring of Kerry for breathtaking scenery, without the throngs.

Tractor transport

County Kerry

The Kerry landscape has a full measure of everything one thinks of as Irish: remote, moody glens, rugged mountains, heather-tinted moors, little sea-misted fishing villages, miles of wave-beaten coast, stone-walled fields lapping at the green foothills, and a warm people full of quixotic wit.

Water seems to make its presence felt everywhere: along the deeply rived western peninsulas that splay like an open hand into the Atlantic, in the rivers and glacial lakes which have brought Kerry so much of its fame, and, of course, in the mercurial clouds and rain. The county's position at the southwest corner of Ireland means that it catches the full effect of the warm Gulf Stream, which explains how gardens here support such startling aliens as mimosa, tree ferns, eucalyptus and magnolia. Everywhere, too, great palisades of fuchsias line the roads, dripping blossoms of pink and lipstick-red.

But the element that seems to strike so many visitors, whether they're fully aware of its influence or not, is the quality of Kerry light. The fey, luminous, pewter light, refracted through the mild air, slants across the rugged mountains and valleys, softening their contours and magnifying the beauty.

John Millington Synge was one of many who have fallen in love with western Kerry. He visited each summer from 1903 to 1907, tramping along the byways and talking with the country folk. Intoxicated with the glorious scene he beheld from the end of the Dingle Peninsula, he rhapsodized:

It is a place of indescribable grandeur, where one can see Carrantuohill and the Skelligs and Loop Head and the full sweep of the Atlantic, and over all, the wonderfully tender and searching light that is seen only in Kerry. . . . One wonders in these places why anyone is left in Dublin or London, or Paris, when it would be better, one would think, to live in a tent or hut with this magnificent sea and sky, and to breathe this wonderful air, which is like wine in one's teeth.

Killarney and the Lakes

Visiting Killarney at the height of the summer season, it's hard not to conclude that the town has struck some Faustian bargain with that old divil, Tourism, and bartered its soul for material success. As early as the 1750s a contemporary observer noted that "a new street with a large commodious inn was designed to be built here, for the curiosities of the neighbouring lake have of late drawn great numbers of curious travellers to visit it".

Great numbers of curious travellers Killarney still draws; so many that, along with the nearby lake country and Ring of Kerry scenic drive, it's the most visited place in all of Ireland. The small town (population 8,000) is thick with bed-and-breakfasts, cafés, pubs, restaurants, craft shops with harp Muzak tinkling from unseen speakers and braces of jaunting cars driven by vociferous jarveys.

In late spring, Killarney hosts Pan-Celtic Week, a singular convocation of artists, musicians, dancers, filmmakers and others hailing from Scotland, Wales, Brittany, Galicia and the Isle of Man, as well as Ireland, Scotland and Wales. Details are available from the well-stocked tourist office, in Main Street. In May, July and October the popular Killarney Races attract punters and horse buffs from all over.

Still, the town is no great end in itself, but rather a convenient centre from which to visit the justifiably famous mountains, lakes and woodlands. For a foretaste of the splendours, get up to the seventh-century church on **Aghadoe Hill**, five kilometres (three miles) north of town. In 1844, the writer Catherine M. O'Connell described the populous cemetery with "skulls and bones lying about" as a "cheerful burying place, if one can imagine this seeming contradiction". One can, for the views of the lakes and mountains are superb.

The real reason to come to Killarney is **Killarney National Park**, 25,000 extravagantly scenic acres (100 square kilometres) of rough mountains, ancient woodland and lakes poured out like silver in the glacier-carved valleys. Lough Leane (the Lower Lake), the largest of the Killarney lakes, lies just west and south of Killarney town; to its south are Muckross (the Middle Lake) and the Upper Lake. Sir Walter Scott declared the lakes of Killarney the grandest sight he'd ever seen, and Tennyson, Wordsworth and Thackeray could not but concur.

Along the lower slopes of the mountains and in the valley bottoms, luxuriant virgin woodlands—dominated by ancient oaks but also thick with arbutus, holly, birch and mountain ash—have somehow eluded the axe's bite. The dense rhododendrons flourishing throughout the park would be the envy of most gardeners, but here they are the enemy, and the foresters must constantly fight them back like rapacious weeds lest they take over everything. Over a hundred species of birds thrive in the area, and the park is home to native red deer as well as a herd of sika deer introduced from Japan. The arbutus, or Kerry strawberry tree, which grows here is remarkable in that, except for this enclave, its northern limit is the south of France.

Opposite the Cathedral of St. Mary of the Assumption in Killarney stand the gates to the vast estate of the Brownes, earls of Kenmare. In the 1700s, the Penal Laws decreed that every Catholic landowner had to divide his property among all his male heirs. The Brownes got around this ruinous statute for a century by spawning just one son in each generation, and so managed to hold their lands intact.

It's a pleasant two-kilometre (1.2-mile) walk through the demesne (now known as the Knockreer Estate) to **Ross Castle**, on a peninsula jutting into Lough Leane. The setting inspired Tennyson to gush purple, Victorian effusions in *The Princess*:

> *The splendour falls on castle walls*
> *And snowy summits old in story:*
> *The long light shakes across the lakes,*
> *And the wild cataract leaps in glory.*

Ross was the last Munster stronghold to surrender to Cromwell's armies, in 1652. The English general Ludlow, aware of a prophecy that the castle would never be captured by land, sailed his army down the lake instead. The defenders of course knew the legend, too, and they lay down their arms as soon as the boats came in sight. From the castle, water-buses leave regularly during the summer for tours of Lough Leane.

A local legend tells that where the lake now spreads was once a splendid city in the midst of a rich valley, ruled by a prince of the O'Donoghues named Domhnall. In the valley there flowed a spring, unequalled for sweetness. The magic of the spring, it was said, required that each night it should be capped with its heavy stone lid, lest it flow out and inundate everything around. But the proud prince doubted the warning. In his cups after a night's revelry, he ordered that the lid be left off.

In the small hours, the spring overflowed as foretold and covered the valley, the city and all its inhabitants. But the water was magical, and so no one drowned. Even now, on still evenings, fishermen may glimpse the turrets and

"Turf accountant"

houses of the city and its people still going about their business beneath the surface of the lake. Once every seven years, Prince Domhnall himself appears, and his coming augurs a year of contentment and plenty. Dressed in red and sporting a three-cornered hat, sometimes he rides over the waves on a white mare or in a boat, or he may even come ashore to play hurling with the boys or join in dancing.

The glass-roofed tour boats pass but do not stop at **Innisfallen**, largest of the three dozen small islands sprinkled around Lough Leane. It's worthwhile to hire a small boat from Ross Castle to explore the abbey and other monastic ruins among the thick evergreens and holly. King Brian Ború got his learning at this pre-eminent scholastic community, which thrived for a thousand years, from the sixth century until the coming of Cromwell. Between about 950 and 1380, the monks compiled the *Annals of Inisfallen,* an important chronicle of Irish and world history, which is now preserved at Oxford.

At the Killarney Races

The 44-square-kilometre (11,000-acre) Muckross Estate, beginning some five kilometres (three miles) south of Killarney, forms the heart of the national park. The splendid and well-maintained **Muckross Abbey**, on the eastern shore of Lough Leane, was founded as a Franciscan friary by Donal MacCarthy in 1448. Elizabeth I had the place destroyed, but the friars clung on, and they completely rebuilt it by 1626. General Ludlow, however, torched it for good in 1652.

Tradition says that the magnificent yew in the cloistered inner courtyard was planted at the abbey's founding. Four of Kerry's last and greatest Gaelic poets—Egan O'Rahilly, Pierce Ferriter, Geoffrey O'Donoghue and Owen Roe O'Sullivan—were buried here in the early 1700s, having outlived the days when their class was venerated and succored by the Irish nobility. After the Cromwellian scourges, O'Donoghue looked about and saw his country in ruins, plagued by a foreign invader that could not be dislodged. He wondered aloud:

Why does Ireland falter?
What is the cause of her bondage?
Isle of brown trees, ancient jewel,
Wherefore this desolation?

Farther on is **Muckross House**, looking for all the world—with its peaked gables, mullioned windows and many chimneys—like an original Elizabethan manor, but actually it was built only in 1843. Much of the splendid house has been transformed into a very rewarding museum of Kerry folklore, with locally made furniture, tools and workshops demonstrating pottery making, bookbinding, weaving and blacksmithing, among other trades. Formal gardens surround the house, and trails lead through the woods to the lakeshore.

Close by is the Old Weir Bridge and the lovely spot called the Meeting of the Waters, where the Upper and Middle lakes flow together amid bosky thickets of arbutus and rhododendron. Just south of Muckross House, the 20-metre (66-foot)-high Torc Waterfall spills off Torc Mountain. Farther south, the highway winds up to the **Ladies' View**, a superlative panorama overlooking the Upper Lake which delighted Queen Victoria and her ladies-in-waiting when they visited in 1861.

The **Gap of Dunloe**, west of the Killarney lakes, makes a wonderful walk or bicycle ride. This stony defile fringed with dark tarns winds for 11 kilometres (seven miles) between Macgillycuddy's Reeks and the Purple and Tomies mountains. The mouth of the gap starts at Kate Kearney's Cottage, a heavily touristed tea shop off the Killorglin road, and continues through the steep, craggy gorge to Moll's Gap on the Kenmare road (N71). Late afternoon is the best time for this trip, when the sky is at its most lustrous and the crowds are at an ebb. Alternatively, plunge in for the full treatment: a day-long package that combines a carriage ride through the gap with a boat journey down the three lakes to Ross Castle, then by jaunting car back to Killarney.

The Ring of Kerry and Skellig Islands

Without any stops or detours, this 180-kilometre (112-mile) circuit around the ravishing Iveragh Peninsula can be driven in about four hours. But that's a ridiculous proposition. The constantly varied scenery demands to be lingered over. The route clings to the coast mainly, sometimes riding over the shoulders of Macgillycuddy's Reeks and other mountains which dominate the peninsula's interior. The reeks rise up to 1,041 metres (3,414 feet) on Carrantuohill, highest point in Ireland.

Following the ring counter-clockwise, from Killarney through Killorglin and around to Kenmare, is the preferred direction, as it shows off the views to best advantage.

The best time to visit **Killorglin**, a hilly town above the River Laune, is August 10–12, during Puck Fair. This riotous three days of drinking, dancing and mayhem—wrapped around the excuse of a livestock sale—is an unrepentant vestige of pagan fertility festivals, thought to have grown out of worship for the Celtic god Lugh. King Puck, a beribboned wild goat captured in the mountains for the occasion, presides over the crowds until he is set free at sunset of the third day.

Following the ring west, the highway runs through the little resort village of Glenbeigh and soon tremendous views open up across the shimmering bay to the mountainous Dingle Peninsula. Just before the busy small town of **Cahirciveen**, the western Iveragh Peninsula's main shopping centre, the road passes ruined Carnan House, where Daniel O'Connell (see below) was born in 1775. The story behind Cahirciveen's surprisingly grandiose police barracks is that the building plans were intended to be sent to India but ended up here through a bureaucratic mix-up.

Notched cleanly from the peninsula's western end, hilly **Valentia Island** in the 17th and 18th centuries harboured French and American privateers, including John Paul Jones. Today it's a very quiet getaway, with spectacular views of the surrounding land and sea. The handsome fishing port of Knightstown is linked to the mainland by ferry; a short bridge joins the island to Portmagee, farther west. Basking fully in the Gulf Stream, Valentia supports bursts of fuchsias as well as yuccas and other semitropical flora.

(following pages) Stairway up to Skellig Michael monastery,
with Little Skellig in background, Co. Kerry

West of Bolus Head, and visible from Valentia and other points around the peninsula, are islands of an entirely different character. The Irish word *sceilig* ("splinter of stone") perfectly describes the **Skellig Islands**, a stark pair of jagged rock triangles lying 13 kilometres (eight miles) offshore. Forbidding and unremittingly inhospitable, the larger island, 217-metre (714-foot)-high Skellig Michael, nevertheless supported a monastic community for centuries.

Some 1,400 years ago, St. Finian and a company of monks hacked a stairway up the face of this sea-mountain to the only conceivably habitable spot, a minuscule plateau 160 metres (528 feet) above the sea. They dedicated their little community, appropriately, to St. Michael, patron saint of high places. In an astonishingly good state of preservation today, remains on the island include a half-dozen beehive-shaped stone huts, two peak-roofed corbelled oratories, and stone crosses and cross-inscribed slabs in the cemetery.

During the winters, when violent Atlantic storms can drive waves 60 metres (200 feet) up the island's windward side, the monks would be utterly marooned for months at a time—just themselves, God and the elements. Clinging like limpets to their stony world, fasting, praying and tending their melancholy garden plots through the brief summer, life for the men of Skellig Michael was a distillation of the most rigorous kind of Irish Christianity.

"Skellig", wrote G.B. Shaw, "is not after the fashion of this world". Ideal for eremitical seclusion it was, but not otherworldly enough to keep the Vikings from raiding in 812 and again in 823, though there could have been but scant plunder. In 956, however, a Norse prince, Olaf Trygveson, was baptized here and then went on to introduce Christianity to Scandinavia.

Up until about a century ago, Skellig Michael was a retreat for penitents, who sailed out to perform the island's Stations of the Cross. The most perilous of these involves squeezing though a narrow aperture called the Eye of the Needle and then clambering out along a sliver of rock 200 metres (660 feet) above the turbulent sea in order to kiss a cross pecked into its tip.

Excursion boats from the **Skellig Experience**, an interpretive centre on Valentia Island, circle but do not land on the Skelligs. Alternatively, it's possible to make private arrangements for a fishing boat in Ballinskelligs, Cahirciveen, Knightstown or Waterville. Landing is not permitted on Little Skellig, a bird sanctuary; but the proscription seems a mere formality, as it's next to impossible anyway—unless you happen to be one of the thousands of gannets, fulmars or gulls which roost upon the unwelcoming rock. Landing on Skellig Michael is only just possible in the best of conditions.

South of Cahirciveen, the Ring of Kerry runs inland for a spell, while minor roads lead west out to wild, wave-battered cliffs and to **Ballinskelligs**, a favourite locality for Gaelic-speaking students. Across Ballinskelligs Bay, and

Daniel O'Connell, "the Liberator"

Born in 1775 into a shrewd old Catholic Gaelic family, which prosperously survived the Protestant Ascendancy through trading and smuggling, Daniel O'Connell studied law and entered politics. In 1823, he organized the Catholic Association, which had the backing of the clergy and the grass-roots support of small landholders and tenant farmers. The association's membership dues of a penny a month earned O'Connell the derisive nickname of the King of the Beggars, but it was a canny strategy. The pennies accumulated into a huge war chest and fueled a potent new political force. Even British Prime Minister William Gladstone acknowledged him as "the greatest popular leader the world has ever known".

In the 1828 parliamentary elections—a time when Catholics still were barred from public office—Clare elected O'Connell with such a staggeringly lopsided majority that Westminster didn't dare refuse to seat him. In a stroke, O'Connell had swept away the severest impediment to Catholic emancipation.

Daniel O'Connell

A clochan, Dingle Peninsula, Co. Kerry

firmly back on the ring route, is **Waterville**, a resort town on a golden beach that has been popular since Victorian times. Charlie Chaplin was quite fond of the sportfishing here, and he was a frequent visitor. Irish legend also records that—because the Ark was full—Noah's son Bith, with two other men and 50 women, sailed into Ballinskelligs Bay in 2958 BC to escape the Great Flood. The three men apportioned the women among them, but Bith and another man died soon thereafter. The last fellow, Fintán, overwhelmed by his responsibility, ran away.

After Waterville the highway climbs steadily, through a wilderness of grey stone tumbled about on the heathy mountains, up to the Pass of Coomakista, which offers spacious views over Ballinskelligs Bay and the Skelligs.

Tiny **Caherdaniel** sits in the midst of the exceptionally lovely coastal scenery of Derrynane National Historic Park. In addition to good bathing beaches, rockbound bays, golden dunes and a riotously overgrown nature reserve, you'll find Derrynane House, home of Daniel O'Connell. It's now a museum full of period furnishings and memorabilia of "the Liberator".

Derrynane Harbour received a rather surprised visitor in August 1992. A 71-year-old American sailed solo from Maine in a ten-metre sloop, intending to visit his brother in Scotland. Somehow he had taken a wrong turn in the mid-Atlantic and landed here instead, mistaking the locals for Scotsmen with a curious accent.

On the side of Eagle's Hill, three kilometres (two miles) up a rough lane northeast of Castlecove, is **Staigue Fort**, dating from about 1000 BC. Many consider this almost perfectly preserved Iron Age stone cashel, with its six-metre (20-foot)-high walls, interior stairways and fairly sophisticated masonry, to be the finest and most impressive of its kind in Ireland.

The tidy village of **Sneem** sits below Knocknagantee Mountain, where Kerry's ancient breed of lithe, terra-cotta-hued cattle graze among the furze bushes. Sneem is mainly a tourist shopping opportunity, but it's a pretty spot nonetheless, with a frothing river crashing right through and fine beaches close by. The houses are painted in a palette of Impressionist colors, so that—claim local wags—inebriated residents can find their way home after a spree.

Southeast of Sneem is **Parknasilla**. There's safe swimming in the sheltered coves and good walks to be had in the surrounding lush woods. This was a favourite holiday getaway for George Bernard Shaw, and he wrote part of *Saint Joan* here.

The end (or beginning) of the Ring of Kerry is the pleasant village of **Kenmare**, which is well stocked with cafés, pubs, restaurants and craft shops. It also has a wonderful location, where the River Roughty empties into the Kenmare River (not really a river but a long, narrow estuary) and the jumbled Derrynasaggart Mountains pile up behind it. The Killarney-Bantry road (N71) runs through, and Kenmare makes a good base from which to explore the wild lands of the Beara Peninsula to the southwest. To finish the Ring of Kerry, continue north up to Moll's Gap (see page 144) and on to Killarney.

Dingle Peninsula and the Blaskets

Most parts of Ireland's west coast have their partisans, but for scenery and atmosphere it's hard to beat the Dingle Peninsula. A cloud-hung spine of sandstone mountains runs its length and high cliffs gird much of its shoreline, which is notched with bays and golden beaches. West from Dingle Town is a Gaeltacht district, with troves of monastic and pre-Christian antiquities that would take months to explore seriously. If the scenery seems familiar, it may be that you recognize it from *Far and Away*, filmed here in 1991.

Two routes lead into the peninsula: the southern, fuchsia-bordered route (described below) follows the long blue furrow of Dingle Bay, while the northern approach skirts the lush coastal plain of Tralee Bay in the shadow of the dark Slieve Mish Mountains.

From Castlemaine, the southern route (R561) runs to **Inch**, located at the foot of a curious anomaly—a long white sand-spit hanging down more than halfway across the bay. Evidence of very early human habitation has been uncovered among the dunes. Today it's mostly the haunt of turnstones, oyster-catchers and other seabirds, and has some of the area's best beaches.

With its excellent, nearly landlocked harbour, **Dingle Town** was Kerry's chief port in the 14th and 15th centuries, and later did a brisk business as a haven for smugglers. Now the lovely fishing village (population 1,400) has found a thriving new trade. Every day in summer the tourists pour in by bus, car, bike and thumb—many of them young French, Germans and Americans who flock to the village like returning swallows. Somehow Dingle avoids being overwhelmed and has managed to hold on to its great charm.

With its back to the high sweep of treeless mountains inland, Dingle turns to face south across the rocking boats in the bay.

Fishing is central to the local ecomony, but a quirky boon arrived in 1984 in the form of Fungi, a bottlenose dolphin who appears regularly in the bay. This lone male—treated with almost mystical veneration by many—seems to bask in the attention of tour boats and divers who visit him.

Dingle is a welcome exception to the peculiar Irish situation of not being able to get a fresh fish meal in a fishing port. Lord Blake's, Beginish and Doyle's, all on the pricey side, have earned high marks for their seafood cuisine. A popular alternative is An Café Liteártha, a café-cum-bookshop serving hearty soups, baked goods and other inexpensive fare, and stocking a worthy selection of local-interest titles.

O'Flaherty's has a traditional session on most evenings, though the pub may be too jammed to get in. An Droichead Beag also has music regularly, as do several of Dingle's many other pubs. Just ask around.

Since the days when the arrival of an itinerant dancing master was an event in a village, there has been a robust tradition of dancing in Kerry. Arthur Young, writing near the end of the 18th century, noted that even parents who could afford no other luxury endeavoured to have their children tutored in the latest steps.

Set dancing, something like American square dancing, is still a popular social pastime in Ireland. It's not unusual to happen on an out-of-the-way Kerry pub with music ringing to the rafters and packed with stoical farmers and fishermen and their wives swirling like dervishes into the small hours. Stop in at Dingle's Hillgrove Hotel on a Thursday night, and you'll have an idea of what the poet James Lyman Molloy was remembering when he mused, "O, the days of Kerry dancing . . ."

From Dingle, the narrow inland road climbs through the interior between steep Slievanea and Ballysitteragh mountains, cresting at 456-metre (1,496-foot)-high Conor Pass. When the pass isn't shawled with clouds, the views south over Dingle Bay and north to the bays of Brandon and Tralee are magnificent.

The coastal road (R559) from Dingle to Slea Head wraps around Ventry Harbour, another fine port that formerly overshadowed Dingle in importance, before rising over the flanks of Mount Eagle and into **Fahan**. Hereabouts lies scattered Ireland's richest congregation of *gallans* (standing stones), sculpted crosses, ring forts and *clochans* (beehive-shaped stone huts). Most of the remains date from the sixth to tenth centuries, but the mortarless stone domes, sprouting like hundreds of mushrooms over the hillsides, were still being built until fairly recently (local farmers even now use them for storage) and in a style so changeless that it may take an expert to determine whether a *clochan* was built 150 or 1,500 years ago.

Mighty Dunbeg occupies a spectacular promontory surrounded by water on three sides. Erosion over the course of 2,000 or so years since the fort was built has crumbled the outer walls into the sea. The views along the coast from here out to Slea Head are fantastic: savage cliffs, solitary cottages and swaying green fields, all suffused in the misty sea-light that distorts perspective and renders the end-of-the-world vastness of the place even more unreal. J.M. Synge was moved to declare the peninsula's resplendent beauty "almost a grief in the mind".

If you have ever seen *Ryan's Daughter* you might recognize the coast hereabouts. Don't look for the fictional village of Kirrary, though; it was constructed near Dunquin for the film but was torn down after the shooting was done.

The clutch of seven islands and rock stacks that make up the **Blasket Islands** are Europe's most westerly outposts. They're often called "the next parish to America", for there's nothing between them and Boston but the blue Atlantic. Fishing communities once flourished here, and the islands were a last refuge for starved, evicted mainlanders during the 19th century; it's recorded that the population of the Blaskets doubled as a result of the 1840s famine. But emigration took its share, and in 1953 the depleted population of barely one hundred finally deserted the Great Blasket after a run of poor fishing seasons. The crochet of fields above their abandoned village can still be clearly discerned from the mainland.

The voluptuously curved hills of the Great Blasket give it the look of a seal lolling on the water, not half a league offshore. It looks almost close enough to

Pipe band at Puck Fair

skip a stone across, but the frequently stormy and treacherous Blasket Sound kept the islanders cut off. The isolation, however, helped to preserve Gaelic custom and nourished a surprising lode of native literature. In the 1930s and '40s, just as the island way of life was fading forever, it was vividly pictured by Peig Sayers (1873–1958) in *An Old Woman's Reflections*, Maurice O'Sullivan (1904–50) in *Twenty Years A-Growing*, and by Tomás Ó Crohan (1855–1937) in *The Islandman*—all written in Irish and later translated into English. At the end of his autobiography, Ó Crohan wrote, "Somewhere there should be a memorial of it all . . . for the like of us will never be again".

In summer, boats to Great Blasket depart the pier at Dunquin, weather permitting. Like as not, the craft that carries you out will be a *naomhóg*. Also called a Blasket canoe, the boats are constructed of tarred canvas stretched over a wooden frame, like the *curraghs* of Galway and Mayo, though the longer Kerry version, with its tapered stern, is considered the most elegantly proportioned and seaworthy of all the canvas-skinned vessels.

Unlike the *curraghs* of the northwest, though, which have been in use since before memory, the style wasn't introduced to the Dingle area until the middle of the 19th century. Blasket Islander Tomás Ó Crohan wrote that in his youth only wooden boats were used, and he recalled the marvel the first *curragh* in the district aroused. The *naomhóg*'s lightness and shallow draft make it easy to

Young farmers at Puck Fair, Killorglin, Co. Kerry

launch from a sandy beach, and so it's more useful here than a wooden boat, because—in the marvelous description one fisherman gave to J.M. Synge —"a canoe will swim in a handful of water". They're still built nearby in Ballydavid.

The population of Irish-speaking **Ballyferriter** swells in summer with students enrolled in Irish-language schools. They can also glimpse what 19th-century life was like here at the heritage centre. Ballyferriter was the birth-place of the 17th-century poet and patriot Pierce Ferriter. His family home, the now-ruined Castle Sybil, is about three kilometres (two miles) northwest of the village, just above Ferriter's Cove. The castle takes its name from Sybil Lynch of Galway, who eloped with Pierce. When her father arrived to reclaim her, Sybil hid herself in the cave beneath the castle, where she was drowned by the rising tide. Pierce himself was later hanged for his insurgency by the Cromwellians.

Another tragedy was played out a few years later at the nearby Dún an Oir. With papal backing, an invasion force of Italian, Spanish and Irish troops landed here in 1580 to foment rebellion against Queen Elizabeth. English troops, however, besieged and quickly overwhelmed the fort. Sir Walter Raleigh oversaw the massacre of all 600 of the surrendered garrison, while the poet Edmund Spenser witnessed the slaughter with righteous approval.

Across Smerwick Harbour, near Ballydavid, is one of the most important early Christian buildings in Ireland, the remarkable **Gallarus Oratory**. This tiny, one-room church, shaped like an overturned boat with its keel to the sky, is thought to date from as early as the eighth century. The design represents a transition between round beehive huts and later rectangular churches. Though sagging a bit in the roof, Gallarus is the best preserved of some 20 such orato-ries found at monastic sites around the country. Built without mortar, its stone walls and corbelled roof are a marvel of masonry, so expertly laid that the church is still sound and watertight after 12 centuries.

Shadowy Brandon Mountain, frequently obscured by clouds, dominates this part of the peninsula. At 953 metres (3,127 feet), it's the second-highest peak in Ireland. A pilgrim's path zigzags up from Kilmalkedar, near the Gallarus Oratory. From the summit you might descry—as did the mountain's name-sake, St. Brendan—the enchanted island of Hy-Brasil, away off to the west.

County Limerick

As the namesake and supposed birthplace of that most democratic of poetic forms, the earthy sonnet of the *hoi polloi*, the name of Limerick has probably circulated far more widely on the metre of its literary invention than it would have on the strength of its own modest rural attractions alone.

The limerick's rhyme scheme, *aabba*, seems uniquely predisposed to sardonic and—more often—bawdy lyrics. What the haiku is to concise elegance, the limerick is to double-entendre and carnal excess. It was probably the 19th-century English writer Edward Lear who did the most to popularize the limerick, but no less luminescent literati than Huxley, Rossetti, Swinburne and Auden were also attracted to its loping cadence, and even Joyce found the humble form worthy of a little dabbling. But by far the limerick's most prolific master must be the redoubtable and seemingly inexhaustible Anonymous, to whom the following specimen is attributed:

> *There was a young fellow of Lyme,*
> *Who lived with three wives at one time.*
> > *When asked: "Why the third?"*
> > *He replied: "One's absurd,*
> *And bigamy, sir, is a crime".*

Bounded on the north by the Shannon, the interior of County Limerick, crosshatched by shaggy hedgerows, tends to be flattish, while the southern and eastern borders are hemmed by the Mullaghereirk, Ballyhoura, Galtee and Slievefelim mountains. Limestone and glacial deposits beneath the undulating plains make the county's rich pastures superb for the grazing of cattle and the breeding of horses.

Outside of Limerick City, the countryside is only infrequently interrupted by trim houses and the occasional village, giving the county quite a spacious feeling. "For miles and miles", wrote Seán O'Faoláin of Limerick, "not a sound but that soughing wind that makes the meadows and the wheat fields flow like water. All over the plain, where a crossroads is an event, where a little, sleepy lake is an excitement. Where their streams are rivers to them. Where their villages are towns".

As evidenced by the intricately wrought Ardagh Chalice, unearthed in a ring-fort near Newcastle West, the fertile lower reaches of the Shannon were generous to the numerous monasteries which grew fat and rich throughout the estuary region. They made easy pickings for the Vikings, who plundered the area time and again before deciding they liked it well enough to settle down here.

Limerick City

In modern Limerick there remains a reverberation of the name the invaders gave to the place—Hlymrekr, after the marshy lowlands here. On Inis Sibhtonn, a small island in the tea-brown Shannon where there had long been an important ford, the Norsemen founded an outpost, now Limerick City, in AD 922.

Brian Ború reclaimed the settlement for the Irish in 1000, making it the capital of Munster. Following the death of Dónal Mór O'Brien, king of Munster, in 1194, the Normans moved in and began a building spree that has left the county with over 400 castles. The chief family among them, the headstrong Fitzgeralds, or Geraldines as they and their vassals were called, were an independent lot who chafed under Tudor rule. Their doomed revolt against Elizabeth in 1571, however, brought devastation to Munster and an end to their dominion.

Limerick Town would figure significantly in the ongoing struggle against the English. Cromwell spent a full year hammering the town before it capitulated in 1650. And 40 years later it was to the haven of this walled city that rebel Irish forces repaired for the final defence after their critical defeat at the Battle of the Boyne. Two sieges ensued, in 1690 and 1691, before the Protestant troops of William of Orange forced the Irish to their knees. Patrick Sarsfield was able to negotiate a reasonable surrender for the Catholic Irish, though the terms were largely abrogated after he and 10,000 troops exiled themselves to France as part of the agreement. The Treaty Stone, upon which the broken Treaty of Limerick is said to have been signed, now stands at the west end of Thomond Bridge.

These sorrowful events are remembered in two poignant airs, "Lament for Limerick", commemorating the city's fall, and "The Wild Geese", which refers to the flight of Sarsfield and his men.

Being only 24 kilometres (15 miles) from Shannon Airport, Limerick is the initial destination for many visitors to Ireland. It also could well be the place that Limerick-bred novelist Kate O'Brien had in mind in describing "that grey smudge of a town called Mellick" in *Without My Cloak*.

Ireland's rather colourless fourth-largest city (population 65,000) is somewhat reminiscent of an English industrial town, though some sections, with their bright gardens and tawny brick houses, wouldn't be out of place in the

Cotswolds. The city fathers from time to time cry foul over what guidebook writers have to say about their fair city, and they do seem to have taken some pains in recent years to make Limerick more attractive. Everything worth seeing is concentrated on the east side of the Shannon, easily covered on foot.

One of the city's most touted attractions is the newly restored **King John's Castle**, whose massive gatehouse and round towers dominate what's now called King's Island, site of the Vikings' original settlement. Within the walls are siege engines, excavated pre-Norman dwellings and interpretive displays. Stone-arched Thomond Bridge, built in 1840, replaced the fortified span erected by King John in the 13th century.

Just around the corner, at Nicholas and Bridge streets, **St. Mary's Cathedral** looks stout enough itself to be a castle rather than a house of God. Built in 1172 by Dónal Mór O'Brien, the cathedral is worth a visit for a close look at the carved 15th-century oak misericords (the last of their ilk surviving in Ireland) and other monuments; *son-et-lumière* performances are held on summer evenings.

Excluded from English Town on King's Island, the native Irish established their own community across the River Abbey, a small Shannon tributary. The

Brother and "sister" at home, Co. Kerry

signposted walking tours through the old English and Irish districts are complemented by leaflets available at the Tourist Office, by the river at Arthur's Quay just west of Patrick Street.

South of the winding streets of the old town is the geometric grid of Georgian Limerick, begun in the mid-18th century, as the ancient walls of the city were being pulled down. (Fragments of the wall can still be seen along Lelia Street near St. John's Hospital.) The once-fashionable area around **St. John's Square**, dating to 1751, is seeing a revival. The **Limerick Museum**, on the west side of the square, exhibits an impressive collection spanning the Neolithic era through modern times. The 86-metre (282-foot) spire of neo-Gothic **St. John's Cathedral**, just off the square, is Ireland's highest.

During the 19th century, some 900 young women in Limerick were employed in the production of lace. The factory is gone, but delicate lace is still made and sold at **Good Shepherd Convent** in Clare Street.

The **Belltable Arts Centre**, at 69 O'Connell Street, presents plays, art exhibits and music and runs a café. A short walk east along Mallow Street leads to the green oasis of **People's Park** and the **City Library and Art Gallery**, which features a permanent collection of 18th- to 20th-century Irish art, as well as visiting exhibits.

Five kilometres (three miles) east of the city centre, off the Limerick-Dublin highway (N7) at the University of Limerick, the **Hunt Museum** displays perhaps the finest assemblage of Celtic and medieval antiquities outside of Dublin's National Museum. Also there is a tribute to self-reflection—the **National Self-Portrait Collection**, with paintings by Ireland's foremost artists.

A number of Limerick venues offer **entertainment**; see the *Limerick Leader* or the Tourist Office for extensive listings. For Irish music, try Nancy Blake's in Denmark Street, Foley's at 2 Lower Shannon Street, the Vintage Club in Ellen Street, or, occasionally, The White House, corner of O'Connell and Glentworth, which also serves a hearty lunch and superior Guinness.

West toward Kerry

Ireland's prettiest village, many will tell you, is **Adare**, 16 kilometres (ten miles) southwest of Limerick on the N21. Its location along the wooded banks of the River Maigue, the meticulously thatched cottages along either side of the broad main street, and a number of ecclesiastical and feudal remains make it nearly storybook-perfect. The soaring Tudor Gothic–style Adare Manor, former seat of the earls of Dunraven built in the mid-19th century, has been restored as a luxury hotel. Its extensive gardens on the 3.4-square-kilometre (840-acre) estate are open to the public. The Augustinian Friary, founded in 1315, is noteworthy for its stone carvings. Restored in 1807, it is still used by the Church of Ireland. Check at the office of the Adare Manor Golf Club before visiting the well-preserved ruins of the romantic **Franciscan Friary**, founded in 1464 and ravaged by parliamentary forces 200 years later. Ruins of the lofty 13th-century Desmond Castle, standing beside the Maigue, include the square keep, great halls, bakery and stables.

The late composer, musician and Adare native Seán Ó Riada—who was instrumental in bringing together the Chieftains and in helping to revive Irish music in the 1960s—is remembered with a plaque on the 1840 limestone courthouse, where musical sessions are held of an evening. In July, the ambitious Adare Festival stretches over two weeks with classical, jazz and pop performances.

Restored **Castle Matrix** is open to the public 13 kilometres (eight miles) southwest of Adare. The square keep was erected around 1440 by the seventh earl of Desmond, one of the earliest Normans to write poetry in Irish. The Elizabethan poets Edmund Spenser and Walter Raleigh first met at Matrix, in 1580, and here Lord Southwell cultivated Ireland's first potatoes, brought back from the New World by Raleigh. Castle Matrix, whose unusual name comes from Matres, the Celtic goddess of love and poetry, also houses an important collection of documents relating to Patrick Sarsfield and the Wild Geese.

A number of ruins merit exploration around **Askeaton**. Fifteenth-century Desmond Castle dominates the village from its rocky islet in the River Deel, and some exceptional carvings survive in the 1389 Franciscan friary downstream. Alongside the Shannon estuary, **Foynes** was the terminus of the transatlantic seaplane service from America in the 1930s and '40s. The era is recalled in the GPA Foynes Flying Boat Museum. Foynes also hosts a week of sailboat racing in June and July. Farther west is the attractive village of Glin, where nearby **Glin Castle** and its beautiful gardens, still the home of a scion of the Fitzgeralds, open to the public in late spring.

Limerick's hilly western borderlands offer some good walking opportunities south of Glin; the area is also noted for traditional music, particularly in the villages of Athea and Abbeyfeale. Two kilometres (one mile) south of Abbeyfeale, the ruined walls of Portrinard Castle stand as a crumbling monument to *amour,* for this was the seat of the sixth earl of Desmond, a love-struck lord who forfeited lands and title for Catherine MacCormick, the peasant girl he loved.

The South and East

It was in **Croom**, on the comfortable banks of the River Maigue south of Limerick City, that the celebrated 18th-century Filí na Máighe spun a large body of love songs, patriotic ballads and other poetry in the Irish language, including the form now known as the limerick. One of their company, Aindrias MacCraith, cast out from Croom for his philandering by the parish priest, counted his painful losses in "Slán le Máigh" ("Farewell to the Maigue"), concluding with:

> *And farewell beyond all others to one who will be nameless,*
> *The lady-like, soft-lipped, joyous fair one,*
> *Who banished me once to a life of wandering.*
> *The love of my heart, but for Ireland I'll not tell her name.*

Students of modern Irish history might consider a stop at Bruree, just east of the Mallow road (N20), for a visit to the **De Valera Museum**, housed in the small school that the late independence fighter, prime minister and president attended as a lad.

At **Kilmallock**, the fortified Blossom Gate and portions of the town wall remain from the reign of the Fitzgeralds. The once lovely and prosperous town was in former times one of the foremost in Munster, but today the attraction is the roofless 13th-century Dominican friary. The carvings and delicate windows—especially the five-lancet east window—are unusually fine.

County Clare

With the "dark mutinous Shannon waves" to the south, the serpentine banks of Lough Derg to the east, and Galway Bay and the restless Atlantic to the west and northwest, County Clare is a great recumbent peninsula, moated on three sides.

From the flattish lowlands bordering the Shannon estuary, Clare swells up 300–500 metres (1,000–1,600 feet) in the Slieve Bernagh and Slieve Aughty mountains in the east and in the north to the bony limestone uplands of the Burren. In between, it's mostly rolling dairy country, dotted with dozens of smallish loughs well regarded for their good fishing. Cliffs rim miles of Clare's western edge, but nowhere else with such abrupt finality as at the Cliffs of Moher, between Liscannor and Doolin.

Above all, Clare is known as a mecca for traditional music. Distinct from the crisp dance cadences of adjacent Kerry's polkas and slides, the Clare style slows the music down a little. The Clare player seems to linger a bit over each note, gracing it with unhurried ornamentation; yet its flowing, irresistible pulse keeps the music ever in motion, undulating like the plains at the county's heart.

Ennis and Thereabouts

Some quarter-million visitors each year first set foot to Irish terra firma at Shannon International Airport, sited where the island-crowded Fergus estuary joins the River Shannon. "It may not be a radiant starting point", novelist Kate O'Brien wrote, "but first impressions need not dazzle; and a slow approach is wise where true acquaintance is expected". The main highway (N18) runs past the airport, connecting Limerick City with Ennis.

In fact, all roads in Clare seem to lead to **Ennis**, the hub of commerce, administration and transport. This county seat (population 8,000) astride the River Fergus, with its narrow twisting streets, still retains a medieval cast. The Tourist Office in Bank Street publishes a useful walking-tour map.

The town in 1828 saw the historic election of Daniel O'Connell to Parliament, the first Irish Catholic to be seated in Westminster. The statue in O'Connell Square, site of O'Connell's nomination, commemorates the Great Liberator and his startlingly enlightened credo: "The greatest political advantages are not worth the shedding of a single drop of human blood". Eamon de

Valera, elected to Parliament for Clare in 1917, is remembered too with a statue outside the grand Palladian courthouse, and with the De Valera Museum and Library in Harmony Row.

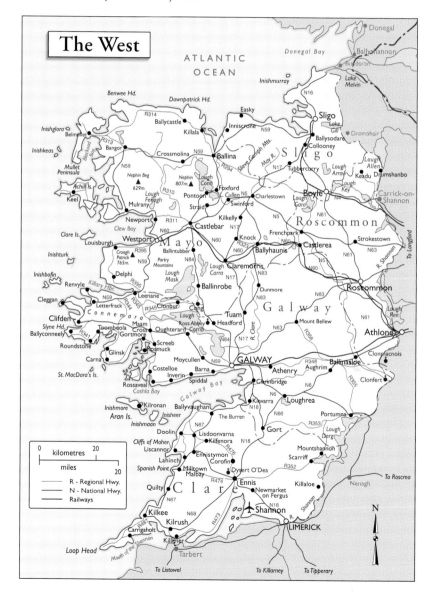

Ennis Abbey in Francis Street was founded in 1250 as a Franciscan friary by the O'Briens, who around 1300 made some striking additions. Notable are the soaring east window and a good deal of stone carving within, while the tower, with its speartip parapets, is an oddly incongruous 15th-century addition.

Music is one of Ennis's strongest draws. For a taste of the sweet Clare traditional style, try Kelly's pub at 5 Carmody Street, Brogan's and Brandon's in O'Connell Street, or May Kearney's on Newbridge Road for sessions, or the Cois na hAbhna, a kilometre (one-half mile) north of town for more formal entertainment. There's also jazz regularly at the Old Ground Hotel in O'Connell Street. In late May, Ennis hosts the Fleadh Nua, a weekend of dance and music, and a tamer alternative to the no-holds-barred Fleadh Cheoil na hÉireann.

In the fields outside the village of Quin, east of Ennis, is the almost perfectly intact **Quin Abbey**. This 15th-century Franciscan friary grew out of the ruins of a Norman castle. To the left of the high altar is the final resting place of one "Fireball" MacNamara, the redoubtable duellist. He christened his deadly pistols Bas Gan Sagart ("Death without the Priest"), and with them he felled 45 opponents before his own death (by natural causes) around 1500. Take in the broad expanse of surrounding countryside by climbing the spiral stairs up one of the towers. Five kilometres (three miles) on is **Knappogue Castle**, a 1467 MacNamara stronghold. Medieval banquets are offered on summer nights in the restored castle, set amongst craft workshops and gardens.

Just north on the Newmarket on Fergus–Moymore road is the **Craggaunowen Project**, a showpiece of historical presentation centred on another MacNamara tower house. Buildings here span some 2,000 years of Irish history. In a tree-fringed lake squats a *crannóg*, a man-made islet with Iron Age–style thatched dwellings, encircled by a wattle fence and accessible via a short causeway. Within the reconstructed ring fort—a usually more domestic than defensive enclosure—is a souterrain, an underground chamber in which the early Irish stored food, or took refuge in times of danger. Also at Craggaunowen, the *Brendan,* the leather-hulled *curragh* in which Tim Severin and crew replicated St. Brendan's voyage to America (see page 166), has found a final berth.

The Irish Discover America: The Voyage of Saint Brendan the Navigator

Many of Ireland's early Christians were of a distinctly eremitical persuasion, men whose craving for solitude drew them to the island's outermost reaches, to such lonely outposts as the forlorn Skelligs off the Kerry coast. For some pious ascetics, even that was not remote enough from society's distractions, and by the end of the eighth century a number of Irish anchorites were leading lives of holy deprivation on the bony coast of Thule (Iceland) and even, perhaps, the eastern shores of North America.

Those distant beachheads of Christianity, according to legend, were first spied some two centuries earlier by St. Brendan, the most celebrated of Ireland's seafarers. Born in AD 484 in Fenit village, on a sea-girded isthmus in Tralee Bay, the religious-minded lad was immersed in the maritime arts and lured by the murmuring sea. After his ordination, he founded a monastery close by, at Ardfert, but the restless young priest yearned for a greater seclusion that would bring him closer to divinity.

In a vision one night, an angel promised to guide Brendan to a wondrous island the priest had beheld across the western sea. Gathering a crew of 17 like-minded monks, Brendan built a boat, wood-ribbed and sheathed in ox hide (nearly identical to the lightweight *curraghs* still used 15 centuries later), and laid in provisions for a 40-day journey.

The voyage that followed is recounted in the tenth-century *Navigatio Sancti Brendani*—a medieval best-seller that saw translation into numerous languages. While full of clearly fanciful embellishments, the *Navigatio* is also illuminated by many tantalizingly factual references, enough to convince some scholars that Brendan was the first European to reach America—a thousand years before what's-his-name took a notion to sail the ocean blue.

According to the tale, Brendan and his crew sailed first to Inishmore, to receive the blessing of St. Enda, thence westward, "over the wave-voice of the strong-maned sea, and over the storm of the green-sided waves, and over the mouths of the marvelous, awful, bitter ocean, where they saw the multitude of the furious red-mouthed monsters, with abundance of the great sea-whales".

Among their landfalls was an island where "hideous furry mice" the size of cats devoured one of their members. In the middle of the sea the travellers came upon the penitent Judas, perched upon a stone and doomed to endure horrible torments until Judgement Day. As Eastertime arrived with no land in sight, a fish of mammoth proportions surfaced, offering its back as temporary terra firma upon which the holy men could celebrate Mass.

Nearing what could have been the volcanically active environs of Iceland, the monks were vouchsafed a glimpse of what they took for the edge of Hell: a mountain rising out of the sea "shooting up flames into the sky" with "the noise of bellows blowing like thunder".

A number of other geography-specific references lend credence to the *Navigatio* as an essentially factual account. One passage, for example, describes Brendan's awe at a massive iceberg, an encounter most likely to occur west of Greenland. A thousand leagues to the south, the Irishmen found themselves becalmed for three days on a sea "like a thick curdled mass", an apt description of the seaweed-choked Sargasso Sea east of the Bahamas.

At last, after seven years and many other adventures, the mariners found Brendan's promised land, a capacious, abundant country "thickly set with trees, laden with fruits", and rich in precious stones. For 40 days they explored without reaching the ends of it. A youth they met there prophesied, with uncanny acumen, that "after many years this land will be made manifest to those who come after you".

continues

St. Brendan celebrates Mass on the back of a great fish.

Their goal accomplished, Brendan and his men then sailed straightaway for home. The saint went on to found monastic sites in Munster and Connacht, most notably at Clonfert, where he now lies buried in the cathedral.

The hyperbole aside, the glowing accounts of this new world in the *Navigatio* could describe just about any place along the eastern seaboard of North America, which frustrates scholars trying to pinpoint the precise whereabouts of "Hy-Brazil", Brendan's fair isle. Some even speculate that Brendan was welcomed in Mexico as Quetzalcoatl, the tall, fair-skinned god from across the sea, whose coming Aztec myth had foretold.

To later European explorers, the *Navigatio Sancti Brendani* was no mere literary curiosity; its text was scrutinized for clues about navigating the mysterious Atlantic. Even as late as 1865, Hy Brazil would appear on nautical charts. In the 1490s, it is said, one of the book's most avid readers, Christopher Columbus, visited Ireland's west coast in hopes of uncovering additional details of Brendan's epic voyage, and he took pains to include several Irish sailors on his own journeys west.

In May 1976, British adventurer Tim Severin and a crew of 12 sailed from Ireland in a wood-and-leather *curragh* to prove that the sixth-century monks could actually have made the crossing. In the 11-metre (36-foot) craft, christened the *Brendan* and fashioned according to ancient methods, they re-created Brendan's route, sailing north to the Hebrides and the Faeroes, and then west via Iceland and Greenland, to make landfall at Newfoundland a year and six weeks later. The redoubtable *Brendan* is now displayed at Craggaunowen in County Clare.

Some sort of fortification has stood on the site of **Bunratty Castle** since the 13th century, but this splendidly restored Norman-Irish tower house was constructed in 1460 by the MacNamara branch of the O'Brien clan. The castle is best known these days for its exceptional collection of 14th- to 17th-century furnishings and for its simulacrum of a medieval banquet. On the castle grounds is Bunratty Folk Park, where an agglomeration of cottages and other buildings re-create 19th-century village life. Wander among the shops, blacksmith's forge, school, weaver's shed, and craft shops to witness demonstrations of basket-weaving, butter-making, and other traditional skills that were a fundamental part of Irish life in bygone days.

A few kilometres east, 307-metre (1,007-foot)-high Woodcock Hill anchors the southern extremity of the Slieve Bernagh range. On its flanks grow the darkly mysterious Cratloe Woods, a vestige of the great sea of oak forest which once covered Ireland. Richard II plundered these woodlands for their mighty timbers—some seven metres (24 feet) long and a metre (three feet) thick—with which he built the hammer-beam roof of London's Westminster Hall in 1399.

Lough Derg and the Lakelands

Lough Derg, largest of the Shannon lakes, forms most of Clare's eastern border. Along its west bank, a few villages cater to boaters, anglers and water-skiers. Where the land pinches together at the foot of the lake, the pleasant village of **Killaloe** huddles on a lazy S of the river below the rounded Slieve Bernaghs. The 13-arch stone bridge spanning the Shannon at this important fording place is the last opportunity to cross before Portumna, some 65 kilometres (40 miles) by road to the northeast.

This was unmistakably O'Brien country since before the tenth century, and the clan left a number of monuments. Among them is the 13th-century St. Flannan's Cathedral on the riverbank, a simple building with a sumptuously carved Romanesque doorway and, in front of it, the Thorgrim stone. Inscribed around AD 1000 with both *ogham* and runic inscriptions—an extreme rarity—

Early crosses, the Burren, Co. Clare

this fragment of a larger cross is a sort of Irish Rosetta stone that invokes, across the centuries, "A blessing upon Thorgrim", the inscription's author.

Crowning the hilltop above the town, the Catholic church is believed to occupy the site of Kincora, Brian Ború's now-vanished palace. It was this native son of Clare who in 1002 ascended to the high-kingship of Ireland and in 1014 gave the Vikings a mortal thrashing at Clontarf. But Brian also died that day when a retreating Viking discovered the aged king unguarded in his pavilion. Bitter was the lamentation of Mac Liag, Ireland's chief poet and Brian's adviser:

> Oh where, Kincora, is Brian the great,
> And where is the beauty that once was thine,
> Oh where are the princes and nobles that sate,
> To feast thy halls and drink the red wine,
> Where, O Kincora?

> They are gone, those heroes of royal birth,
> Who plundered no churches, who broke no trust;
> 'Tis weary for me to be living on earth,
> When they, O Kincora, lie low in the dust,
> Low, O Kincora.

The road north alternately hugs the lakeside and mounts the hills for good views over Lough Derg. Just beyond Tuamgraney is Drewsboro House, birthplace of the brilliant contemporary novelist Edna O'Brien.

Neatly tended **Mountshannon** commands the high ground above a broad arm of Lough Derg. A popular port of call for lake cruisers, this is also the place to hire a boat out to **Holy Island** (Iniscealtra), where a Christian settlement founded by St. Caimin thrived from the seventh to 13th centuries. A 24-metre (80-foot)-high round tower, graveyard, five churches and other monastic buildings remain. Though Caimin established the monastery here for the purpose of pious isolation, the island was even then plagued with visitors.

Feakle, west of Scarriff in the southern foothills of the Slieve Aughty Mountains, employed Brian Merriman (1749-1805) for a time as school master. The poet chose the old chuchyard (where his bones now lie) and the wooded shores of nearby Lough Graney as the settings for his only known work, the satirical Cuirt an Mhean Oíche (The Midnight Court). In this 1,200-line poem, the last major work in Irish to be written before the Famine (and the only poem ever banned in Ireland), the narrator finds himself standing trial before the Queen of the Fairies. His offense? Recalcitrant bachelorhood.

Postponing marriage—even into one's 40s or 50s—was a peculiarly Irish solution to the problem of subdividing family lands into uselessly small allotments. But among the consequences was a shrinking population:

> *The Court considered the country's crisis,*
> *And what do you think its main advice is—*
> *That unless there's a spurt in procreation*
> *We can bid goodbye to the Irish nation;*
> *It's growing smaller year by year—*
> *And don't pretend that's not your affair.*

The poem goes on to bemoan the unhappy fate of tender brides wedded to reluctant old codgers while the "primest beef" of Irish manhood is wasted in the celibacy of priesthood! In the proper spirit of the bard, various Clare towns host the Merriman Summer School each year, a week-long confabulation where revelry is taken at least as seriously as literary edification.

The restored white cottage of **Biddy Early** stands atop a brushy knoll south of Feakle. It was from this copper-haired healer and practitioner of white magic that Lady Gregory derived much of the material for *Visions and Beliefs of the West of Ireland*. Biddy outlived three husbands and married a fourth— "a fine young man"—when still just a slip of a girl herself in her 80s. The parish priest, naturally, took a dim view of her doings, and upon her death he cast her fortune-telling bottle into the nearby tarn of Kilbarron, where it remains to this day.

Between Feakle and Corofin, 35 kilometres (22 miles) to the west, lies the broad swath known as the Clare Lakelands, a sparsely settled area that's excellent for trout and pike fishing. A shattered round tower and remains of a church stand in lonesome isolation at **Dysert O'Dea**, south of Corofin off the Ennis road. Above the church doorway, 19 grotesque stone heads arch mutely in a Romanesque semicircle. The severed human head was central to early Celtic mythology, a talisman of extreme potency capable of foretelling the future and averting evil. The great champion Cuchulain brandished precisely the same number, nine heads in one hand and ten in the other, to chill the hearts of his enemies. Perhaps the 12th-century carvers at Dysert O'Dea, with this memory of remote paganism in mind, placed these heads here to turn away the enemies of Christianity.

Atop a grassy rise is the tall 12th-century White Cross of Tola, intricately carved with zoomorphic patterns, the figure of the crucified Christ, and below him a crosier-bearing bishop—perhaps St. Tola himself. In 1318, Muircheartach O'Brien defeated Richard de Clare in a mighty confrontation here and expelled the Normans, leaving this ancient kingdom of Thomond to its own devices until Henry VIII reasserted English dominion in the 1530s.

The shell of marvelous **Leamaneh Castle**, eight kilometres (five miles) northwest of Corofin, bridges the transition from 15th-century fortified tower to 17th-century mansion. Legends of the iron-willed lady of the house, Máire Ruadh (Red Mary) MacMahon, have grown with the telling. According to one story, following her husband's death at the hands of the Cromwellians in 1651, she immediately wed an English soldier in order to save her lands from confiscation. Her purpose achieved, the new bride pushed him out of a tower window when she objected to some remark he made concerning her late husband.

The Burren

In Clare's northwestern corner, the county's primeval limestone skeleton is exposed in the enigmatic, starkly beautiful landscape of the Burren. Over the eons, the remorseless action of rain has eroded the porous limestone, etching an otherworldly surface of stony pillows, deep fissures and corrugations made as if by a harrow. Deep below it all spread labrynthine networks of fantastic caverns. Another feature, *turloughs,* or disappearing lakes, form as rainwater gathers in the hollows, only to seep away within a few days into the hidden veins of the earth. This karst topography spreads over 500 square kilometres (124,000 acres) of Clare and across the sound to the Arans, which are composed of the same limestone strata.

Cromwell's General Ludlow, a man of finite imagination, dismissed the Burren as "a country where there is not water enough to drown a man, wood enough to hang one, or earth enough to bury him". But these hills and plateaus of grey stone are not the sterile moonscape they might at first appear. From the seams sprout brilliant saxifrages, cranesbills, Delft-blue gentians, maidenhair ferns, orchids and scores of other arctic, alpine and Mediterranean species which fascinate botanists—not least because they have no business growing together in such inexplicable proximity. Blooms usually peak mid-May to June.

Those who take the time to explore the Burren will be at it a good long while before they exhaust its surprises. The Burren Display Centre in **Kilfenora** offers an introduction to the area's natural and human history; another useful resource is Tim Robinson's outstanding map of the Burren, available at the centre and bookshops. Also in Kilfenora, don't miss the small, 12th-century "cathedral" of St. Fachtnan. The roofless chancel is full of strange stone effigies, and on the grounds are several high crosses, most notably the four-metre (13-foot)-high Doorty Cross, depicting a bishop and other figures in bas-relief.

Poulnabrone Dolmen, the Burren

As inhospitable to human habitation as the Burren may appear, the region was in fact once densely populated, as the profuse littering of dolmens, ring forts, cairns and other constructions attests. The stone ring fort of **Cahermacnaghten**, seven kilometres (four miles) northeast of Kilfenora on the west side of the road to Corkscrew Hill, marks the site of O'Davoren's Town. This was Ireland's most important school of Brehon law (the ancient Gaelic legal code, abolished under James I), which thrived as late as the 17th century. Now the high walls and some foundations are all that remain, but the sense that these abandoned hills once hummed with human endeavour gives the Burren a haunted feeling.

One of the most photographed of the Burren's monuments is the stone table of **Poulnabrone Dolmen**, which marks the burial place of a Stone Age Irishman who died around 2500 BC. It's just east of the road a kilometre or so north of Caherconnel. Three kilometres (two miles) north is the well-preserved Glenisheen wedge tomb, and then comes **Aillwee Cave**, discovered in 1944; it's not the most impressive of the Burren's numerous caverns, but it is the only one developed for tourism.

The pretty village of **Ballyvaughan** at the Burren's northern border looks out on Galway Bay. Look in at Monk's Pub or the Ballyvaughan Inn for music on weekends. From here, you can continue in three directions. East along the Galway road, the handsome grey ruin of 12th-century **Corcomroe Abbey**, with a delicately vaulted choir and narrow lancet windows in the east wall, slumbers in a placid valley. Yeats used this locale as the background for *The Dreaming of the Bones*. In the play a modern revolutionary encounters the ghost of Dermot MacMurrough (see page 231) seeking forgiveness for all the troubles he brought on Ireland. Not far from here, at Burrin pier, G.B. Shaw set some scenes of his *Back to Methuselah*.

The coast road west from Ballyvaughan via Black Head opens on unimpeded views over the Aran Islands and across the bay to Galway, where the blue mountains of Connemara run up and down the horizon like a graph. The inland route to Lisdoonvarna, across the layer cake of **Corkscrew Hill**, loops higher and higher, playing hide-and-seek with Galway Bay. On a clear day the vista is spectacular.

Visitors have been taking the waters since the early 1800s at **Lisdoonvarna**, Ireland's principal mineral-springs spa. Among other events throughout the summer, the town hosts a folk festival in mid-July, and, through the month of September, the famous matchmaking festival, which brings hopeful ladies from around Ireland and abroad for dancing, music and introductions to eligible Irish bachelors.

The West Coast

Any traveller with an interest in Irish music will have heard about **Doolin** (marked as "Fisherstreet" on many maps) long before coming anywhere near it. The tiny hamlet eight kilometres (five miles) west of Lisdoonvarna is hugely popular with young French and German tourists, who swell its several hostels till they must outnumber residents three to one. The attraction is good Clare music, supplied most evenings in Doolin's trio of often-crowded pubs. Doolin is also the place to catch a boat, weather permitting, for the 30-minute passage to Inisheer, the nearest of the Aran islands. Around the quay, the pocked limestone shelves of the Burren slip beneath the waves, returning to the sea from which they came.

The scenic coastal road south from Doolin arrives at Aill na Searrach (the "Cliff of the Colts"), the northernmost reach of the **Cliffs of Moher**. The renowned precipice stretches eight kilometres (five miles), around Hag's Head almost to Liscannor, reaching their highest elevation (about 200 metres/660 feet) at O'Brien's Tower near the northern end. Along the cliffs' dark bands of shale and sandstone, shorn away vertically by the sea-knives of the implacable Atlantic, seabirds—puffins, choughs, kittiwakes, gulls—nest on impossible clawholds.

Continuing south from the cliffs, pass the Ionic pillar of O'Brien's Monument, erected in modest tribute to himself (at the expense of his reluctant tenants) by the selfsame Cornelius O'Brien who put the tower on the Cliffs of Moher. Close by is **St. Brigid's Well**, a humble west Ireland Lourdes to which hopeful pilgrims come for its reputedly curative waters. The spring, along with the Irish themselves, made the seamless transition from paganism to Christianity, for in earlier times its holy properties were attributed to an ancient Celtic goddess before she was supplanted by the saint. (St. Joseph's Well has a similar shrine on a steep, wooded bank at Stackpoole's Bridge, two-and-a-half kilometres [1½ miles] southwest of Milltown Malbay.)

A gaunt 16th-century tower guards the fishing village of **Liscannor**. One of several scattered like broken teeth along this billowy coastline, this tower kept vigil against a Spanish invasion which never came. The reef at the mouth of Liscannor Bay, according to legend, marks the submerged location of the city and church of Kilstephen. John P. Holland, born in Liscannor in 1840, gets the credit for inventing the submarine. Although some might think this contribution of dubious value to human evolution, the U.S. Navy felt sufficiently grateful to donate a commemorative stone to the harbour in 1977.

Across the bay is the small seaside resort of **Lahinch**, where, according to the beloved songwriter Percy French, "the sea shines like a jewel". A pair of 18-hole golf courses spread above the broad, tawny beach, safe for swimming and among Ireland's few surfing spots. From here a short road connects inland with **Ennistymon**, an agreeable market town straddling the cascading River Cullenagh, amid hilly countryside of cattle pasture and wooded valleys. Among the town's colourfully painted shopfronts is one Nagle's, whose sign identifies it—without a suggestion of irony—as both bar and undertaker, an ingenious combination which surely must violate some Irish antitrust statute. The poet Brian Merriman was born here in 1749 (see page 170). There are fine walks and views along the river (notice the tiny hydroelectric station with which the riverside Falls Hotel generates its own power) and music in the

Cliffs of Moher, Co. Clare

pubs (try O'Malley's, Cooley's House, the Matchmaker's Shack, Carrigg's or Phil's Place).

The coast road south from Lahinch follows the cliff-sides along the bay before turning briefly inland to **Milltown Malbay**. The little town comes alive in early July during the Willie Clancy Summer School (named for the much-loved local piper), when musicians from all over the world arrive for lectures, *ceilis*, recitals, and tuition in *sean-nós* singing, flute, pipes, accordion, fiddle and other instruments. Every other doorway in Milltown seems to house a pub, and from every other one music emanates. The sessions linger later and later into the summer nights as the nine-day festival draws toward its climax, the big Saturday night concert. The Fiddler's Inn generally has music on weekends year-round.

There's safe swimming nearby at **Spanish Point**, named for the unfortunate crew of a Spanish warship who survived the wrecking of their vessel in 1588 only to be executed by the high sheriff of Clare.

Fishing is quite good at **Quilty**, both from the beach and offshore in hired boats. The great heaps of seaweed gathered on the shore here will be processed into fertilizers and food and beverage additives; it's the ingredient, for example, that gives stout its creamy head.

The road turns inland again here, not touching the coast again until **Kilkee**, a Victorian-era resort on a crescent strand wrapped around Moore Bay, a brief interruption in the spectacular cliffs which palisade so much of this coast. From Kilkee the N67 veers sharply to the east, but the long westerly tongue of land culminating at Loop Head calls for a detour. The signposted Sli na Mara coastal route around the peninsula takes in natural bridges, sea stacks, sea caves and cliffs. En route, the little grey church at Moneen preserves a strange carriagelike contraption known as the **Little Ark**. It's a testament to the determination of the Catholic Irish to practice their faith against stacked odds. Used from 1852 to 1857, when Catholicism was still suppressed and neither land nor church was available for services, the Little Ark would be wheeled to the coast where, in the no-man's-land between the high and low tides, the priest and his parishioners could celebrate Mass unmolested by Protestant authority.

At land's end, **Loop Head** (or Leap Head) takes its name from a curious legend. The mighty Cuchulain, fleeing the amorous attentions of a witch named Mal, leapt from the point to the large sea stack called Diarmuid and Gráinne's rock offshore. Mal matched his feat, but when Cuchulain leapt back to the mainland, she fell short, plummeting into the roiling channel. The current swept her body northward, coming ashore at the bay that now carries her name.

Along the Shannon

From the fine beach at Carrigaholt, the road (R473) skirts the expansive sheet of the Shannon estuary to the busy market town of Kilrush. Author Kate O'Brien had strong opinions about the river: "The Shannon is a formidable water; nothing parochial about it", she said in *My Ireland*, "nothing of prattle or girlish dream. It sweeps in and out of the ocean and the world according to the rules of far-out tides, and in association with dangerous distances".

In summer, from the nearby harbour of Cappagh, it's possible to find a boat out to the abandoned monastic settlement on **Scattery Island**. According to legend, the dauntless St. Senan slew the island's only inhabitant, a dragon, before founding this sixth-century settlement, which was intended—in true hermit fashion—to be free from all females, including cows, hens, sows and, of course, women. The 35-metre (115-foot) round tower (unusual in that its door is exposed at the ground level rather than elevated out of harm's reach) dominates the five churches and other ruins on this barren island. That any structures survive is surprising, as the monastery was plundered time and again by Vikings. Take a pebble with you from the shore of this holy island; they are said to have the power to protect the bearer from shipwreck.

Nine kilometres (six miles) east of Kilrush is the Clare terminus of the **Killimer-Tarbert car ferry**, a convenient shortcut to Kerry that avoids the long detour through Limerick. The R473 continues, however, up the Shannon and northeast along the Fergus estuary into Ennis.

Sunrise behind Ballinskelligs Abbey,
Co. Kerry

County Galway

"There's something in the core of me", wrote Oliver Gogarty, "that needs the West to set it free". As the heart of Ireland's wild west, Galway also inspired Yeats, Lady Gregory, Synge and others during the creative nationalist awakening of the Celtic Revival. With its magnificent landscapes and still-Gaelic culture, it was to them (and it remains) a potent symbol of an authentic old Ireland.

Ireland's second-largest county, Galway stretches from the tattered hem of its Atlantic coast, along the deep bight of Galway Bay, eastward to gentle pasturelands bordering the Shannon. It's a model of the country as a whole, embracing austere valleys, peat bogs, tiny hamlets, lively Galway town and the blue immensity of the Twelve Bens tumbling along the spine of Connemara. Ireland's most extensive Gaeltacht survives in County Galway, where half the population still speak a soft, swaying Irish as their first language.

Galway City

Sited on the narrow isthmus between Lough Corrib and the bay, Galway is the natural gateway to Connemara, the Joyce Country and the Arans. It's not surprising then that this strategic location on the salmon-silvered River Corrib has been settled since pre-Christian times, first by fisherfolk and later by traders and merchants. In 1226 the covetous Normans under Richard de Burgo wrested the village and fort here from the O'Flahertys. They fortified their settlement to keep the unwashed masses at bay, but before the century was out, as so often happened, Irish ways had seduced the outsiders: the name de Burgo was Hibernicized to Burke, and their loyalty to the English king evaporated.

The renegade Burkes soon found themselves displaced, however, by Welsh and Anglo–Norman settlers bolstered by royal patronage. Fourteen merchant families—among them Blake, Browne, Joyce, Morris and especially Lynch—rose in prominence and came to dominate the town, ruling it with jealous resolve like a private fiefdom. Their walled town became an Anglo-Norman enclave deep in hostile Irish territory. Fearful throughout the Middle Ages of attack from the dispossessed natives, they crafted a variety of statutes intended to keep the bellicose Connachtmen out, one declaring that "neither O nor Mac should strutte ne swagger thro the streets of Galway". And above one of the town's 14 gates they placed the famous invocation: "From the fury of the O'Flahertys good Lord deliver us".

Through brisk trade with the Continent, Spain in particular, the port town and its reigning oligarchy grew prosperous. In addition to wines and other imports, Spanish influence extended to local architecture, reflected in round-arched doorways and houses built around an interior courtyard. When the Cromwellians arrived in the 1650s, they found these frontier English families not quite English enough, deriding them as the "tribes" of Galway. For nine months, Sir Charles Coote besieged the staunchly royalist town, which at last capitulated in 1652. Galway took a beating again in 1691 from Williamite guns, and the once-proud city declined into a provincial backwater until this century.

Today Galway is the metropolis of western Ireland, the Republic's third-largest town (and some think its most *Irish*), with a rapidly growing population of over 50,000. Galway City's bayside location and robust cultural life have drawn some comparisons with San Francisco. While it's hardly a Hibernian Babylon by the Bay, affable Galway is decidedly a thriving centre for theatre, music, education and Irish culture.

University College, for example, is a magnet for Irish studies, with courses taught in both English and Irish; it's also a UNESCO archive for spoken material in all the Celtic languages. Irish is celebrated as well at **An Taibhdhearc** (pronounced "on THIVE-yark") **Theatre** in Middle Street, founded in 1928 as the national theatre for plays in the Irish language. The summer season leans toward traditional music and folk presentations, some bilingual, so that you need nary a smidgen of Gaelic to follow and appreciate the productions. The well-regarded **Druid Theatre**, in Chapel Lane off Shop Street, concentrates on new works by Irish playwrights.

Galway is not large, and walking is the best way to get around the town. At its centre is **Eyre Square**, and within it the sloping greensward of John F. Kennedy Memorial Park. The president was warmly received here during his visit to Ireland in 1963, a few months before the fateful day in Dallas. It's just the place for people-watching and snatching a few moments of the fickle Galway sunshine. The Browne Doorway, at the edge of the park, was once the main entranceway to the 1617 Browne mansion in Upper Abbeygate Street. Moved to the square around 1900, the stone portal, though stripped of context here, makes a strangely congruous junction between two eras.

Nearby, the gnomish statue of Galwayman Pádraic Ó Conaire (1881–1928) sits in eternal bemusement. Ó Conaire, a prolific writer of short stories, novels and plays, helped to revive the Irish in Irish literature. His few works translated into English reveal something of the inventiveness with which he used his native language. When the two estranged sisters quarrel in his story "The Woman on Whom God Laid His Hand", Ó Conaire writes: "The words went from mouth to mouth between them like sharp poisoned knives till the two of them were severely wounded".

Williamsgate Street leads off the top of the square, right into the marvellous old commercial district. Narrowing, it becomes William Street and then Shop Street, lined on each side with jewellers, butchers, pubs, gift stores and relics of 17th- and 18th-century merchant houses. At the intersection with Abbeygate Street is four-storey **Lynch's Castle**, one of Ireland's finest examples of an urban tower house and the last intact survivor from the ascendancy of the Galway tribes. A row of arched window embrasures and a doorway help soften the severe lines of the 16th-century building; above, carved lion crests and a frieze of canine and quasi-human gargoyles decorate the walls.

A short way farther on, Shop Street forks: toward the right is the **Collegiate Church of St. Nicholas**. Founded in 1320 and enlarged over the centuries, it's Ireland's second-largest medieval parish church. The Irish say that Columbus bent a knee here in 1492, beseeching the good favour of Nicholas of Myra, patron saint of sailors, before heading west to parts unknown. Local tradition also maintains that a Galwayman, Rice de Culvey, signed on for the ride.

Behind the church, in Market Street, the **Lynch Memorial**, a Gothic doorway surmounted by a skull and crossbones, commemorates a persistent but probably apocryphal legend concerning the mayor of Galway, James Lynch FitzStephen. The story goes that in 1493 his son Walter murdered a Spanish merchant's son for having stolen his fiancée. As magistrate, FitzStephen felt bound to uphold the law, and he pronounced a sentence of death on his own son. So popular was Walter, however, that no one could be induced to carry out the execution. The mayor, a tragic prisoner to his duty, then launched the lad into eternity himself, hanging him from a nearby window.

Just off Market Street, No. 8 Bowling Green is a station for Joyceans: the **Nora Barnacle House**, now a small museum, where Joyce's companion and constant inspiration was born. At her grandmother's simple bungalow around the corner at No. 5 Nuns' Island, Nora was staying the rainy night her young sweetheart, Michael Bodkin, left his sickbed to sing her a farewell. It was his swan-song performance, for he soon worsened and died, and now lies buried not far away in Rahoon Cemetery. Joyce used the episode in the poignant conclusion of "The Dead", as Gretta Conroy weeps herself to sleep with the memory of it:

> "The night before I left I was in my grandmother's house in Nuns' Island, packing up, and I heard gravel thrown up against the window. The window was so wet I couldn't see so I ran downstairs as I was and slipped out the back into the garden and there was the poor fellow at the end of the garden, shivering".

All around this part of town there's pleasant walking along the several channels of the Corrib. To the north you can't miss the looming hulk of the **Catholic cathedral**, built in the 1960s in a dizzying farrago of styles: Romanesque arches, a green Renaissance dome, Gothic rose windows, etc. Close by, the river comes sluicing out of Lough Corrib at the Salmon Weir. In summer, salmon "thick as paving stones" returning from the Atlantic pass under the bridge, en route to spawning grounds far upstream in the Connaught interior.

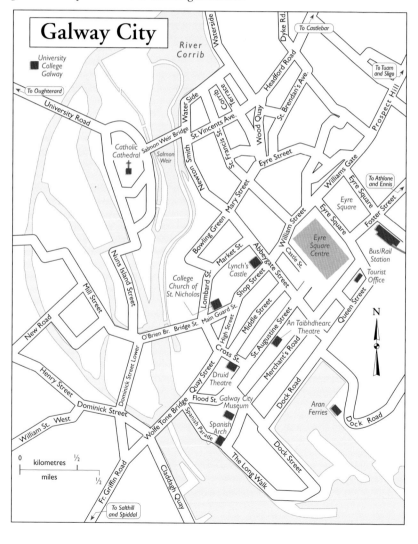

Kenny's Bookshop, in High Street, is the nicest sort of bookstore, stuffed to bursting with both hoary curiosities and crisp new editions, with a leaning toward items of Irish interest. The tables groan under teetering piles, unexpected gems wait on every shelf, and everywhere hang signed photographs of the literati who have passed through. The art gallery in back holds changing shows of sculpture and paintings, while the print room upstairs offers the largest remaining collection of luminous hand-colored block prints by Jack Yeats and others from the now-defunct Cuala Press. A must for bibliophiles of all stripes; ask to see the fine bookbinding work by the owner's son.

Continue along busy High Street, which becomes Quay Street. At its foot the Corrib rushes past the **Spanish Arch**. Actually, it's a pair of stone arches, an extension of the city wall built in 1594 to safeguard the quays where the Spanish merchant ships docked. Adjacent to the arch is the small Galway City Museum, and in front stretches the riverside Spanish Parade, where grandees of old were said to have promenaded as their ships' holds gave up their wines and spices.

Until the 1930s, across the River Corrib from the English town spread the **Claddagh**, the ghetto to which the Irish fisherfolk were banished. In his episodic memoir, *Lovely Is the Lee*, Robert Gibbings encounters a Galway character one evening who boasts of how things were in the old days, before the Claddagh fell to the scythe of progress:

> *"Come down with me now and I'll show you the Claddagh," he said. "Well, you can't see it; but we'll walk through it. 'Tis as well for you that you can't see it, for what is it now but slates and stones, and all the houses in straight lines. Planning, they calls that. There was a time when there were eight thousand in the Claddagh and they all fine healthy fishermen, and now there isn't five hundred. I tell you, the vests they wore in them days would make coats for men today. And they had their own king and queen, and not one of them would marry outside of the Claddagh, and they had their own wedding ring, the Claddagh ring, with the two hands catching hold of the crowned heart. And the houses were thatched, and warm in winter and cool in summer, and they didn't know what disease was, for no man died but by the will of God. And today, what with the damp out of the concrete floor under their feet, and the cold out of the slates over their heads, 'tis only one sneeze they need give and they drop dead."*

Gone now are the whitewashed cottages, but the Claddagh ring remains, ubiquitous in Galway jewellery shops and indeed throughout Ireland and upon the finger of many an Irish exile. The device of the heart gingerly clasped between encircling hands is thought to have been adopted from Spanish traders.

Apart from Galway's sights and historical and literary connections, the main reason to come is just to hang out, walk along the river and the bustling lanes, eat and drink, and soak up the lively atmosphere. There's a particularly nice buzz in the city all summer long, with buskers up and down the narrow streets wheezing away on old accordions or doing close-harmony singing, and music leaking out of most every pub you pass. Almost solidly from May through September there is something on, either in town or nearby. Make a point of stopping in at the Tourist Office just off Eyre Square for an events schedule.

The fortnight of the **Galway Arts Festival** in July brings together a cosmopolitan program of music, theatre and film. For six giddy days at the end of July, the subject is horses at Ballybrit Racecourse, three kilometres (two miles) east of town. Races are held here July through October, but the fever peaks during **Race Week**—a fascinating slice of Irish life.

In late September, the **Galway International Oyster Festival** is a must for lovers of the succulent mollusks. It's one of the biggest shindigs in these parts all year, with music, dances and food, climaxing in the world championship oyster-opening competition.

There's no dearth of music in Galway; check the *Galway Observer* or *Galway Advertiser* for listings. There are discos in town and just west at the somewhat tatty Salthill resort area. The King's Head pub and the Great Southern Hotel offer jazz. Galway seems to have attracted more than its share of traditional musicians, and they play with passion. Befitting Galway's long history as port of call, the local music scene has produced some exotic hybrids. Don't be surprised to find a bongo or even a didgeridoo being played alongside the fiddle and banjo. The Quays on Quay Street, Tigh Neachtain (Naughton's) close by on Cross Street, and the Crane Bar across the river on Sea Road are reliable venues for a spirited session. There are many others; finding them is part of the adventure, so ask around and follow your ears.

Lough Corrib and the Joyce Country

The inland route (N59) through Connemara angles northwest from Galway and offers occasional, tantalizing glimpses of Lough Corrib. Around **Moycullen** are quarries of Connemara marble, a lustrous metamorphic stone ranging in colour from cream to deep trout-green. Three kilometres (two miles) beyond is a turnoff to the right which skirts Ross Lake and Ross Castle (not open to the public). This was the birthplace of Violet Martin (1862–1915)—better known by her pseudonym, Martin Ross—one-half of the literary duet of Somerville and Ross (see page 136).

A few kilometres up the highway, the stout, well-restored **Aughnanure Castle**, on a streambound island just beside Lough Corrib, is open to the public. An oft-told legend of this O'Flaherty stronghold relates that a certain flagstone in the banquet hall floor was hinged downward, like a gallows trap-door; by simply sliding a bolt, the lord of the manor could dispatch an unwelcome guest, pitching him into the stream which flowed through a cavern below. This was the fate of one young man who had come to demand the rent owed on the castle. Nature played the last trick, however, for the entire hall has since collapsed, its foundations undermined by the subterranean stream.

Lough Corrib is Ireland's second-largest lake, covering 176 square kilometres (68 square miles). Low hills checquered with hay-fields and woodland kneel down around its convoluted shoreline, and hundreds of green islands break its surface. Europe's greatest free fishing waters, the Corrib is beloved for its salmon and brown trout; seasons are 1 February–30 September and 15 February–30 September, respectively. A good introduction to the lower end of the lake might be a cruise on the *Corrib Princess*, which departs from Galway's Wood Quay, above the salmon weir.

Oughterard (pronounced "OOK-ter-ard"), the last sizable town before Clifden, is a popular centre for river and lake fishing. It's in an attractive setting, with a grove of green beeches and the River Owenriff threading right through it.

Turn off the main highway here for a drive or walk along Lough Corrib, with lush views out across its great blue sheet. On the largest of the lake-isles, lonely, wooded **Inchagoill** ("Island of the Devout Foreigner"), stands the Stone of Lugna. The small obelisk bears Europe's oldest known Christian inscription (dating to the era of St. Patrick), after the Roman catacombs. One Sunday each July, worshippers from all around the lake sail out to the island to celebrate Mass in the tenth-century ruins of Teampall na Naomh, the Church of the Saints.

Between the northwestern end of Lough Corrib and the Maumturk Mountains spreads the **Joyce Country**, a glorious, little-visited domain named for the Welsh clan which ruled here from the 13th to 19th centuries. One of the jewels of this countryside is **Lough Nafooey**, set in a bewitched glen at the foot of 673-metre (2,207-foot)-high Maumtransa.

The isthmus between Lough Corrib and Lough Mask was a causeway across which the warring plains tribes from east Galway and Mayo poured, only to be repulsed by the ferocious O'Flahertys and Joyces. From the clamour of many battles it came to be known as the Gap of Danger. Deep in antiquity, the hosts of the Fir Bolg assembled atop Mount Gable before their final confrontation with the Tuatha Dé Danaan in the legendary Battle of Moytura. It's a bit quieter now, the haunt of fishermen who base themselves in Clonbur and Cong.

Connemara

West of Galway City and Lough Corrib spreads one of Ireland's most memorable regions. Connemara is a wilderness of brown and golden boglands, the mountainy heights of the Maumturks and the Twelve Bens, and, everywhere, the glitter of water: from rivers and streams, small lakes set in the granite hollows of the hills, rain pooling in the black rectangles of turbaries where turf has been dug out, and the deeply scored coastline scattered with islands.

But its beauty may well be the most generous of Connemara's scant resources. Most of the soil here is hopelessly unproductive; that fact, combined with desperate overpopulation in the 18th and 19th centuries, made this one of the country's wretchedest corners. The Famine hit hard in Connemara, killing many thousands among the tenant farmers and opening the floodgates of exodus to America and England. Everywhere along the once-congested south coast are reminders: roofless, crumbling shells that once were cottages, and their adjacent fields, heartbreakingly tiny and long abandoned. Government programs, however, have helped to improve the local economy and encouraged people to stay, though life is still hard.

Two main roads lead into Connemara from Galway, both unfolding with increasing scenic drama as they move west. The sky grows expansive over the unpeopled countryside of wild moorland, silver outcrops of granite, rising mountains and shreds of little lakes. For miles and miles you may find yourself alone, with nothing to break the stillness but the stray breeze bearing the sparkle of birdsong and the bog's damp earthen fragrances.

There's little more to the oft-signposted crossroads of **Maam Cross** than a pub, shop and petrol station, but everyone travelling through western Galway ends up here sooner or later. To the south are Rossaveal and the broken inlets off Galway Bay, to the north the Joyce Country and County Mayo. Continue west to the hamlet of Recess, a pretty oasis after the emptiness of central Connemara. Between Recess and Clifden, 16 kilometres (ten miles) distant, are gorgeous Glendalough, Derryclare and Ballynahinch lakes, looking-glasses to the fringing trees and ever-changing sky.

The southern route from Galway enters **Iar-Chonnacht**, the vaguely defined region reaching inland along Galway Bay. Along this seaboard most of the county's Irish speakers are concentrated. The first section, through Barna,

Connemara cottage, Co. Galway

Furbo and Spiddal, is disappointingly built up, with modern houses and a surplus of traffic. Still, you're in the Gaeltacht now; here's your chance to try out a phrase or two of Gaelic you've been practising diligently. Spiddal hosts curragh races each summer, and boats depart from the quay out to the Arans.

Farther west, the road turns sharply northwest where the coastline begins to break apart at Cashla Bay. Rossaveal also has regular boat service to the Arans. Costelloe is the headquarters for Radio na Gaeltachta, the national Irish-language broadcasting network. In these parts, even the sheepdogs answer only to Irish: *"Suigh síos!"* Follow the signposted lane near here to the Coral Strand. The brilliant white beach, like others around Connemara, is composed not of sand but of fine calcareous fragments of a kind of coral-like seaweed.

A branch road snakes from Costelloe out through the stony archipelago of Gorumna and Lettermore islands, joined to the world by the tenuous nexus of causeways between them. Out in the bays, more islets seem to rise and fall with the tide, like green-backed sea beasts.

In 1905, the *Manchester Guardian* commissioned J.M. Synge to travel through the most depressed areas of Ireland and report on the conditions he observed. His companion was Jack Yeats, hired to illustrate Synge's essays with line drawings. At the time, the parish of Carraroe was reckoned to be poorest of the poor. Many eked out a living here by cutting turf and sailing it to the Arans, which have no fuel resources of their own. "One feels", Synge wrote, ". . . that it is part of the misfortune of Ireland that nearly all the characteristics which give colour and attractiveness to Irish life are bound up with a social condition that is near to penury".

But hard times can also foster a gritty entrepreneurial spirit. An 18th-century French visitor remarked on the bustling commerce carried out here in what was jauntily called "the smuggling business". And this part of Connemara has long been famed *poitín* country, where the isolated islands and hidden bays shelter the illicit moonshiner from the searching eyes of the authorities. With a little persistence and discreet enquiry, you might find a drop of the fabled elixir yourself: the best can warm you like the flush of young love, while the worst, distilled from God-knows-what, would stiffen a tinker. A taste of *poitín* brings to mind a colourful description from John L. O'Sullivan: "A torchlight procession marching down your throat". From time to time the proposal is put forward to legalize the stuff, with the rationale that legalization would drive the inferior varieties off the market and at the same time bring tax revenues from this black-market trade into the above-board economy.

The inland road (R336) continues north at Screeb, rising and falling through quiet, barren lowlands to Maam Cross and beyond, while the coastal road (R340) circles the marvelously varied indentations of Camus and Kilkieran bays. At Gortmore, a road dangles south down the peninsula to Rosmuc, where Patrick Pearse, martyred leader of the Easter Rising, had a holiday cottage. (It's now a national monument, open to the public.) Here he wrote poems and plays, both in English and Irish, believing the fate of the nation to be bound up inextricably with its language. On Easter Monday in 1916, Pearse read aloud the declaration of an Irish Republic from the steps of Dublin's General Post Office. The rebellion ended in ashes; on the eve of his execution before a British firing squad, he wrote a few lines on the transient pleasures of this life, and thought, perhaps, of Connemara:

> *The beauty of the world hath made me sad,*
> *This beauty that will pass . . .*
> *Some quiet hill where mountainy man hath sown*
> *And soon would reap; near to the gate of Heaven;*
> *Or children with bare feet upon the sands*
> *Of some ebbed sea, or playing in the streets*
> *Of little towns in Connacht . . .*

The coast road (R340) loops deeply along the fretted coastline through **Carna**, terminus of the summer curragh races between here and Spiddal. This is a likely locality, in the sanctum of the Gaeltacht, in which to seek out the strange, melancholy singing called *sean-nós* (literally, "old style")—a sound almost as intoxicating, and elusive, as *poitín*.

Uninhabited **St. MacDara's Island** draws pilgrims each 16 July to the restored, steep-roofed stone oratory, the island's sole structure. Boatmen from the area ferry people over from the mainland in their claret-sailed hookers, refusing payment for the passage in deference to the saint. In times past, fishermen would dip their sails thrice when passing the island lest misfortune strike. Along this coast there was a time when it was also considered most unlucky to save a man from drowning. "The sea must have its due", was the superstition, and if cheated, it might well take you or one of your family instead.

Galway hookers are still made around **Mweenish Island**, just offshore from Carna. The lyrical curves of the hull make these sailboats extremely sturdy and seaworthy. You can see these lamp-black workhorses plying the west coast transporting turf and other supplies.

Following the R342 around Bertraghboy Bay, you come to Toombeola. A short

Sean-nós Singing

The singer's voice, solo and unaccompanied, is the instrument, with which she or he ornaments the words in a quavering, somewhat nasal tone. The songs (in Irish) may be lovelorn outpourings or lengthy accounts of fishermen lost to the sea, or may consist of a few simple lines repeated in constantly improvised variation. In any case, the lyric and metre become fluid, ductile, drawn out in long curling lines or broken by momentary caesura at the singer's whim. In a standing position, or bolt upright in a chair, the performer may seem impassive and utterly detached from the emotional content of the song, with eyes closed or fixed on eternity. There's no crescendo, no climax, and the song ends abruptly, breaking the spell with a jolt.

Sean-nós exploits the innate musicality of the Irish language, employing internal rhyme that's difficult to translate intact into English. The Tyrone-born novelist William Carleton recorded that his mother, when asked to sing the English version of "Bean an Fhir Rua", replied, "I'll sing it for you, but the English words and the air are like a quarrelling man and wife—the Irish melts into the tune but the English doesn't".

Shearing the sheep

distance north stands **Ballynahinch Castle**, ancestral seat of the "kings of Connemara", the eccentric Martin family, who ruled most of Connemara for two centuries. One of the clan, Richard Martin, bore the memorable sobriquet of Hairtrigger Dick for his duelling successes. Demonstrably fonder of animals than of his fellow humans, this member of Parliament ran a private gaol in which he punished tenants who mistreated their livestock. He's also known for his efforts at founding the Royal Society for the Prevention of Cruelty to Animals in 1824, for which King George IV rechristened him Humanity Dick. The great fortune of the Martins—one of the rare landowning families who gave a damn—was broken in trying to relieve the suffering of the Famine. The castle has since been converted into a hotel.

William Makepeace Thackeray thought the countryside about **Roundstone** "one of the most wild and beautiful districts that it is ever the fortune of the traveller to examine". This fishing village lies under 300-metre (987-foot) Errisbeg Mountain beside the much-photographed Dog's Bay. Though Thackeray was right regardless of what the spot is called, somehow the bay's original name, Port na Feadog ("Bay of the Plover"), seems more fitting than the rude English mistranslation. Stop in at the crafts complex on the outskirts of the village; at Roundstone Musical Instruments, Malachy Kearns fashions *bodhráns*, flutes and other instruments. Other studios include a pottery studio and Folding Landscapes, which produces the wonderful regional maps.

The intoxicating, breezy route west and north from Roundstone, called the "brandy and soda road", passes fine beaches along Ballyconneely and Mannin bays and a welter of small loughs inland. En route, **Derrygimlagh Bog** is the unlikely site of two historic firsts. Radio pioneer Guglielmo Marconi established a wireless station here, from which he sent Europe's first radio messages to America. One fine Sunday morning, 15 June 1919, John Alcock and Arthur Whitten Brown completed the first west-to-east flight across the Atlantic—by crashing their Vickers Vimy biplane nose-first into the bog.

The so-called capital of Connemara, sheltered at the head of Clifden Bay, **Clifden** is one of the west's handsomest towns. With a population of only about 1,400, it's nevertheless the largest settlement hereabouts and the perfect base for launching excursions around the area. Salmon, lobsters and other seafood are a specialty here. The distinctive skyline—backed by the brooding jumble of the Twelve Bens and pierced by the twin spires of the Protestant church and the Catholic cathedral—makes Clifden a postcard publisher's dream.

The Connemara pony is a sturdy, diminutive horse well adapted to farmwork in this rough mountain and bog country. A 14th-century French traveller described them aptly: "They are small, hairy, unkempt little creatures who scout the hills and valleys and they are fleeter than deer". You can see them up close in August, when Clifden hosts the Connemara Pony Show, where these shaggy-coated beasts are judged and sold, against a country fair atmosphere of music and craft and cooking competitions. The September Community Arts Festival features poetry, set-dancing, music and usually a smattering of Irish luminaries.

The mansion of Clifden's founder, John D'Arcy, stands in a cattle pasture about ten minutes' walk west of town. It's just a shell now, yet the remains are a romantic's picture of precisely what a castle should be—soaring square keep, crenellated round towers, notched battlements and a commanding view. But it's all show. Built in 1815, well after the need for real fortifications, the "castle" wouldn't have long withstood a siege by querulous schoolgirls, let alone a determined army.

By all means take the signposted **Sky Road**, a precipitous scenic loop above Clifden and Streamstown bays. To the north is Omey Island, which can be walked to at low tide; pony races are held on the hard-packed strand in August.

The busy fishing port of Cleggan is the place to get the mail boat out to **Inishbofin**, a relaxed place with friendly people and good beaches embraced by clear, clean water. St. Colman, the abbot of Lindisfarne, hied himself to this "Island of the White Cow" after a raging dispute with the church in AD 664 over the method for reckoning the date of Easter. Hundreds of students flocked to the settlement he founded to learn the monkish arts of calligraphy and illumination.

Grace O'Malley (see "Clare Island", page 209), the self-made pirate-queen of the west coast, fortified the island in the 16th century. But Inishbofin surrendered to the Cromwellians in 1652; they built up the star-shaped fortress above the harbour, where they billeted troops and imprisoned captured priests. On a rock in the harbour, visible at low tide, they chained an unfortunate bishop and watched him drown by degrees as the sea returned.

From Cleggan, follow the fuchsia-lined road east and north into the Renvyle Peninsula, where there are some wonderful beaches. In the village of **Renvyle** the writer-physician Oliver St. John Gogarty—the model for Joyce's "stately plump Buck Mulligan" in *Ulysses*—had a summer home. Now the Renvyle House Hotel, it remains as Gogarty described it in his autobiography, *As I Was Going Down Sackville Street:*

> *My house . . . stands on a lake, but it stands also on the sea. Water-lilies meet the golden seaweed. It is as if, in the faery land of Connemara at the extreme end of Europe, the incongruous flowed together at last; and the sweet and bitter blended.*

Until it was exorcised some time ago, the house enjoyed a reputation for being haunted. Mr. and Mrs. William Butler Yeats, much given to mysticism, honeymooned here as Gogarty's guests and spent an evening trying to summon up the shade of Athelstone Blake, son of the original owners. Years later, a chambermaid spotted the restless ghost of W.B. himself floating through the hallways.

The comely mission settlement of **Letterfrack**, founded by the Quakers in the 19th century, is the gateway into 15-square-kilometre (3,800-acre) **Connemara National Park**. A number of walks have been laid out; get a breathtaking overview of the surrounding countryside by walking to the 445-metre (1,460-foot) summit of Diamond Hill.

Rising from the rhododendron-fringed shore of Kylemore Lough, the extraordinary pale limestone **Kylemore Abbey** appears altogether too, well, English, for this wild part of Ireland. In fact, this monumental neo-Gothic mansion *is* English, sort of. It was built in the middle of the 1860s—at the then astonishing sum of £1 million—by Liverpool shipping magnate Mitchell Henry. Since the end of World War I the estate has been in the possession of Benedictine nuns, who run it as a convent and girls school. A restaurant, a crafts shop and the grounds are open to the public, though the abbey proper is not.

The R344 branches to the south past Kylemore, curving through the austere Inagh Valley to connect with the Oughterard-Clifden highway (N59) near Recess. To the northeast, a drowned glacial valley forms the long, slender inlet of **Killary Harbour**, the only true fjord in Ireland. One of the world's safest anchorages, the entire British navy once sheltered here during the First World War. Across the water the barren, folded slopes of the Mweelrea Mountains thrust up directly from the sea. At Lough Fee, near Salruck just south of the harbour, Oscar Wilde often fished with his brother, Willie, during the summers of their boyhood.

Near the head of Killary Harbour, **Leenane** huddles under the shadow of the 648-metre (2,125 foot)-high mass of the Devil's Mother. *The Field,* based on John B. Keane's tragic play, was filmed here in 1989 with Richard Harris, John Hurt and a number of villagers.

The Aran Islands

In May 1898, after abandoning his ambition to become a concert violinist, John Millington Synge (1871–1909) followed the advice of W.B. Yeats and boarded a steamer across Galway Bay. "Go to the Aran Islands", Yeats had urged him. "Live there as if you were one of the people themselves; express a life that has never found expression".

Synge came and was enchanted by the Arans and their sea-haunted people. "No two journeys to these islands are alike", he wrote, and he would return each autumn for the next four years, staying mainly on Inishmaan, recording in a quiet, perceptive voice his experiences there, which he published as *The Aran Islands* in 1907.

The stoic self-reliance and dignity of the islanders particularly impressed the young writer. Many of their insular customs and beliefs had developed undiluted by the mainstream of Irish life; during the period of Synge's visits, he found the people in transition to modernity, their Christian veneer still undergirded by vestiges of ancient paganism.

Inisheer (the east island), Inishmaan (the middle island) and Inishmore (the largest and most westerly island) curve away from Clare in a brief arc, like Beardsley's signature birds, across the mouth of Galway Bay. Seamus Heaney described these three lonely sentinels as "stepping stones out of

Inisheer, Aran Islands

A Burial on Inishmaan

After Mass this morning an old woman was buried. She lived in the cottage next mine, and more than once before noon I heard a faint echo of the keen. I did not go to the wake for fear my presence might jar upon the mourners, but all last evening I could hear the strokes of a hammer in the yard, where, in the middle of a little crowd of idlers, the next of kin laboured slowly at the coffin. To-day, before the hour for the funeral, poteen was served to a number of men who stood about upon the road, and a portion was brought to me in my room. Then the coffin was carried out sewn loosely in sailcloth, and held near the ground by three crosspoles lashed upon the top. As we moved down to the low eastern portion of the island, nearly all the men, and all the oldest women, wearing petticoats over their heads, came out and joined in the procession.

While the grave was being opened the women sat down among the flat tombstones, bordered with a pale fringe of early bracken, and began the wild keen, or crying for the dead. Each old woman, as she took her turn in the leading recitative, seemed possessed for the moment with a profound ecstasy of grief, swaying to and fro, and bending her forehead to the stone before her, while she called out to the dead with a perpetually recurring chant of sobs.

All round the graveyard other wrinkled women, looking out from under the deep red petticoats that cloaked them, rocked themselves with the same rhythm, and intoned the inarticulate chant that is sustained by all as an accompaniment.

The morning had been beautifully fine, but as they lowered the coffin into the grave, thunder rumbled overhead and hailstones hissed among the bracken.

In Inishmaan one is forced to believe in a sympathy between man and nature, and at this moment when the thunder sounded a death-peal of extraordinary grandeur above the voices of the women, I could see the faces near me stiff and drawn with emotion.

When the coffin was in the grave, and the thunder had rolled away across the hills of Clare, the keen broke out again more passionately than before.

This grief of the keen is no personal complaint for the death of one woman, but seems to contain the whole passionate rage that lurks somewhere in every native of the island. In this cry of pain the inner consciousness of the people seems to lay itself bare for an instant, and to reveal the mood of beings who feel their isolation in the face of a universe that wars on them with winds and seas. They are usually silent, but in the presence of death all outward show of indifference or patience is forgotten, and they shriek with pitiable despair before the horror of the fate to which they are all doomed.

Before they covered the coffin an old man kneeled down by the grave and repeated a simple prayer for the dead.

There was an irony in these words of atonement and Christian belief spoken by voices that were still hoarse with the cries of pagan desperation.

A little beyond the grave I saw a line of old women who had recited in the keen sitting in the shadow of a wall beside the roofless shell of the church. They were still sobbing and shaken with grief, yet they were beginning to talk again of the daily trifles that veil from them the terror of the world.

When we had all come out of the graveyard, and two men had rebuilt the hole in the wall through which the coffin had been carried in, we walked back to the village, talking of anything, and joking of anything, as if merely coming from the boat-slip, or the pier. . . .

Before we reached the village, rain began to fall in large single drops, and as we walked slowly through this world of grey, the soft hissing of the rain gave me one of the moods which we realise with immense distress the short moment we have left us to experience all the wonder and beauty in the world.

—J.M. Synge, The Aran Islands, *1907*

John Millington Synge, pencil sketch by Jack Yeats, 1905

Europe". In a sense though the islands lead not out but inward, as Synge and subsequent visitors have discovered, into the lingering and sometimes palpable past.

Though they've been inhabited for 50 centuries, life on the Arans has probably never been easy. Their sole resources are reduced to the utterly elemental: the ever-present sea, stone upon countless stone, and the fierce tenacity of the islanders themselves. "A wilderness of stone and stone walls", Synge wrote of the islands, nearly treeless echoes of the limestone Burren. Everywhere, the shaky grey weave of the walls defines a filigree of tiny fields. Every inch of soil here is the product of back-bending toil, composed of manure and sand and seaweed carried up from the shore and combined into a fertile loam atop the naked bedrock.

Old-timers claim the islands have changed irrevocably since Synge's time. The artfully knit Aran sweaters, of course, are everywhere, but only rarely, and mostly on Inishmaan, will you see other traditional island garb: the heel-less cowhide *pampooties,* the women's heavy handwoven shawls and red-flannel skirts, the unbleached wool vest called a *bainin,* or the colorful woven *crios* with which the men cinch up their thick homespun tweed trousers. Tourists have replaced fish as the most important economic resource. Thatched roofs have given way to corrugated tin and television aerials. But much remains intact: Irish is still the people's first language, men still brave the sea in their canvas-shelled *curraghs,* and the islands are still as starkly lovely and indelible as ever, fascinating relics of preindustrial Europe.

The three islands can be reached by plane from Carnmore Airport, near Galway, and the new Connemara Airport, at Inverin; Aer Arann proudly advertises that its flight is "now only six minutes" from Inverin to the Arans. Why one would want to travel in such haste to arrive at a place where time has passed so slowly is a mystery. Rather, a boat from Galway, Spiddal, Rossaveal or Doolin seems the proper way to go, attuned to the tides and subject to the delays of uncooperative weather. Smell the sea scents, roll on the long swells, and taste, as Synge did, the "bay full of green delirium". But don't forget the Dramamine. It's a long three hours or so from Galway (or about 45 minutes from Rossaveal to Kilronan or from Doolin to Inisheer).

For really exploring in detail, you can do no better than to obtain Tim Robinson's detailed map of the islands, or read his thoroughly engaging book, *Stones of Aran,* which concentrates on the largest island.

Inishmore holds about 900 of the Arans' 1,450 people, and it takes the brunt of the growing tourist traffic. The little port of Kilronan, where the ferry docks, is the islands' main village, with pubs, shops, a hostel, bicycle rentals and other amenities. A road running the island's length connects Kilronan

Inisheer, Aran Islands: "A wilderness of stone and stone walls".

with the other main villages, Killeany to the southeast and Kilmurvy near the western end.

In summer at the parish hall, Halla Rónáin, you can see *Man of Aran*, filmed in 1932–34 by the pioneer documentarian Robert Flaherty. Though nominally a documentary, the film now looks rather stagey and mawkish. Flaherty portrayed the lifestyle of a century earlier and was not above bending the facts to heighten the drama. All the cast members were island folk, but for the climactic shark hunt, for example, fishermen had to be brought in from Achill Island, as no Aran men had hunted the giant basking sharks in at least a generation. As an old man who had played a barefoot child in one scene told Tim Robinson, it was "the exaggeratingest film ever made!" *Man of Aran* remains a compelling cinematic landmark nonetheless, and what better place to see it?

The novelist and short-story writer Liam O'Flaherty (1896–1984) was born in the hamlet of Gort na gCapall, close to Dun Aengus. His terse, plain-spoken prose seems to owe a debt to Hemingway; or perhaps 'twas the other way around.

Among the many monastic ruins on Inishmore is steeply gabled sixth-century **Teampall Bheanain**, atop the hill above the village of Killeany. One of the smallest churches in Christendom, its interior measures a bit over three by two metres (11 by seven feet). **Teampall an Cheathrair Álainn** ("the Church of the Four Comely Saints"), near the village of Cowrugh, is named after

Fursa, Conall, Bearchán and Breandán of Birr, whose gravesites are marked by large, plain slabs; they were just four of the 120 saints who lived and were buried on Inishmore, making the Arans famous throughout the early Christian world as Ara Sanctorum, "Islands of the Saints". Close by is a holy well, where an old man related the tale to Synge of a miraculous well on which the writer based his play *The Well of the Saints*. The eighth- to tenth-century **Teampall Bhreacáin**, popularly misnamed the Seven Churches, lies just east of Eoghanacht village, toward the island's west end; among the complex of ruined domestic buildings are only two churches, and scattered about are fragments of several high crosses.

Clinging to a high coastal promontory south of the Kilronan-Killeany road is **Dun Dubh Cathair**, the Black Fort. Two thousand years ago, this was the largest of the island's ring forts, but much of it has since crumbled into the sea along with the eroding cliff. The vistas from here, as along much of the island's uptilted rim, are breathtaking in every direction.

But Inishmore's most spectacular attraction—indeed one of the most remarkable prehistoric monuments in all of Europe—is **Dun Aengus**. It's south of Kilmurvy, about six kilometres (four miles) west of Kilronan, at the very brink of the sheer, 90-metre (300-foot) palisade of the southern coast. The massive Iron Age fort is named for Aengus (or Aonghus), chief of the legendary, pre-Celtic Fir Bolgs, who are credited with its construction, sometime between 800 BC and AD 400. The three roughly concentric, semi-circular walls, reaching nearly six metres (18 feet) high by four metres (13 feet) thick, enclose an area of .4 square kilometres (11 acres). Between the middle and outer walls spreads a fearsome *chevaux-de-frise*, a crippling thicket of jagged, waist-high limestone splinters. With its back to the sea-cliff, Dun Aengus may have been intended as a defense of last resort, from which there was no retreat. No one seems to know for certain, however, just what invaders the Fir Bolgs were expecting to come calling.

On **Inishmaan**, still the most traditional of the Arans, Synge wandered restlessly, listened intently to the story-tellers, and spent countless hours in solitary contemplation. Here he found inspiration and material for his three best-known plays—including *Riders to the Sea*, called by some the most perfect one-act play in English.

The island's 300 inhabitants still wrest a living from the sea. Fishing has always been a precarious livelihood, and an old-timer's words to Synge hold as true today: "A man who is not afraid of the sea will soon be drownded, for he will be going out on a day he shouldn't. But we do be afraid of the sea, and we do only be drownded now and again". *Curraghs* are in common use here, transporting heavy loads that belie their frail appearance. Tricky craft to master, they're rowed with bladeless oars, or sometimes fitted with an outboard motor. On the waves, they bob as lightly as gulls; on shore, you may see them overturned on the strand, their tarred canvas hulls glistening blackly like beetle carapaces in the sun.

The principal monument on Inishmaan is **Dun Conor**, the best-preserved and largest stone fort in Ireland. With walls six metres (20 feet) high and nearly as thick, the massive oval stands on a rocky shelf at the island's highest point.

Inisheer, just three kilometres (two miles) across, completes the archipelago, lying just a few kilometres from the Clare coast. As you approach the island, a 15th-century O'Brien castle stands out against the sky, built within the confines of Iron Age Dun Formna atop a limestone promontory. The diminutive tenth-century church of St. Gobnait, a short walk west of the boat slip, is dedicated to the only woman suffered to live in the Arans by the saintly misogynists who ruled them for a time. Inisheer also has a pair of good sandy beaches.

The Belfast-born poet Derek Mahon thought of Inisheer as "a dream of limestone in sea light". There's a slow, wistful air named for the island, and if you hear it played late one night in the public house you may find the tune returning to you long after you've gone, reminding you of this place.

Eastern Galway

Inland from Galway City, the county is mostly tame pastureland and limestone plains that are a marked contrast from the dramatic west. Southeast of Galway, **Clarinbridge**, famed for its oysters, celebrates its own Oyster Festival each mid-September. Around the bay on the road to Ballyvaughan (N67), the handsome fishing village of **Kinvarra** makes a very pleasant stop for lunch or tea, and the quay may offer a close look at traditional Galway hookers—boats, that is, not fallen ladies.

Just before Kinvarra, completely restored **Dunguaire Castle** stands at the water's edge. This was the home of seventh-century King Guaire, who, it was said, entertained with such generosity that his right arm, his "giving arm", grew longer than the left. The medieval banquets held here are reckoned by some to be a more satisfying experience than others around Ireland. Irish music follows dinner, along with readings from writers with local connections. Continue west from Kinvarra and you're soon in the Burren.

Southwest of Gort, the main market town for south Galway, **Kilmacduagh** commands an impressive site above a reedy lake, with good views of the

Burren. The most conspicuous feature of the sixth-century monastery is the intact, 36-metre (about 120 foot)-high round tower, tallest in Ireland; an Irish Tower of Pisa, it lists noticeably to one side.

Three kilometres (two miles) north of Gort is **Coole Park**, the erstwhile estate of the tireless folklorist and dramatist Lady Augusta Gregory (1852–1932). With W.B. Yeats and her neighbor Edward Martyn, she founded the Irish Literary Theatre, subsequently the Abbey, to which she herself contributed 40 plays, including probably her best known, *Spreading the News*, which inaugurated the Abbey in 1904.

Unforgivably, her Georgian mansion, which had frequently hosted so many of her important contemporaries, was pulled down in 1941 for the reuse of the stone. What remains, though, is the great copper beech autograph tree, a virtual index of Irish literary giants—among them G.B. Shaw, Seán O'Casey, W.B. Yeats, Violet Martin, Douglas Hyde—who carved their initials into the bole. The luxuriously wooded 3.5-square-kilometre (894-acre) expanse has been operated as a national forest and wildlife preserve for the past 60 years, and in 1992 the renovated stone barn was opened to the public as a visitor centre.

In 1915, W.B. Yeats bought himself—for the bargain price of £35—an ivory tower of sorts, quite close to Coole Park. It was a square Norman keep from the 16th century, which he spent the next three years making habitable for himself and his new bride. Standing by an arched stone bridge across the elm-shadowed Cloon River, and with a flame of ivy consuming one corner, **Thoor Ballylee** is a most fitting poet's eyrie. Sylvia Plath thought it "the most beautiful and peaceful place in the world". Yeats lived in the tower until 1929, and he invoked it as a powerful emblem in several poems:

> *An ancient bridge, and a more ancient tower,*
> *A farmhouse that is sheltered by its wall,*
> *An acre of stony ground,*
> *Where the symbolic rose can break in flower . . .*

Now a museum, Thoor Ballylee houses a few Yeats first editions and other rarities, interpretive exhibits, and a tea shop.

Far out on the county's southeastern corner, at the head of Lough Derg, the market town of **Portumna** sits at the edge of a four-square-kilometre (1,000 acre) forest park and wildlife sanctuary, the former demesne of the earls of Clanrickarde. Near the lakeshore the impressive shell of Dutch-influenced Portumna Castle, one of the finest 17th-century manor houses in the country, stands amid geometric, manicured gardens.

After his voyage across the Atlantic, St. Brendan returned to Ireland and, in AD 563, founded a monastery at Clonfert, in a crook of the Shannon 24 kilometres (15 miles) northeast of Portumna. The establishment fared exceedingly badly, being twice sacked by Vikings and four times destroyed by fire between 844 and 1179. A later church, **Clonfert Cathedral** is on the whole nothing special. But what's noteworthy is its 12th-century west doorway, fashioned from russet sandstone and considered the finest example of Romanesque architecture in Ireland.

Six orders of pillars support as many rounded arches, each embellished with carved foliage, animal faces, zoomorphic interlacing, beads, etc. Surmounting this is the most unusual feature, a triangular pediment from which a choir of disembodied human heads gaze out morosely across the plain. Like Dysert O'Dea in Clare, Clonfert's entranceway seems to mark a strange spiritual hyphenation between the waning paganism of the Celts and ascendant Christianity. In contrast to the severity of this portal is an unexpectedly whimsical carving inside of a mermaid, clasping a comb and mirror and smiling the enigmatic smile of the Mona Lisa.

North again, where the Galway-Dublin road fords the River Suck, is **Ballinasloe**, famed for its eight-day Horse Fair held each October. Beyond is Athlone, a much-fought-over town straddling the Shannon. Eight kilometres (five miles) southwest of Ballinasloe, the course of Irish history was decided in July 1691. Along the ridge at **Aughrim**, Williamite troops overcame the combined French and Irish army of 14,000 men, who scattered following the death of their commander, the French general St. Ruth. The battle followed the Catholic defeat at the Boyne the previous year and was, in the simple words of the old Irish lament, "a great disaster".

Farther west, 24 kilometres (15 miles) east of Galway, **Athenry**, the centre of Norman power in the county, boasts the best-preserved fortifications in Ireland. Extensive portions of the town walls and five of the original six towers survive.

Northwest of Headford, just west of the Galway-Cong road, **Ross Abbey**, also known as Ross Errily Friary, is an exceptionally large and well-preserved Franciscan establishment founded in the 14th century. This is the burial place of the Galway families of Burke, Browne, Kirwan and Lynch. Cromwell sacked the monastery in 1656, but the tenacious monks continued on here for another hundred years. It's a marvellous ruin, dramatically silhouetted on the plains above Lough Corrib.

County Mayo

You'd hardly know from seeing it now, but 150 years ago Mayo teemed with people. It was to this rough corner of Ireland that Cromwell drove the natives of the rich midlands and the east when he banished them "to hell or Connacht". In spite of the mostly unresponsive lands here, these "bog Irish" managed to thrive and multiply, mainly on the strength of a single crop—the nutritious but dangerously unreliable potato.

The famines of the 1840s and 1870s, of course, changed all that, and much of the county nowadays seems empty, haunted by absences. There are deserted beaches, silent valleys and vast spaces of mountain and bog where the only signs of life are the white flecks of sheep moving among the hills. When inhabitants are asked where they come from, they've been known to reply, "Mayo, God help us".

Yet it would be a great mistake to think of Mayo as too bleak to bother with. On the contrary, though many travellers bypass it altogether, the county holds some of Ireland's loveliest scenery. The pace of life seems slow and unhurried here, even by Irish standards. It's in the back-of-beyonds of Mayo, as in Connemara to the south, that you're still likely to round a corner and find snug whitewashed cottages with a spindle of turf smoke rising, as perfectly idyllic as a movie set.

Cong to Castlebar

The fact that the name **Cong** is actually Irish—from *cunga*, an isthmus—doesn't dispel its faintly exotic resonance. Apart from its enviable location between Loughs Corrib and Mask—which makes it a good headquarters for seekers of salmon and trout—Cong has made its reputation on the strength of its Technicolor appearance in that boisterous late-show chestnut, *The Quiet Man*. This 1952 John Ford film helped to fix in the popular imagination the stereotype of Ireland as a land peopled mainly by good-natured but pugilistic rustics. Fans may recognize the placid village of Cong as the fictional Inishfree; pony carts can be hired for guided tours of local film sites.

At the top of the village are the remains of Cong Abbey, founded in AD 624 by St. Feichin and expanded by Turlough Mór O'Conor in the 1100s. (It was Turlough, too, who in 1123 commissioned the Cross of Cong to encase a piece of the True Cross; the oaken shrine, elaborately chased in silver and bronze, is now displayed in the National Museum.) Enough of the tiny faces, floral capitals and other ornamental stonework on the abbey chancel survives to testify to the skills of the 12th-century craftsmen who worked here.

One of the curiosities at the abbey is the monks' fishing house, a stone hut built in the River Cong. Fish swimming under it were trapped in a chamber; as they struggled they would touch a wire which in turn rang a bell in the monastery kitchen, summoning their own executioner.

Following his submission to the Welshman Strongbow and his Norman army, Turlough's son Rory O'Conor secluded himself at the abbey. Here he remained until his death in 1198, knowing, perhaps, that he had been the last of the high-kings of Ireland and that with his defeat the old Gaelic world had begun to sink beneath the waves of foreign invasion.

Cong Abbey at its height thronged with some 3,000 people, but now an air of sad abandon pervades the place. It stands open to the sky, cloistered by the lacing elms, the murmuring streams its only choir.

Everywhere you walk through the leafy solitude around Cong there seems to be water, where chortling coots and whistling grebes fish among the reedy banks. The waters of Lough Mask plunge into the earth a few kilometres to the north, reappearing at Cong in a phenomenon known as the Rising of the Waters. During the 1840s the notion was conceived to cut a canal to link Mask with Lough Corrib. The purpose was twofold: to make work for the unemployed, and in order that persons of leisure might sail their boats from lake to lake. Five hundred men laboured on the project for over four years at fourpence a day to complete the canal and five locks—still reckoned to be a fine piece of workmanship. The porous limestone through which the channel was dug, however, won't suffer a drop of water to stand in it, and the canal is dry to this day.

Cong borders the 12-square-kilometre (3,000-acre) demesne of **Ashford Castle**, a stunningly extravagant neo-Gothic Victorian fantasia built by the Guinness family. Now a luxury hotel, it's an exemplum of the adage, If you have to ask "How much?" you can't afford it.

By the eastern shore of Lough Mask, not far from Cong, is the former house of Charles Boycott, who gave the English language a new noun and verb. Failures of the potato crop in the late 1870s had reduced the peasantry once again to destitution. In 1878 and 1879, evictions for nonpayment of rent were carried out by the thousands. To the Irishman, this threat held more terror than starvation; in order to make the rent, a hungry farmer would sell his crops rather than eat them. As a further cruelty, the law required the dispossessed to relocate themselves not less than 20 miles away.

Nowhere were evictions carried out with such cold efficiency as on the lands of Lord Erne. His agent, Captain Boycott, refused even partial payment of rents, but soon in turn found himself the target of the social agitation of the Land League. In 1880 its president, Charles Stewart Parnell, urged an ingenious, nonviolent retaliation: complete ostracism.

You must show what you think of him . . . by leaving him severely alone, by putting him into a sort of moral Coventry, by isolating him from the rest of his kind as if he were a leper of old, you must show him your detestation of the crime he has committed.

Tradesmen refused to deliver goods, the farrier would not shoe his horses, and come autumn, when Lord Erne's corn waved ripe in the fields, no tenant would lift a hand to help with the harvest. Boycott was last seen with his family and furnishings trundling away in a wagon bound for England. The successful tactic was widely copied; over the next few years genuine land reform—including redistribution and the establishment of Land Courts to fix fair rents—was finally passed by Parliament.

At **Ballintubber** (or Ballintober), St. Patrick baptized fifth-century converts in a holy well and founded a church. In defiance of the traumas of the past

800 years—among them Cromwell and the repressive Penal Laws—Mass has been held at the site without interruption since the early 13th century.

On an overgrown estate a few kilometres to the southeast is the burnt-out shell of **Moore Hall**. Notwithstanding the pedigree of the Moores, a Catholic gentry family which had been active in the 1798 Rising and the 19th-century land-reform movement, the IRA torched the house in 1923. As was the fate of Oliver Gogarty's Renvyle House, this was retribution for author George Moore's support of the Anglo-Irish Treaty, a compromise the all-or-nothing Republicans wouldn't brook. Nor did locals appreciate that Moore used Lough Carra as the venue of his anticlerical novel, *The Lake*. When he died ten years later, local boatmen refused to row mourners across the lake to Castle Island, where his ashes were to be buried.

At **Castlebar**, the main town for County Mayo, the Irish had one of their all-too-rare successes in the struggle against the British. In the summer of 1798, the French general Humbert landed with about 1,100 soldiers in Killala Bay. Joining with a ragtag force of Irish volunteers, they managed to rout a superior English army, which retreated in such haste that the event has been gleefully remembered as the Races of Castlebar ever since. In the heady optimism of the moment, John Moore, an ancestor of George, was proclaimed president of the newborn Republic of Connacht. The Irish, however, couldn't long savour the taste of victory: massive English reinforcements soon extinguished the rebellion; Moore was subsequently captured and died in Waterford Gaol. The remains of the first and last president now lie, with a commemorative plaque, in Castlebar's tree-lined Mall. The town hosts the popular International Song Festival each October.

The Southwest

Just before the River Erriff empties into Killary Harbour, its peat-stained waters fold over **Aasleagh Falls**. Niagara it isn't, but it's a fine sight nonetheless in a glorious golden-walled valley between 700-metre (2,297 foot)-high Ben Gorm to the west and the Devil's Mother to the southeast. The falls formed the backdrop to the ill-fated fight scene in *The Field*. From the wooded vale of Aasleagh, two scenic routes bring you to Westport.

The N59 follows the Erriff—a river very popular with salmon anglers—through the pretty, quiet valley between the Sheffrey Hills and the steep-sided Partry Mountains. The R335 hugs the north side of the harbour before turning sharply northward, passing through a lonesome glen with three roadside loughs and luxuriant growths of rhododendrons. One of the flamboyant marquesses of Sligo built a fishing lodge at Fionnlough, rechristening the place with the most un-Irish name of **Delphi**. The brooding valley reminded him of the home of the Greek oracle, which he had visited in 1811 with his friend Lord Byron. To the southwest are the Mweelrea Mountains, highest in Mayo, which slide into the fjord below.

Near the corner of Clew Bay is another place with a less-than-Irish name, the quaint fishing village of Louisburgh. A small interpretive centre here presents a few details on the life and times of the pirate-queen Grace O'Malley (see page 209). Sandy beaches line much of the south coast of Clew Bay as far east as Murrisk. Seven kilometres west of Louisburgh, boats depart Roonah Quay for Caher Island, Inishturk and Clare Island.

Clare Island

Clare Island is the dark hulk guarding the mouth of Clew Bay. Much of Clare is dominated by Knockmore, which rises up 461 metres (1,512 feet) from the island's western half. The slopes fall away in sea-cliffs which ring most of its perimeter, though there are some good beaches as well. This is a quiet place, with fuchsia-bordered lanes, about 160 inhabitants and just one small hotel. From the massive square keep near the harbour, the pirate-queen Grace O'Malley ruled the west coast of Connacht. It's said she slept here with a rope tied from her big toe down to her flagship, so that she'd be wakened for her raiding forays at the first shift of the tide. Grace may be among the O'Malleys who are interred nearby at the 15th-century Clare Abbey, where a carved coat of arms boasts, "O'Malley invincible on land and sea". Notice the trace of fresco painting on the plaster of the vaulted ceiling, one of the few examples to survive the ruinous damp of the Irish climate.

Croagh Patrick

Visible from points all throughout the region, the dark cone of Croagh Patrick, popularly known as the Reek, rises up 765 metres (2,510 feet) from the southern shore of Clew Bay. This is Ireland's holy mountain, which St. Patrick ascended at the approach of Lent in AD 441. At the grim summit he fasted, like Christ and Moses, for a biblical 40 days and 40 nights. From here he banished the evil crawling things—including snakes—from the holy ground of Ireland.

Afterward, an angel appeared to the saint to ask what he desired of God in return for abandoning the peak. Five times the angel came and went, and each time Patrick—as shrewdly obstinate as an Irish horse-trader—increased his demands. All his wishes were granted, but not, as Brian de Breffny describes, before he delivered God his ultimatum:

> The Angel asks Patrick what he will accept. 'That is not hard to say,' Patrick replies, 'seven persons out of Hell on Doomsday for every hair on my chasuble.' The Angel, not yet fully exasperated, grants this, and for the sixth

time tells Patrick to leave the reek. When Patrick refuses this time the Angel threatens him with force, but Patrick boldly answers that even though the High King of Seven Heavens should come, he will not leave until he is fully satisfied, so the Angel asks him what else he wants. Patrick asks that on the Day of Judgment he, himself, should judge the people of Ireland. The Angel tells him that assuredly that blessing cannot be obtained from the Lord. 'Unless it is got from Him,' Patrick says to the Angel, 'there is no way that I shall leave the reek before Doomsday.'

Stumbling out before dawn every year on Reek Sunday, the last Sunday in July, thousands of pilgrims follow in Patrick's footsteps to celebrate Mass at the tiny chapel on the summit. The view on a clear day—to Clare Island, the smoke-grey cliffs of the Corraun Peninsula, and across the green constellation of islets in Clew Bay—could convert a pagan. Clouds, however, frequently arrive to wring themselves out along the rough slopes, drenching stone and pilgrim with equal indifference. The cruel-edged shards of quartzite scree along the steepening route are punishing enough for the boot-clad hiker, but some pilgrims ascend the holy mountain barefoot.

For the unrepentant climber, there's a salvation of sorts—a homespun and most welcome little pub back at the foot of the Reek, where you can assuage your chilled bones with the creamiest stout you've ever tasted.

Westport and around Clew Bay

Westport was laid out around 1780 by James Wyatt for the marquess of Sligo. It's one of the rare planned towns in the west of Ireland, yet still it's charmingly idiosyncratic, with hardly a right angle to be found among its walkable network of streets. There was clearly a Continental sensibility at work in the design of the sycamore-shaded avenue called the Mall, running along both sides of the canalized Carrowbeg River. Climb Tubber Hill Street for an excellent overview.

The town of about 3,500 people spreads out from the Octagon, with traffic swirling around its now-truncated central plinth. Guidebook writers, for reasons unknown, seem compelled to mention that it was a statue of a banker, George Glendenning, which, once upon a time, capped the Doric pillar. Why George came to be thus commemorated—or how his likeness came to disappear—are greater mysteries which no one seems to know anything about.

The stone quay and abandoned warehouses at Westport Bay are reminders that the town once cherished hopes of becoming a great trading centre, but the arrival of the railway in the 1800s diverted the expected shipping trade. Westport is no Killarney yet, but the town has grown quite popular among tourists in the past few years. They're catered to by a rash of restaurants, gift shops and hotels.

Annual summer events include the Sea Angling and Ceol na Mart (traditional music) festivals in June, the week-long open-air (bring your bumbershoot!) Street Festival in July, and the big Westport Arts Festival (music, theatre, art exhibits) straddling September and October.

Heneghan's is a rustic pub in Bridge Street where there's likely to be New Orleans-style jazz or other music of an evening. Matt Molloy's, a couple of doors down, is the namesake of the nonpareil flute player from the Bothy Band, Planxty, and currently a little ensemble called the Chieftains. The place is frequently jammed, but if you can squeeze in you may get a glimpse of himself performing his publicanly duties, or perhaps even his flute, in the spirited session.

A little to the west of town is one of the few symbols of patrician opulence to escape the retribution so liberally meted out around the time of the Civil War. Now open to the public, the stately Palladian showpiece **Westport**

Clew Bay, Co. Mayo ·

House, seat of the marquesses of Sligo, was built in 1730 and subsequently enlarged and redecorated by Wyatt. Guests at the estate have included Thomas de Quincey (author of *Confessions of an English Opium Eater*) and William Makepeace Thackeray. The dun-coloured limestone mansion is appointed with period furnishings, family portraits (including two by Sir Joshua Reynolds), old Irish silver and Waterford crystal.

Grace O'Malley, Queen of Connacht

Such extravagant legends have accrued around the memory of Grania ni Mhaille, the great iron-breasted pirate-queen of Connacht, that it's hard to pierce the thicket of myth obscuring the historical figure. Islands up and down the coast of Galway and Mayo have associations with her, and, according to lore, nearly every seaside castle in Connacht must have passed through her possession at one time.

Grania, Granuaile, or, more pronounceably, Grace O'Malley, was born around 1530, the daughter of a Connacht warlord. At the age of 15 she was married off to an O'Flaherty chieftain, whom she came to master in every way—in courage, in leadership and in the arts of war. When he died, though Celtic law forbade his title from passing to her, O'Flaherty's soldiers pledged fealty to his doughty widow.

Grace took up the vocation of piracy, and from her base in Clare Island she made seaborne raids along the western coast, expanding her domain and her power. One story told about her is that she wed her second husband, Richard Burke, with the prenuptial understanding that the union might be dissolved after one year with the simple declaration, "I dismiss you". Grace used the time busily garrisoning his castles with her own loyal men. After 12 months, she did curtly dismiss him, slamming the door of Carrigahooley Castle in his face. Burke woke up rudely from the honeymoon and realized that most of his property was in his ex-wife's possession.

In another tale, Grace arose from childbed (on-board ship, of course) in the midst of a ferocious battle that was turning against her. Seizing a blunderbuss, she shot the enemy captain dead. Her sailors, freshly inspired, rallied to victory.

Scourge of the Elizabethans, the uncrowned queen of Connacht bitterly resisted the encroaching English. In 1593, seven years before her death, following a furious sea battle against Connacht's English governor, indomitable Grace sailed her corsair to England and up the Thames to Greenwich for a parley with Queen Elizabeth. Elizabeth offered to confer the title of countess upon her, but Grace declined the honour, replying with regal hauteur that she was already nothing less than a queen in her own right.

A good catch in Mayo

Up the bay from Westport is her country cousin, **Newport**. The little town lacks the tidy prosperity of its larger neighbour but still has its own sense of pride. The beautifully placed, speckled grey ruins of **Burrishoole Abbey** overlook Newport Bay three kilometres (two miles) to the northwest. Close by stands the well-preserved **Carrigahooley Castle** (also called Rockfleet Castle), where wily Grace O'Malley supposedly gave her artless hubby the gate.

Lovely Feeagh and Furnace loughs lie just north. Beyond them spreads the gloriously wild and unpeopled expanse of the **Nephin Beg Range**. From the youth hostel at the top of Lough Feeagh, foot trails branch out across the wilderness, one reaching as far as Bangor. The flanks of Nephin to the northeast, tallest in the range, are a dark jumble of red sandstone, schist and gneiss, while the glimmering 807-metre (2,648-foot)-high cone is of snowy quartzite. It's a grand sight to behold these great mountains, blue in the hazy distance, when the clouds crack open and the sunlight pours down on Mayo through the rain-washed air like a benediction.

In "The Brow of Nephin", gathered by Douglas Hyde in *The Love Songs of Connacht,* the nameless folk poet lifts his thoughts to the mountain, a refuge from his life's troubles:

> *Did I stand on the bald top of Nephin*
> *And my hundred-times loved one with me,*
> *We should nestle together as safe in*
> *Its shade as the birds on a tree.*

The highway follows the island-littered northern shore of Newport Bay. The hundreds of little islands—one, some say, for every day of the year—are submerged drumlins, the debris left by advancing and retreating glaciers 10,000 years ago. At Mulrany, the **Corraun Peninsula** has kept a short ligature with the mainland. The road forks to encircle this mountainous knuckle of land, with tremendous views all around, and meets again on the far side.

Achill Island

A bridge across the narrow sound tethers the Corraun to Achill Island, largest of Ireland's offshore satellites. Because it's accessible by road, and not solely via a queasy boat ride, it's also the most touristed island. From the village of Achill Sound, just over the bridge, the signposted Atlantic Drive makes a hair-raising loop around the island's precipitous southern end. En route, you'll pass a square tower house, yet another of Grace O'Malley's coastal fastnesses.

Keel and Doogort have good beaches, and tramping possibilities are plentiful among the island's camelback hills and valleys. A rented bicycle makes a good way to get around, but there's a good deal of up and down. Pick up a map of the island at one of the shops. One easy walk is to follow the road up the skirts of 670-metre (2,198-foot) Slievemore, the mountain rising behind Keel. There's an eerie deserted village partway up, almost invisible among the stony slopes until you're near it. The view from here is mighty, taking in the sparkling amethyst quarry on Croaghaun mountain to the west, across the sweep of heathery bogs and the white flecks of sheep below you, and over the green bay to Clare Island. The 600-metre (2,040-foot) cliffs on the seaward side of Croaghaun are the highest in the British Isles.

Because nearly all its attractions are out-of-doors, you'll want good weather when you visit Achill. "In winter rain, mist and storm sweep over its wild desolate bogs, the sea raves incessantly among the rocks", wrote R.L. Praeger in 1937. "Frost and snow are rare visitors, but the whole island lies soaked and hopeless". Fifty-five years later, when this writer visited—in summer—the weather wasn't much improved. "The worst summer in memory", the locals intoned, with a sad shake of the head and what seemed to be a well-practised facility with the phrase.

Atlantic beach

North to the Mullet

Back at Mulrany, the highway shoots northward through extensive tracts of bog and into Mayo's Gaeltacht, where Irish speakers cling to the county's northwestern edges. If it's lonesome isolation you're after, you're getting warmer. Five thousand years ago, all of Ireland—including this barren region—was densely wooded. Deforestation and intensive agriculture, however, coupled with an increasingly wet climate, led to serious environmental degradation, and the region turned to bogland. In recent years, turf cutters here have revealed settlements and the neatly combed furrows of Neolithic farmland, arrested in time under more than a metre of peat bog.

From gloomy **Bangor** (sometimes called Bangor Erris) a secondary road branches straight off to the northwest past Carrowmore Lake. The mystical poet Æ (George Russell) wrote:

> It's a lonely road through bogland to the lake at Carrowmore,
> And a sleeper there lies dreaming where the water laps the shore;
> Though the moth-wings of the twilight in their purples are unfurled,
> Yet his sleep is filled with music by the masters of the world.

Beyond the lake lies the remote **Mullet Peninsula**. The deeply scalloped contours of Blacksod Bay give the flat, wind-raked Mullet the look of a seahorse on the map; the slenderest of causeways spears it near the middle, joining it to the mainland. Walk the Cliffs of Erris, along the northern end, for the most dramatic vistas.

Early monks found that the peninsula and its several little islands offered just the hardscrabble deprivation they were seeking; the islands are unpopulated today, but monastic remains are plentiful enough among the sheep and tussocks of grass, as are colonies of phalaropes, kittiwakes, mergansers and other seabirds, especially on the two Inishkeas. Until 1931, North and South Inishkea were inhabited by communities of Norwegian whalers, each island with its own king. Tiny **Inishglora** (the "Island of the Voice"), just west of the Mullet, is where the legendary Children of Lír, transformed into swans by their spiteful stepmother, came ashore when they heard the bell of St. Patrick (see page 265). Passage to the islands can be negotiated with local fishermen.

Eastern Mayo

High, dizzying cliffs rim much of the north coast of Mayo from Benwee Head east to Downpatrick Head, where St. Patrick wrestled the Devil. In their mighty thrashing, a piece of the headland broke away. To this day the layered sea-stack called Doonbristy—with an ancient stone fort dramatically perched on top—looms offshore as evidence of the fray.

Into the broad cleft of **Killala Bay** General Humbert sailed his three warships and some 1,100 men on 22 August 1798. The long-awaited French liberators had arrived. From Kilcummin they moved south and quickly took Killala, where Humbert set up headquarters at the bishop's palace; the Union Jack came down and in its stead was unfurled the Irish banner—a golden harp floating in a green field, bearing the legend *Erin go Bragh*—"Ireland Forever".

Humbert and his Irish allies enjoyed other initial successes, at Ballina and Castlebar (see page 205), but the tide soon turned against them. The planned national uprising had been betrayed, its leaders arrested; the scattered insurrections which flared were quickly snuffed out.

Yeats chose a peasant cottage in Killala, at the moment of the Frenchmen's arrival, for the setting of his play *Cathleen ni Houlihan*. As the villagers are heard cheering for them down at the bay, a stranger appears at the Gillane cottage. She is Cathleen ni Houlihan, the poor old woman "that goes through the country whatever time there's war or trouble coming". She is Ireland, and in that symbolic aspect her words are a cipher, doubly meaningful and laden with portent on the eve of battle against the English. "I have my hopes", she says. "The hope of getting my beautiful fields back again; the hope of putting the strangers out of my house".

After she departs, the youngest son returns to the cottage. Did he see an old woman going down the path, the family asks. "I did not", the son replies, "but I saw a young girl, and she had the walk of a queen".

Years later, Yeats would wonder aloud if the play had helped set in motion the tragic events of the Easter Rising:

> Did that play of mine send out
> Certain men the English shot?

Sights in the handsome little port include a restored round tower built of pale blue and green limestone; at 26 metres (85 feet) it's the highest and finest in Mayo. Southeast of Killala are two romantically ruined 15th-century Franciscan friaries, built unusually close to one another beside the bay: **Moyne Abbey** is three kilometres (two miles) from Killala; look inside for the sailing ships scratched into the nave plaster 400 years ago by some idle friar, dreaming, perhaps, of a more adventuresome life. A little farther on is superb **Rosserk Abbey**, the finest and best-preserved site of its kind in Ireland.

The road south soon reaches **Ballina**, a pleasant-enough market town and fishing centre grown up beside the River Moy. To the southwest is large Lough Conn, and below it, separated by a narrow isthmus, smaller Lough Cullin. Pontoon and Foxford make good bases for fishing holidays on the lakes.

Kilkelly is an unprepossessing little place on the plains southeast of Swinford. But through the words of his dirgeful song "Kilkelly", Peter Jones has let the village represent all the keen sorrow of the Irish exile's experience, a story told a million times over. Jones based the words on a bundle of letters he found, written by his great-great-grandfather in Kilkelly to his son, who had emigrated to America and whom he would never see again. The song compresses 30 years of births and deaths, bad harvests and hard times, and the pain of separation into five poignant verses.

> *Kilkelly Ireland eighteen and sixty, my dear and loving son John,*
> *Your good friend and school master Pat McNamara so good as*
>   *to write these words down.*
> *Your brothers have all gone to find work in England, the house is*
>   *all empty and sad,*
> *The crop of potatoes is sorely infected a third to a half of*
>   *them bad.*
> *Your sister Bridget and Patrick O'Donnell they're going to be*
>   *married in June,*
> *Your mother says not to work on the railroad and be sure to come*
>   *on home soon.*

County Roscommon

Roscommon is Connacht's only landlocked county, but in recompense for its lack of a dramatic coastline it got the west's most fertile lands. An arch of lakes forms the county's northern boundary, while the Shannon delineates its long eastern edge.

Tame Roscommon has been disparaged as Ireland's most boring county, but that's not quite fair. The southern portions are unexciting, but the scenery in the north is quite handsome. The region was among the earliest in Ireland to be inhabited, and an abundance of ring forts, megalithic tombs and burial mounds remain to be explored.

Castlerea to Keadue

The main reason to visit the small market town of Castlerea is **Clonalis House**, a Victorian mansion in a small estate close by to the west. This is the last vestige of the ancestral properties of the storied O'Conor clan, the oldest recorded family in Europe. The O'Conors can trace their lineage back to AD 75, with Feredach the Just. All told, 35 kings have issued from the O'Conors, including Ireland's last two high-kings, Turlough Mór and his son Rory. The last direct heir to the kingship of Connacht took Jesuit vows in the 19th century, leaving no descendants and thus breaking the venerable line.

The elegantly appointed house—stuffed with family portraits, Victorian furnishings, and documents pertaining to O'Conor genealogy—is a rarity among Ireland's great houses in being owned by a Gaelic family. Among the treasures stored here is the harp of the brilliant blind composer O'Carolan (see page 218).

The first president of the Republic of Ireland lies buried in the Protestant churchyard at **Frenchpark**, northeast of Castlerea. Douglas Hyde was born at the nearby rectory in 1860, and in his younger days he tramped throughout the western counties, recording and translating the stories and songs of the deep Gaelic oral tradition. His several published collections, including the best known, *Love Songs of Connacht*, helped to awaken a wider appreciation for Ireland's native lyricism and prepared the ground for the flowering of the Irish Literary Revival.

In 1893, Hyde and others founded the Gaelic League with the aim of revivifying the Irish language and culture. From 1938 to 1945, Ireland was one of the only modern nations to place a poet in high office by electing Hyde to the presidency—prefiguring Czechoslovakia's remarkable election of Vaclev Havel by more than half a century.

The handsome little town of **Boyle** sits at the base of the Curlew Mountains, midway between two beautiful loughs, Gara and Key. Centrepiece of the town is the Cistercian Boyle Abbey. Founded in 1161 but not completed until 1220, its mix of styles illustrates the architectural transition occurring at that time, from the rounded Hiberno-Romanesque arches to the pointed forms typical of early Gothic. Considering the litany of indignities the abbey has suffered over the centuries, it remains in surprisingly good repair, especially the choir, nave and transept, built of fawn-colored stone.

Flanking the southern shore of the lake east of Boyle, **Lough Key Forest Park** offers camping, boating, swimming, picnicking and walks amid the luxuriant woodlands. On one of the lake-islands, the dove-grey turrets of a MacDermott family castle rise above the trees, storybook-perfect.

Of the many songs gathered by Douglas Hyde, one of the most widely known and best loved concerns Lough Key and a pair of star-crossed lovers, Úna MacDermott and Thomas Costelloe. Because their two families, like Irish Capulets and Montagues, had taken opposing sides during the Cromwellian upheavals, the MacDermotts refused Thomas's proposal of marriage to Úna. A true romantic heroine, Úna died of her thwarted love. Before Thomas followed her—dead too, of a broken heart—he composed the passionately tormented love song, "Úna Bhán" ("Fair Úna"). One version runs to 45 verses, but the single stanza below conveys something of its flavour:

> O Úna Bhán, it was you who drove me mad;
> O Úna, 'twas you and your beauty tore me from God;
> O Úna, I was ruined by the view of your fine fair head,
> And if I could choose, I'd sooner be blind or dead.

The lovers were buried side by side, in the shadow of the abbey on Lough Key's Trinity Island; two ash trees grew from their graves and twined above the sweethearts, together at last.

"Our great solace in our great need", reads the tombstone of Turlough O'Carolan, the last and greatest of Ireland's harper-bards, whose earthly remains lie in the cemetery of **Kilronan Abbey**, between the villages of Keadue and Ballyfarnan. Well beloved in his lifetime, hundreds mourned him at the wake, which carried on for four days. Now modern harpers and other musicians celebrate his life and music here each August in the ten-day O'Carolan Festival.

Roscommon Town and Thereabouts

In the centre of the county, on the plain all around **Rathcroghan**, are ring forts, tumuli and other reminders that this was the capital and burial place of the ancient royalty of Connacht. Queen Maeve had her palace here on the flat-topped Hill of Rathcroghan. It was this semi-mythical, first-century queen who set in motion the epic battle between the armies of Connacht and the legendary Ulster champion Cuchulain over possession of a mighty brown bull. The story is found in the *Táin Bó Cuailgne* (*Cattle Raid of Cooley*), the central event in the Ulster cycle of heroic tales (see page 251).

Close by is the Graveyard of the Kings, and three kilometres (two miles) south of Tulsk is another mound, called Carnfree, where the kings of Connacht were crowned.

The graceful Palladian **Strokestown Park House** stands behind the castellated wall at the end of the country's widest main street, in the planned village of Strokestown. Built in 1730, the mansion has the last galleried kitchen in Ireland, from which the lady of the house could supervise the activities of her cooks without having to descend and mingle with the scullery maids.

The county capital, **Roscommon**, is at the north end of a long udder of luxuriant pastureland hanging southward. On the town square, the former county gaol holds the curious distinction of having once employed a female executioner, a woman with the seemingly benign sobriquet of "Lady Betty". Under sentence of death herself for murder, Betty escaped the noose by assuming the unwanted job of hangman (hangperson?). The massive stone building now houses the tourist information office.

In Roscommon's 13th-century Dominican friary are the effigy its founder, King Felim O'Conor, and a 15th-century tomb bearing the images of eight *gallowglasses*, fearsome Scottish mercenaries brought over by Gaelic chieftains to help square the odds against their Anglo–Norman foes. Immediately north of town is the impressive shell of 13th-century Roscommon Castle. With massive circular towers joined by curtain walls, and lacking a central keep, this Anglo–Norman redoubt is one of Ireland's best examples of a courtyard castle. The addition of numerous mullioned windows in the 16th century helps domesticate the grimly functional profile.

East of Roscommon town the Shannon swells to form Lough Ree, the county's boundary with Longford and Westmeath. Straddling the river below the lake is the market town of **Athlone**, a place much fought over since ancient times because of its strategic ford across the Shannon.

Turlough O'Carolan

Since ancient times the Celtic chieftains employed among their retinue one or more bards whose duties were to compose birthday odes and lamentations for the dead, celebrate the master's exploits in verse, and the like. They were accorded high social status and were dreaded by their enemies for the sharp-toothed satire which they could inflict with eminent skill.

Turlough O'Carolan, inheritor of this long tradition, was born in County Meath in 1670, but he spent much of his adult life around Leitrim and Roscommon. An attack of smallpox left him blinded at the age of 22. Having shown an early aptitude on the harp, he took up the instrument as his lifelong vocation.

O'Carolan travelled about the countryside, where he was hospitably welcomed at the great Irish houses. In return, he composed airs and songs, called *planxties*, which lavished the most extravagant praises on his patrons. Only a handful of his verses have come down to us, but over 200 of the melodies have survived and, in fact, his music has been enjoying something of a revival in recent years. The tunes suggest baroque distillations from traditional airs and dances, but the composer was probably more influenced by his Italian contemporaries. There is a fey, plangent quality to an O'Carolan melody, and through even the gayest of them there runs a dark thread of melancholy.

The harper's keen ear and prodigious musicianship have become the stuff of legend. One oft-told story, recorded by Oliver Goldsmith, relates that, upon hearing Vivaldi's Fifth Violin Concerto for the first time, O'Carolan picked up his harp and played back the entire piece without missing so much as a note. He then topped this performance by immediately composing one of his now best-known works, the spirited, elegant "Carolan's Concerto".

When, at the age of 68, death was nigh, O'Carolan called for his two great loves—his harp and his whiskey. From his deathbed he rhapsodized his final dirge, the mournful "Farewell to Music". The whiskey then was held to his lips and, though unable to drink, he declared that "it would be hard if two such friends as he and the cup should part without at least kissing".

Turlough O'Carolan

Clonmacnois, St. Ciaran's sixth-century monastic city, stands over a reedy bend of the river downstream. Despite its fairly remote location, over the centuries Clonmacnois was plundered and burned dozens of times, in turn by Vikings, Normans and English. The monastery flourished in spite of these disasters to become one of medieval Ireland's foremost capitals of scholarship and artistic production. The extensive remains include eight churches, three carved high crosses, two round towers and some 200 gravestones spanning pagan times to the present. The high-king Rory O'Conor was buried here in 1198, along with many others, as remembered by the Irish bard Angus O'Gillan (translated by Thomas Rolleston) in "The Dead at Clonmacnois":

> *There they laid to rest the Seven Kings of Tara,*
> *There the sons of Cairbrè sleep—*
> *Battle-banners of the Gael, that in Kieran's plain of crosses*
> *Now their final hosting keep.*

County Sligo

One of the overlooked corners of Ireland, County Sligo is hand in glove with the name of William Butler Yeats, and one can hardly be mentioned without the other. His poetry is so laden with its place-names and so thoroughly imbued with its atmosphere that his *Collected Poems* could well serve as a sort of map and guidebook to the literary landscape. For his brother, Jack, too, one of Ireland's most talented painters, the county was a deep well of inspiration. "Sligo", he said, "was my school and the sky above it".

To W.B. Yeats this was the "Land of Heart's Desire" and the place that most influenced his life and writings. Though neither born nor bred here, Yeats spent his boyhood summers in and near Sligo Town, where his mother's family, the Pollexfens, owned a merchant shipping concern. From the eyrie of the Watch Tower, at the corner of Wine and Adelaide streets, young W.B. watched his grandfather's ships coming and going in the harbour.

Every year the Yeats International Summer School draws academics and dewy-eyed romantics from all over, well-thumbed volumes clutched to their breasts, who come to mine the seemingly inexhaustible vein of interest in the poet and to visit the sites associated with him.

Apart from its unexpected loveliness, what's most surprising about Sligo is that it's not better known. But that's bound to change as more people discover its cream-white beaches, soft valleys and bold table mountains, all bathed in the "pearl-pale" light that's peculiar to the Irish northwest.

Sligo Town

The approach to the town is dominated by the beetle-browed escarpment of Benbulben, at whose feet W.B. Yeats wished to be buried. Its dramatically upswept, concave face seems to have been pushed up from the coast by the heel of some enormous primeval hand. To the west is the dome of Knocknarea, where Queen Maeve sleeps for eternity under a coverlet of stone.

To anyone arriving after the heavy silences of Mayo, Roscommon or Leitrim, buzzing Sligo Town strikes the senses like a metropolis. With a population of close to 20,000, this old and flourishing town, alive with the hum of commerce, is the largest in Ireland's northwest. Sligo is full of satisfied-looking, well-kept Victorian and Edwardian shopfronts and winding streets, looking little changed when compared with photographs taken a century ago— except that macadam has replaced the mud thoroughfares, and the corner smithy and the mercantile next door now probably deal in stereo equipment and computers.

The locus of activity is around the intersecting web of O'Connell, Harmony Hill, Grattan and Market streets, where the sidewalks are often jammed with shoppers and strollers, and the streets—designed for 19th-century traffic—strain to accommodate two lanes of subcompacts.

Like so many Irish towns, Sligo grew up around an ancient fording place. The River Garavogue, spanned by three bridges, hurries through on its brief journey from Lough Gill to three-lobed Sligo Bay. The castle which once guarded the settlement has disappeared without a trace, but its defences were strong enough that Sligo held out against the armies of King Billy when the other western garrisons had fallen after the Battle of the Boyne.

The sights of Sligo are easily covered on foot (the Tourism Centre in Temple Street sells an annotated walking-tour guide), and the more ambitious can hike out to Carrowmore, Knocknarea and other destinations close by. A fine short walk leads east from Hyde Bridge along Kennedy Parade, following the river to **Doorly Park**; the rewards are splendid views of Lough Gill and the surrounding mountains.

One of the town's only medieval relics is the elegant Dominican priory, known as **Sligo Abbey**. Founded in 1252, it was reconstructed after suffering badly in a fire in 1414, but eight lancet windows in the choir have survived from the 13th-century original. The monks abandoned the abbey permanently after Cromwell's Roundheads sacked it in 1641. Restoration work has saved the cloisters on three sides, each with 18 beautifully worked arches and elaborately coupled pillars.

Across the river, in Stephen Street, the **Sligo County Museum** and adjacent **Municipal Art Gallery** offer an introduction to the brothers Yeats. One room of the tiny museum has a rather higgledy-piggledy assortment of Bronze Age artifacts and rural curiosities from days of yore. The other room is mostly given over to likenesses of W.B. Yeats in various poses, plus some broadsheets, manuscripts, prints by Jack Yeats and a few items pertaining to Countess Markievicz (see page 224). A replica of W.B.'s 1923 Nobel Prize for Literature is proudly displayed. Of interest to Irish-music aficionados is a bruised old fiddle once belonging to the virtuoso Michael Coleman (see below), strung up and ready to be played, but silent as a brick now.

Next door, the art gallery is more rewarding, with pictures by John Yeats (who attempted to make a livelihood as a portrait painter in London when his two sons were boys), Jack Yeats, George Russell (Æ), Nora McGuinness and Paul Henry, among others.

Still on the trail of Yeats, continue west on Stephen Street to the long-legged bronze of the poet (unveiled by his son in 1989), cloaked in his own words and gazing aloofly through pince-nez over the passersby. Cross Hyde Bridge to the **Yeats Memorial Building**, the headquarters for the Yeats International Summer School, held each August since 1956. The building also houses the Sligo Art Gallery, which hosts visiting exhibits throughout the year.

A *must* stop in Sligo for a quiet jar is **Hargadon's**, in O'Connell Street. This is the real McCoy, a Spartan, completely unpretentious old pub, unchanged for a hundred years, panelled in age-darkened wood, with rows of private drinking booths and hardly a nod of acknowledgment to the 20th century.

Keohane's Bookshop in Castle Street is one of Sligo's best, with a solid selection of Irish literature and local history. Sartorially savvy gents come from three continents to be fitted at Joseph Martin's tailor shop in Wine Street. A bespoke suit will set you back about £375–700.

William Butler Yeats, 1908

Each March and April the Feis Cheoil/Feis Shligigh presents traditional music, while the ten-day Sligo Arts Festival in September showcases traditional, jazz and classical music, as well as theatre and dance. The Hawk's Well Theatre, next to the Tourism Centre in Temple Street, stages plays, musicals and concerts throughout the year. For traditional and folk music, stop in at TD's Lounge or McGlynn's, which have something on most every night. On Tuesday nights year-round, the Trades Club in Castle Street hosts a traditional session. Xanadu's Disco and the Oasis Nightclub in the Blue Lagoon Saloon are two of Sligo's major dance venues, while there's frequently jazz at the Silver Swan Hotel. See the Friday edition of the *Sligo Champion* for more entertainment listings.

Around Sligo Town

Sligo holds an astonishing wealth of prehistoric remains, with some 4,500 sites of archaeological interest identified throughout the county. Three kilometres (two miles) southwest of Sligo Town, the cluster of megalithic tombs and other monuments at **Carrowmore** is among the richest concentrations in Western Europe. Though scores of dolmens and passage graves were destroyed here over the past two centuries, about 50 remain. The oldest date back to about 4500 BC, making them already ancient when the Egyptians began thinking about piling up the pyramids at Giza.

Generally the tombs consist of a large stone burial chamber with a roof cap, in which cremated bones were interred, surrounded by a circle of boulders. Most of the tombs originally were buried within a cairn but have since been uncovered.

The cemetery spreads out over a wide area at the base of 300-metre (1,020-foot)-high **Knocknarea**, the great truncated limestone mound that dominates the horizon west of Sligo Town and which loomed large in Yeats's imagination. At night, according to legend, the supernatural, pre-Christian warriors called the Fianna ride out between Knocknarea and Benbulben:

> *The host is riding from Knocknarea*
> *And over the grave of Clooth-na-Bare;*
> *Caoilte tossing his burning hair,*
> *And Niamh calling Away, come away;*
> *Empty your heart of its mortal dream.*

Knocknarea is easily climbed from Grange House, on the southeast side, and the views from the summit are stupendous: to the cliffs of Slieve League in Donegal and, away off to the southwest, Croagh Patrick. The dry historian will insist that the massive stone cairn at the top of Knocknarea was built by Stone Age farmers about 3000 BC. But the more poetic will side with Yeats in believing it was erected as the burial place of Maeve in the first century AD, and a fitting place for the mighty warrior-queen of Connacht it is (see page 217). Carry up a stone with you to add to the pile, lest Maeve one day reawaken.

About a kilometre west of Grange House is the start of the footpath which runs through the **Glen of Knocknarea**, an extraordinary, sheer-walled limestone chasm choked with trees, ivy and ferns. Around the mountain, at the end of the peninsula, the seaside resort of **Strandhill** has a good beach and an 18-hole golf course. At low tide, one can walk out to Coney Island, namesake of the New York amusement park.

A great-uncle of W.B. Yeats owned a mill at **Ballysodare**, eight kilometres (five miles) south of Sligo. Along the river close by there once stood a row of cottages, each with its own "salley" (willow) garden. Salley branches were useful in basket making and for thatching, and the gardens also made an ideal trysting place for lovers. Here Yeats overheard an old man singing a folk air on which he modelled his rueful "Salley Gardens". The Thatch, an old-fashioned, thatch-roofed pub, is renowned for its traditional music nights on Tuesdays and Thursdays.

Among the tree-clad hills just east of Sligo is gorgeous **Lough Gill**. The silver bell from the Dominican priory was cast into its waters centuries ago, and now, it's said, only the pure of heart can hear its tolling. Roads lead around the lake, via Dromahair in County Leitrim, for an unforgettably scenic loop tour, and there are many wonderful walks around the shores. A nice alternative is the two-hour cruise from Sligo on the *Queen Maeve*, which stops at **Innisfree**, the tiny lake-isle that inspired one of Yeats's best-loved poems. When he wrote this bucolic reverie, he was living in the hurly-burly of London, far from the sound of Gill's "lake water lapping . . . by the shore", but dreaming nevertheless of his Land of Heart's Desire:

> *I will arise and go now, and go to Innisfree,*
> *And a small cabin build there, of clay and wattles made;*
> *Nine bean-rows will I have there, a hive for the honey-bee,*
> *And live alone in the bee-loud glade.*

Yeats died in the south of France in 1939. Almost ten years later, in fulfilment of his wishes, his body was brought to the churchyard of **Drumcliff**, "under bare Ben Bulben's head", where his great-grandfather had been rector. He wanted "no marble, no conventional phrase", and his instructions were honoured. A severe grey rectangle, quarried from the limestone heart of Sligo, marks the simple site.

Drumcliff Church was built upon an early monastic settlement founded by St. Colmcille. There's an excellent tenth-century high cross, a sort of stationary Bible, bearing on both faces carvings that illustrated Old and New Testament stories for the unlettered folk: Adam and Eve, Cain slaying Abel, the Crucifixion and other scenes. At the end of the peninsula jutting out to the southwest of Drumcliff is the popular seaside resort of **Rosses Point**, with two very good beaches and a world-class golf course.

From its spacious, forested demesne, **Lissadell House**, home of the remarkable Gore-Booth family, overlooks Drumcliff Bay. Yeats befriended Eva and Constance ("Two girls in silk kimonos, both beautiful, one a gazelle"), daughters of the Arctic explorer Sir Henry Gore-Booth, and was a frequent visitor to the house in 1894–95. In the waning days of the aristocracy, the sisters defied the expectations of their privileged Anglo-Irish class: the poetess Eva (1870–1926) became a labor organizer for women in Britain, while Constance (1868–1927), later Countess Markievicz, having married a Polish nobleman, traded her silks for a uniform and appeared as one of the firebrands in the 1916

Rising. She was condemned to death for her participation but was reprieved. Two years later she became the first woman elected to the British House of Commons, but, like the other members of the nationalistic Sinn Féin party, she refused to take her seat at Westminster, and would serve as minister for labour in the Dáil Éireann when Eamon de Valera formed a government in 1919.

Today the picture of shabby gentility, the neo-classical mansion, still lived in by the Gore-Booths, is open to the public, and one of the most satisfying of the Irish great houses to visit.

Travelling along the coast road between Sligo and Bundoran, you might glimpse **Inishmurray**, six kilometres (four miles) offshore, where St. Molaise founded a monastery in the sixth century. The rocky island was home to such tenacious distillers of illicit *poitín* that a detachment of the Royal Irish Constabulary had to be posted there to stamp it out. The last 50 inhabitants departed the bleak place for the last time in 1947, and now it's left to a breeding colony of eider ducks. Boats sail out on day-trips from Rosses Point, Mullaghmore and Streedagh.

Five thousand years ago, Neolithic builders piled up the enormous stones of the **Creevykeel Court Tomb**, a double-chambered burial monument with a semi-circular courtyard, bounded by upright stones. Known locally as the Giant's Grave, Creevykeel is one of the most accessible megalithic sites and, according to some authorities, the country's finest. The tomb is beside the highway, shortly before the Leitrim border.

Southern and Western Sligo

The road to Boyle (N4) runs through pastoral expanses of wooded hill country, past island-strewn Lough Arrow and into the Curlew Mountains as it crosses into Roscommon. The views are glorious.

The Bricklieve Mountains fold into five parallel limestone ridges, separated by deep valleys, west of Lough Arrow. Sited along the ridgetops is the **Carrowkeel Cemetery**, a complex of 14 cairn-covered Neolithic passage tombs as well as other relics. On the summer solstice, the longest day of the year, the setting sun illuminates the interior of cruciform Cairn K. This arrangement contrasts with Newgrange, in County Meath, where the rays of the rising sun penetrate its inner chamber on the shortest day of the year, the winter solstice. Getting to Carrowkeel requires a stiff uphill walk, but there's enough here for hours of exploration.

West of Boyle lies the musical heart of Sligo, sometimes called the Coleman Country, around **Gorteen** and **Tubbercurry**. Michael Coleman, one of the great celebrated figures in Irish traditional music, was born close by in 1892 in the village of Killavil. A fiddle player of prodigious inventiveness, he never turned a tune precisely the same way twice, but added some subtle variation each time through it. Coleman emigrated to America in the 1920s, where he recorded a number of 78s that enjoyed considerable popularity both there and back home. His playing exerted such a strong influence on other players that the Sligo style—fluid, brisk and almost florid with ornamentation—came to dominate Irish music for decades thereafter, overshadowing Ireland's other regional styles.

Teach Murray in Gorteen holds a Monday-night session where you can hear the echoes of Coleman's style performed by local musicians. In the market town of Tubbercurry (or Tobercurry), the May Queen Lounge and The Traditional regularly have a good bit of *ceol* (Irish music). A local troupe stages the Western Drama Festival each spring and autumn.

The Boyle–Ballina road (R294) continues west through the jumbled metamorphic lumps of the Slieve Gamph, or Ox Mountains. The seaside resort of **Enniscrone** (also called Inishcrone), looking out to Mayo across Killala Bay, has a long sandy beach and an 18-hole golf course. At Lecan Castle north of town a number of early books were compiled from the 14th to 17th centuries by the MacFirbises, a clan of poets and historiographers. Among the most important of these are *The Yellow Book of Lecan* and *The Book of Genealogies of Ireland,* both now preserved in Dublin. Each September the MacFirbis Weekend Summer School presents lectures and historical tours to commemorate the family's accomplishments.

Sea cliffs edge the northwestern corner of Sligo but fade out before **Easky**. Two martello towers face the Atlantic here, still defending the fishing village and sea resort against an invasion by Napoleon. Within a few kilometres the secondary road rejoins the N59, which continues east to Ballysodare via the few hamlets lying between the Ox Mountains and the sea. The **Ladies Brae road**, a popular scenic side trip offering some wonderful views, branches south from near Skreen and runs along tumbling streams and over the flanks of Knockalongy before meeting the Castlebar–Sligo highway.

Goat for sale, Puck Fair

County Leitrim and the Midlands

Quiet Leitrim, least populous of all Ireland's counties, has been largely by-passed by tourism, though its lakes and rivers are well appreciated by anglers and boaters. The soil is mostly thin and poor, so farmers are few, but sheep manage well enough here, nipping the grasses between the rough hedgerows of whitethorn, ash and brier.

The preponderance of place-names with "Drum" (from the Irish word for a low ridge) in them offers a clue to the character of the landscape: the waving hills are the moraines left by retreating glaciers. Southern Leitrim is a sleepy country of gentle hills perforated by a welter of small lakes, while the more mountainous northern reaches squeeze in between Sligo and Fermanagh to claim just a few kilometres of coastline on Donegal Bay. Leaf-shaped Lough Allen—the first in the long necklace of Shannon lakes—nearly divides Leitrim in two at the county's narrow waist.

Southern Leitrim

Drumshanbo, at the southern point of Lough Allen, sounds like a nonce word made up for a limerick, but in fact the name means "the Back of the Old Cow". It's a popular centre for pike fishing. To the east of the lake rise bare-sided Slieve Anierin and the Iron Mountains, from which ore was mined until about 200 years ago, when the neighbouring forests which had fueled the smelters were finally exhausted. Each June the town hosts the enjoyable festival of An Tóstal, with Irish music, dancing and singing.

The twin hills Si Beag and Si Mor ("Little Fairy Mound" and "Big Fairy Mound") rise near Keshcarrigan, among the swath of lakes spreading across Leitrim from Cavan to Roscommon. The blind harper Turlough O'Carolan (see page 218), who lived for a time at Mohill to the south, is said to have fallen asleep near these drumlins and forever after heard fairy music running through his head. Upon waking, he immediately composed the delicate air, named after the hills, which is still commonly played today.

The tackle shops along wide **Carrick-on-Shannon**'s broad main street and the many boats moored in the Shannon give away the *raison d'être* of this easygoing town. But if you're here for neither the fishing nor river cruising, probably the best diversion in Carrick is walking across the six-arched stone bridge which gracefully spans the river to the Shannon View Pub; the tables on the green outside are just the place for a drink and a bit of boat-watching when the weather's fair. Seán's and Burke's bars on Bridge Street have weekly music nights.

Sandwiched between two shops near the top of the high street is the tiny Costello Chapel, reputed to be the second smallest in the world. It was erected by Edward Costello as a mausoleum for his wife, who died in her prime in 1877. He too now lies entombed across the aisle from her.

The Longford road from Carrick-on-Shannon leaves the river for a few kilometres before crossing it again at Jamestown, dating from the 17th-century Protestant settlement of Leitrim. Like Carrick, it was fortified and garrisoned to guard the river ford. Just across a tight loop of the Shannon is Drumsna. In the 1840s, the English author Anthony Trollope worked at various jobs throughout Ireland before he embarked on his true vocation. A mouldering old house in Drumsna, which he encountered in the course of his duties as a clerk for the Post Office Surveyor, inspired the first of his 47 weighty novels, *The MacDermots of Ballycloran*, based on the once-powerful Gaelic landowning family: "The usual story, thought I, of Connacht gentlemen; an extravagant landlord, reckless tenants, debt, embarrassment, despair, ruin".

Into the Midlands

From County Leitrim, the N4 to Dublin passes into the rolling farm and pasture country in the heart of the Ireland Midlands, Counties Longford and Westmeath. William Bulfin, who bicycled around Ireland 90 years ago, felt a special affection for this countyside, but he couldn't help feeling the sense of loss that the departure of the region's people and industry had caused:

> There was a day when the corn mills of Ballymahon were famous, and when from early morning to late at night, through the winter months, long lines of cars crowded the thoroughfares around it waiting to deliver grain. . . . The Inny is capable of turning hundreds of mill wheels, but so far as I know the turbine at Ballymulvey is the only one at work. The great mills of MacGann, of Fagan, of Murtagh and others—all busy centres of industry forty years ago—are tenantless, and the owls and bats alone keep guard over the remains of the rust-eaten machinery. The splendid might of the water power is squandered in play amongst lilies and flaggers and sedges. . . . But although the gentle Inny has been robbed of its industries, its beauty still remains. I have seen the river many times from Ballycorky Bridge to Murtagh's Mills, and it was lovely always.

There's not much in Longford Town to dawdle over, but the southwestern part of the county, spilling over into Westmeath, is pretty enough. It's known as the **Goldsmith Country** after Oliver Goldsmith (1728–74), who was born here in the hamlet of Pallas and who wove the landscape of the Midlands into his writings. Discreet plaques here and there indicate places associated with the author's life and landmarks he described in his poems and plays.

In **Kilkenny West**, Goldsmith's father, Charles, was curate-in-charge at what Oliver called "the decent church that topt the neighbouring hill" in his long poem, *The Deserted Village* (1770), a perennial fixture in English literature anthologies. The young Goldsmith's career as a poet is said to have been born in that church; while listening to his father's sermon, the boy noticed a rat climbing down a rope from the belfry, and he commemorated the moment with the verse:

> *A pious rat, for want of stairs*
> *Came down a rope to say his prayers.*

Opinion seems about equally divided as to whether it's **Lissoy** or **Glassan**, both near Lough Ree's eastern shore, which served as the model for "sweet Auburn, the loveliest village of the plain", the subject of *The Deserted Village*. Both seem likely candidates on a summer afternoon, with their pervading air of sleepy abandonment.

Canal lock, Co. Offaly

In **Ardagh**, southeast of Longford Town, the 16-year-old Goldsmith called in at Ardagh House one chilly night in 1744. Under the mistaken impression that the private home was a public inn, he demanded lodgings and began ordering the residents about. The owners, a Mr. Fetherston and his wife, patiently humoured their unexpected guest until the morning. Years later, Goldsmith enlarged the incident into a great comical set-piece at the centre of *She Stoops to Conquer*. The white Georgian house is now a convent.

The hedge-bordered lanes branching west from the Mostrim–Athlone highway (N55) lead down to beautiful, forested coves. At most of them boats can be hired for exploring the quiet lakeshore and fishing among the many islands. To the west, the green plains of Roscommon rise above the far shore and fade away into the haze.

After a day of recreating on the lake or tracing literary connections, a good way to quench your thirst is with a pint at the Three Jolly Pigeons pub in the village of **Tang**. This is not the original alehouse whose delights were sung in *She Stoops to Conquer*, but it's said that the doorstep was made from the original millstone of "the busy mill" in *The Deserted Village*.

About midway between Athlone and the busy county town, Mullingar, the **Hill of Uisneach** stands out for miles around. This brushy, flat-topped hillock, some 180 metres (602 feet) high, has traditionally been considered the geographic centre of Ireland. It was here too that ancient Ireland's five main provinces (Connacht, Munster, Leinster, Meath and Ulster) intersect, at a crumbling boulder called the Cat Stone (for its resemblance to a pouncing cat). Atop the hill King Tuathal Teachmar erected his royal palace in the second century AD, though scant traces remain today. The hill is not high, but it's a vigorous climb to the summit; on a clear day, you might be rewarded with a distant glimpse of the O'Connell Monument in Dublin's Glasnevin Cemetery far away to the east.

Northern Leitrim

Before the shiring of the countryside in the 1500s, the area now comprising Leitrim was an independent kingdom known as West Breiffni. It was the domain of the powerful O'Rourkes, who maintained strongholds at Leitrim town and at Dromahair. In the middle of the 12th century, Tighernan O'Rourke was the chief ally to Rory O'Conor, last high-king of Ireland, and he supported Rory in his struggles against Dermot MacMurrough, king of South Leinster. When MacMurrough raided Breiffni in 1152—taking with him O'Rourke's wife,

Dervorgilla—he set into action a chain of events that would spell the end of the old Gaelic order and have grave consequences for Ireland right down to modern times.

Whether Dervorgilla was kidnaped or willingly eloped is a disputed footnote among historians. In either case, she was sent back after a year, but instead of returning to her husband she betook herself to the convent at Mellifont. O'Rourke bitterly nursed his wounded honour, and 14 years later he was able to exact his revenge, invading Wexford and driving Dermot MacMurrough to exile in England. There the deposed king recruited a body of Welsh and Norman adventurers to help him reclaim his crown. Chief among them was the earl of Pembroke, Richard de Clare, better known as Strongbow, to whom MacMurrough promised the hand of his daughter and succession to the throne of Leinster.

With a small but disciplined force (including a hundred armoured cavalry-men, hitherto unknown in Ireland), Leinster was recaptured over the next two years, and when MacMurrough died, Strongbow assumed his place.

An Ireland constantly fractured by feuding petty kings had never posed a threat to England, but in 1171 Henry II began to awaken to the danger of a powerful, independent Norman kingdom at his back door. He sailed to Ireland himself to assert his ultimate dominion over the lands newly captured by his vassals. Henry received the obeisance of Strongbow and the kings of Munster and Connacht (though the men of Ulster rebuffed him), and so in a stroke three-quarters of Ireland was startled out of its isolation and brought into the sphere of European politics.

In **Dromahair**, prettily set on the banks of the River Bonet, portions of the banqueting hall of Tighernan O'Rourke's castle remain, though much of the stone was used to construct the adjacent Old Hall 500 years later. It might well have inspired "O'Rourke's Noble Feast", which describes a night of revelry gotten out of hand. Written around 1720 by Aodh Mac Abhráin and set to music by Turlough O'Carolan, the poem was extremely popular in its time:

> O'Rourke's noble fare
>   Will ne'er be forgot,
> By those who were there,
> And those who were not.

The mostly complete, though roofless, ruin of Creevelea Friary stands close by across the river, the last monastery established in Ireland (1508) before Henry VIII brought the hammer down on the religious houses. The eastern end of Lough Gill, so well loved by Yeats, is just a short walk to the north. The thoroughly restored 17th-century plantation house called Parke's Castle looks out from the lakeshore. The heavy fortifications illustrate well the fierce animosity of the native Irish and the insecurity of colonists like Parke. Open to the public, it houses permanent exhibits with information on local history and sites.

Manorhamilton sits at the confluence of five lovely valleys to the northeast. This modest rural town owes its existence to Sir Frederick Hamilton, a 17th-century Scottish landlord. His ruined castle, consumed by ivy, perches on a height overlooking the town. The Bundoran road (R280) leads north through the crag-sided valley of the River Bonet, past Glenade Lough, and finally to the seaside resort of Bundoran.

The Enniskillen-Sligo road runs west, where beautiful **Glencar Lake** lies in a lush green rift between the hills. This place is the setting of Yeats's "The Stolen Child". Above the north side of the lake, the silver sheet of Glencar Waterfall spills into a dark hollow. Below it spread the tiny pools that, the poet wrote, "scarce could bathe a star".

County Donegal

While portions of Donegal are tame pastureland, uneventful bog and heathery moor, the Republic's northernmost county also holds some of Ireland's most glorious landscapes, with a forlorn grandeur borrowed from the Scottish Highlands. The primeval bedrock of schist, gneiss and marble—the oldest strata in Ireland—thrusts up to carve the jagged skyline of the Blue Stacks, the Derryveaghs and other mountains in the interior. The sea-torn coast presents an intricate, constantly varied scape of land and water, heart-stopping cliffs, hidden bays and hundreds of little islands. Donegal also has the country's largest concentration of Irish speakers—about 23,000—spread mainly along the western seaboard.

Donegal's history is closely bound up with the O'Neills and O'Donnells, mighty clans ceaselessly at odds with one another for a thousand years. They finally allied themselves at the turn of the 17th century to fight their common enemy, the English, but by then it was too late.

Culturally, Donegal has always belonged to the ancient province of Ulster, but when Ireland was being divided up in 1921, the majority of Donegal voters were staunchly anti-Union. Fearing that if Donegal were included with the rest of Northern Ireland it would eventually vote itself—and other counties of Ulster—into the Republic, the British cut the county loose.

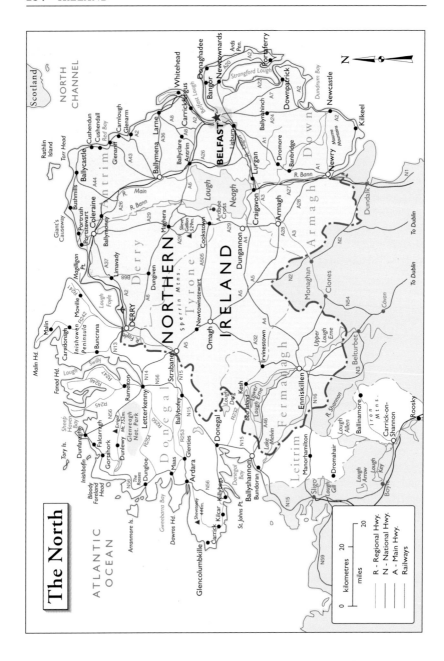

The North

Near Glencolumbkille, Co. Donegal

Really satisfying exploration of anything but the most heavily travelled routes requires a car or—for the waterproof traveller—a bicycle. Public transport rapidly fades outside of the southern parts of the county, but the stirring scenery and character of the north reward the extra effort.

Bundoran to Donegal Town

The boisterous old seaside resort of **Bundoran**, at the county's southwestern corner, makes a rather misleading introduction to a county better known for its misty glens and towering mountains. There are a good beach and a golf course, as well as the usual tawdry agglomeration of souvenir shops and video arcades.

More attractive is the nearby town of **Ballyshannon**, winding up a steep hill above the mouth of the River Erne. The Ballyshannon Folk Festival, one of Ireland's biggest and best, consistently draws the cream of Irish artists the first weekend in August. Ballyshannon's most famous progeny, the poet William Allingham (1824–89), was an early influence on Yeats and a friend to Tennyson, Carlyle and Rossetti—and the author of a good deal of rather doggerel verse. The churchyard of St. Anne's, where he now lies buried, offers a fair vista out over the town.

The Donegal Parian China Factory on the outskirts of town, as well as the more famous porcelain works at Belleek (seven kilometres/four miles up the River Erne, just over border into Northern Ireland), welcome visitors to watch their delicate wares being produced. Northwest of Ballyshannon the long, golden-sand beach at **Rossknowlagh** has a reputation for the best surfing in Ireland.

Of County Donegal's two main towns, Donegal and Letterkenny, smaller **Donegal** (population 2,300) has the more appealing setting. The pretty River Eske slips through, its tree-lined banks a blaze of colour toward autumn, before it meets the little harbour on Donegal Bay. The town centres on the Diamond, the spacious, three-cornered plaza around which cross-county traffic swirls all day long. Shops on all sides sell good-quality Donegal tweeds and heavy sweaters at competitive prices.

Donegal Town makes a good base from which to launch forays out to the county's western reaches, but otherwise there is disappointingly little to see or do here, apart from quiet walks along the riverbanks, leading to some prime

A Pilgrim at Lough Derg

'You will collect me on Wednesday about noon, won't you?'

He looked at her grimly. She looked every one of her forty-one years. The skin of her neck was corrugated. In five years' time she would begin to have jowls.

'Have a good time,' he said, and slammed in the gears, and drove away.

The big lumbering ferryboat was approaching, its prow slapping the corrugated waves. There were three men to each oar. It began to spit rain again. With about a hundred and fifty men and women, of every age and, so far as she could see, of every class, she clambered aboard. They pushed out and slowly they made the crossing, huddling together from the wind and rain. The boat nosed into its cleft and unloaded. She had a sensation of dark water, wet cement, houses, and a great number of people; and that she would have given gold for a cup of hot tea. Beyond the four or five whitewashed houses—she guessed that they had been the only buildings on the island before trains and buses made the pilgrimage popular—and beyond the cement paths, she came on the remains of the natural island: a knoll, some warm grass, the tree, and the roots of the old hermits' cells across whose teeth of stone barefooted pilgrims were already treading on one another's heels. Most of these barefooted people wore mackintoshes. They not only stumbled on one another's heels; they kneeled on one another's toes and tails; for the island was crowded—she thought there must be nearly two thousand people on it. They were packed between the two modern hostels and the big church. She saw a priest in sou'wester and gum boots. A nun waiting for the new views of Donegal Bay and to the ruins of Donegal Abbey on the south side. The town's main diversion, immediately off the Diamond, is the resplendent, newly renovated castle, built in 1474 by the O'Donnells. In 1610 it was incorporated into the fortified three-storey Jacobean house built by the Scottish colonist Sir Basil Brooke, who took possession soon after the Flight of the Earls (see page 245).

The Schooner bar, wonderfully cluttered with things nautical, is the place for Irish music on Tuesdays and Thursdays. On Wednesdays and Fridays the disco in the Abbey Hotel throbs away until the wee hours. On the Diamond, relax with a quiet afternoon jar in the honey-coloured light of the Old Castle Bar. Next door is a good music shop, with recordings on ground level and instruments upstairs; this just might be the place to find that accordion you've been looking for.

The obelisk in the Diamond commemorates the authors of the *Annals of the Four Masters*, a 1,100-page tome that was researched and compiled from 1632 to 1636 by four Franciscan historiographers at the abbey below the town.

---

arrivals at the door of the women's hostel took her name and address, and gave her the number of her cubicle. She went upstairs to it, laid her red bag on the cot beside it, unfastened her garters, took off her shoes, unpeeled her nylons, and without transition became yet another anonymous pilgrim. As she went out among the pilgrims already praying in the rain she felt only a sense of shame as if she were specially singled out under the microscope of the sky. The wet ground was cold.

A fat old woman in black, rich-breasted, grey-haired, took her kindly by the arm and said in a warm, Kerry voice: 'You're shivering, you poor creature! Hould hard now. Sure, when we have the first station done they'll be giving us the ould cup of black tay.'

And laughed at the folly of this longing for the tea. She winced when she stepped on the gritty concrete of the terrace surrounding the basilica, built out on piles over the lake. A young man smiled sympathetically, seeing that she was a delicate subject for the rigours before her: he was dressed like a clerk, with three pens in his breast pocket, and he wore a Total Abstinence badge.

'Saint's Island they call it,' he smiled. 'Some people think it should be called Divil's Island.'

She disliked his kindness—she had never in her life asked for pity from anybody, but she soon found that the island floated on kindness. Everything and everybody about her seemed to say, 'We are all sinners here, wretched creatures barely worthy of mercy.' She felt the abasement of the doomed. She was among people who had surrendered all personal identity, all pride.

—Seán O'Faoláin, Lovers of the Lake

Chronicling 4,500 years of Irish history, from legendary times up to their own era, the *Annals* offers invaluable insights into the Celtic world that was rapidly vanishing under the English onslaught.

Lough Derg

Inland from Donegal Town, remote Lough Derg has been an important destination for Christian pilgrims since at least the 1100s. A pit or cavern on Saint's Island in the lake, called St. Patrick's Purgatory because there the saint had supposedly been vouchsafed a vision of Hell, was believed to be a portal to the underworld. Penitents from all over Europe arrived to fast and pray in the cavern for 24 hours. In 1200, the Welsh chronicler Geraldus Cambrensis wrote that anyone daring to pass the night within would be "immediately seized by evil spirits" and "tortured all night with such heavy pains, and tormented so incessantly with so many grievous and unspeakable torments of fire and water, that with morning there is scarcely any or only the dregs of life surviving in his wretched body". Some unfortunates were never seen again, but those who did emerge alive from the ordeal were cleansed of their sins.

In the 15th century, Pope Alexander VI commanded that the place be demolished. The devout continued to hold vigil among the ruins, but at some point the activities were transferred over to tiny Station Island. In *Traits and Stories of the Irish Peasantry,* William Carleton, writing in the 1830s, told how those who made the daunting pilgrimage brought back a little bag of pebbles from the lake to give as gifts to their families and friends. The pebbles were said to possess "an uncommon virtue in curing all kinds of complaints".

Today, pilgrims by the thousands still come to Lough Derg, seeking not the horrors of Purgatory but the spiritual consolations found in penitential fasting, abstinence and prayer. Participants in the three-day retreat on Station Island, one of most rigorous in Christendom, make numerous Stations of the Cross in bare feet, hold a vigil of 24 hours without sleep, and are restricted to a diet of bread and black tea only.

To Glencolumbkille

The highway west from Donegal passes through gorse-covered hills and woodland, with glimpses out over Donegal Bay. At Dunkineely a minor road

Antrim coastline

follows an extraordinarily long, slender peninsula dangling into the bay, terminating at St. John's Point, where castle ruins guard one of the best beaches in the county.

Before you actually arrive at the outstanding natural harbour of **Killybegs**, your nose may forewarn you that its primary occupations involve fish—and lots of them. In fact, this is one of Ireland's most productive fishing ports. Until recently, Killybegs also enjoyed an international reputation for its exquisite carpets. A factory here wove high-quality carpets for Buckingham Palace and other equally prestigious addresses around the world, but sadly, it has now closed.

Killybegs roughly marks the edge of the Gaeltacht, and it's no coincidence that the landscape to the west also begins to grow more rugged and dramatic: lovely to look at, but suitable mostly for the raising of only the hardiest sheep, which mince over the rocky slopes on black-stockinged legs. Thatched rounded roofs are still common in western Donegal; out here they're usually secured with a netting of straw rope to keep the Atlantic gales from stripping them off the cottages.

Kilcar to the west and **Ardara** to the north are centres for the local woolen industry, with several weaving factories and shops. Carrick marks the turnoff for one of the great natural sights of Ireland: the cliffs of **Slieve League**. Half of the enormous, multi-hued mountain slides right into the Atlantic, forming sea-cliffs 601 metres (1,972 feet) high. Pummelled by wind and rain, the sun battling the flying clouds and the abyss of the grey-green sea churning far below, Slieve League is a Wagnerian overture made gloriously visible. Two paths trace over the clifftops, through clumps of yellow mountain arnica and yarrow; it's possible to follow one all the way out to Malin Beg. Caution is called for, and the mountain should be avoided in foul weather: hikers are occasionally plucked from the cliffs by the ferocious winds and cast into eternity.

Out near the far western tip of Donegal, the village of **Glencolumbkille** crouches in a beautiful valley at the edge of the sea. St. Colmcille (Columba) founded a monastic settlement out here in the sixth century and grappled with the demons that had escaped St. Pat, casting them out forever. The ascetic monks attracted to the place must have been delighted by the poor, stony soil, which only made their lives harder and holier. But Colmcille, poet as well as proselytizer, even then yearned for greater isolation, writing:

> On some island I long to be,
> a rocky promontory, looking on
> the coiling surface of the sea.

To hear the whisper of small waves
against the rocks, that endless sea-
sound, like keening over graves.

Colmcille introduced the Christian gospel to Scotland and converted the king of the Picts. He eventually found the island he sought, Iona, off Scotland's west coast, where he lived out his days.

In the predawn hours each year on 9 June, the saint is commemorated at Glencolumbkille with a five-kilometre (three-mile) pilgrimage around the 15 Stations of the Cross, incorporating some of the valley's many cairns, cross-inscribed stones and other ancient monuments. Climb the wind-scoured headlands north and south of the village for memorable views.

Because of its marvellous setting, Glen has long been a magnet for artists, composers and writers, among them the American painter and illustrator Rockwell Kent, who stayed for four months in 1926, producing a large body of paintings and sketches inspired by the Donegal landscape.

Near the beach the Folk Museum preserves a cluster of period buildings furnished to show how the local people lived over the past two centuries, including a 19th-century schoolhouse and a *shebeen,* where illicit whiskey would have been purveyed.

The Northwest

The coast around the sea-bitten bulge of land known as **The Rosses** (from the Irish for "Headlands") has been shredded into a welter of small islands and inlets. Inland, these stone-strewn, Irish-speaking wilds are scored by streams and over a hundred tiny lakes, famously rewarding for trout and salmon fishermen.

Largest of Donegal's islands is the great knob of **Arranmore Island,** which has some good beaches, seacliffs on the north side, and one hotel and a youth hostel. The 30-minute boat ride, weaving from Burtonport through the thicket of offshore islets, alone makes Arran worth visiting.

Northeast of Dungloe, the silver cone of **Errigal Mountain,** at 752 metres (2,557 feet) Donegal's highest peak, wouldn't be out of place in the Cascade Range of America's Pacific Northwest. The mountain has also been called Ireland's Fujiyama. From Dunlewy Lough, the scramble up the quartzite scree is not too strenuous, and on a clear day you may scan as far as the mountains of Scotland. The **Poisoned Glen,** lying just beyond the roofless white church

two kilometres (one mile) southeast of Dunlewy, earned its ominous name from the abundance of toxic spurge growing in the valley, which makes the water there unfit to drink. Local lore holds that even the birds refuse to fly over it. From Dunlewy, the R251 continues east to Glenveagh National Park (see below).

The coast road north of The Rosses traces a semicircle through the attractive fishing village of Bunbeg and up around the Bloody Foreland. With the country's violent history in the back of the mind, the name conjures images of exceptional gruesomeness, but actually it's the reddish cast of the rocks, heightened by the westering sun, that gave the place its name.

Caprices of the weather permitting, boats leave Meenlaragh and Falcarragh for **Tory Island**, 11 kilometres (eight miles) off Donegal's north coast. In 1884, the gunship HMS *Wasp* foundered off the island while trying to land soldiers and police sent to collect rents. Most of the crew were drowned, and because of this disaster the islanders paid not a penny of rent for several years thereafter. Tory is a treeless, weather-strafed place, and even the pragmatic naming of its two villages as West Town and East Town seems to suggest a tired resignation. In contrast, the island's fishermen have developed a primitivist school of painting over the last 25 years which favours unabashedly bright colours. Dun Bhaloir, the promontory fort at the island's east end, was reputedly the stronghold of malevolent Balor, the Celtic god of darkness who, like the Cyclops of Greek myth, possessed a single eye staring balefully from the middle of his forehead. As preordained by fate, Balor's grandson Lugh (like Odysseus) put out the eye with a burning beam and then relieved him of his head.

Falcarragh, near the eastern extent of the Gaeltacht, attracts Irish-language students every summer. The village makes an ideal base from which to explore Muckish ("Pig's Back") Mountain and the northern beaches and headlands. Boats leave from here for **Inishbofin**, a close-in island of about 150 people that is a stronghold of Irish language and customs.

Like Sligo, Donegal is storied fiddling country and has produced its own share of talented players, notably the late Johnny Doherty. In contrast to the ornate Sligo style, traditional Donegal fiddlers tend toward a clean, vigorous sound with an economy of ornamentation. Pubs in Falcarragh and nearby Gortahork are likely places to find a good session.

The popular seaside resort of **Dunfanaghy**, 11 kilometres (eight miles) northeast of Falcarragh, is surrounded by inviting beaches. A minor road branches north to the wild cliffs of Horn Head, which teem with nesting seabirds in summer.

Turning the hay

From Falcarragh a tertiary road leads southeast to **Glenveagh National Park**. One of the greatest natural areas remaining in Ireland, the park spreads over 16 square kilometres (4,000 acres) between the Derryveagh and Glendowan mountains. The forests and heathy slopes are in virtually pristine condition. Peregrine falcons wheel high over narrow Lough Beagh, and the country's largest herd of red deer browses the woodlands.

But the solitude was bought at a terrible price: John Adair purchased the property in 1857, and soon thereafter "cleared" the valley, turfing out scores of families—every man, woman and child—and levelling their homes. The notorious event still burns in local memory, as if it had happened only last year. In 1870, Adair built the Gothic castle above the lake, its crenellated outline showing above the conifers and rhododendrons which cloak the hillside tumbling down to the water's edge.

In the 1930s an American millionaire, Henry McIlhenny, the grandson of a Donegal emigrant, bought the estate and later bequeathed the lands and castle to the nation. It's open to the public through the summer months.

Just outside the southern edge of the national park lies the surpassingly beautiful area surrounding **Gartan Lake**, where St. Colmcille, a prince of the royal family of Donegal, was born in AD 521. In addition to the community at Glencolumbkille, the indefatigable missionary founded more than 35 monastic churches around Ireland, including those at Derry and Kells. Among the several local sites associated with Colmcille is a flagstone marking the place where the saint was born, on the hillside above the lake. Believed to prevent the pangs of homesickness, the stone was much visited in the last century by folk who were forced to emigrate.

The Regency-style **Glebe House and Gallery**, on the shore of Lough Gartan near Church Hill, displays some surprisingly cosmopolitan art for this part of the world. Represented in the large permanent collection are works by landscape and portrait painter Derek Hill (whose home this was), Picasso, Bonnard, Jack Yeats and Tory Island painters.

Apart from its impressive modern cathedral, there's precious little to see in **Letterkenny**, Donegal's largest town (population 10,000). It is, however, a well-placed travel hub from which to continue into the Inishowen Peninsula and Northern Ireland. The week-long International Folk Festival attracts top performers in August.

With a round tower and massive square keep surrounded by high battlements, khaki-coloured **Doe Castle** stands on a tongue of land running into cerulean Sheep Haven Bay, about 30 kilometres (19 miles) north of Letterkenny. The MacSweeny clan, mercenary *gallowglasses* from Scotland, settled here at the invitation of the O'Donnells, and the castle passed into their hands

The Flight of the Earls

In 1587, 15-year-old Red Hugh O'Donnell was visiting his foster-father at Rathmullan when a ship, purporting to be a wine-merchant's vessel, anchored offshore in Lough Swilly. Young Hugh was lured aboard on the pretext of sharing a drink, but the crew's true purpose, on Queen Elizabeth's orders, was to secure important hostages in order to keep the Donegal chieftains compliant to English will. Hugh was clapped in irons and the ship immediately set sail to Dublin, where he was imprisoned for five years. The future leader of the O'Donnell clan escaped on Christmas Eve, making his way home on foot over the snowy Wicklow Mountains.

In 1601 O'Donnell set aside ancient enmities and joined forces with Hugh O'Neill (who in his youth had also spent years in London as a "guest" of the English queen), to assault the British at the ill-fated Battle of Kinsale (see page 133). Their army was crushed, and O'Donnell subsequently chose exile in Spain over an ignominious peace in Ireland; he died there in 1602 under dubious circumstances.

Five years later, at midnight on 14 September 1607, O'Neill, together with Red Hugh's brother and successor, Rory O'Donnell, sailed out from Rathmullan with their families and retainers for exile in France. This "Flight of the Earls" was a mortal blow to Gaelic Ireland, which in a stroke lost the two leaders who might have guided the nation out of bondage. As the ship heaved away across Lough Swilly, Robin Flower wrote, "a great cry of lament and farewell went up from their followers left behind on the shore". Aindrais MacMarcuis, a poet of the time, summed up the tragedy of the event:

This night sees Eire desolate,
Her chiefs are cast out of state;
Her men, her maidens weep to see
Her desolate that peopled should be. . . .

Her chiefs are gone. There's none to bear
Her cross or lift her from despair;
The grieving lords take ship. With these
Our very souls pass overseas.

Hugh O'Neill

By departing Ireland the two families forfeited their extensive domains, clearing the way for the English plantation of Donegal. In Rathmullan's Battery Fort, the Flight of the Earls Heritage Centre sheds further light on the story.

in the 1500s. When the English attacked Doe in 1650, they reported it was "the strongest in all the province which endured a hundred blows of the demi-cannon before it yielded".

To the east, across Sheep Haven Bay, the **Atlantic Drive** (R245) makes a meandering circuit of the sculpted Rosguill Peninsula, following the coastal headlands and beaches for unforgettable views. To the east, the Fanad Peninsula folds over on itself, nearly enclosing labyrinthine Mulroy Bay; a signposted 72-kilometre (45-mile) scenic tour circles the Fanad as well. Both of these peninsulas are popular with holidaymakers from Northern Ireland.

The Inishowen Peninsula

The rugged land of the Inishowen Peninsula flares into the North Atlantic like an angry rooster's crest, culminating at Malin Head, northernmost point of the Irish mainland. The mountainous spine tumbles down to broad, heathery lowlands brightened with the mustard-yellow blooms of gorse. Cliffs and long ribbons of sandy beach rim much of the coastline. The peninsula has become rather popular with Irish vacationers from both the Republic and the North, who crowd the resorts of Buncrana, Ballyliffin and Moville.

The **Grianán of Aileach**, a monumental stone fort ringed by concentric earthworks atop a 250-metre (820-foot) hill, is the foremost of Inishowen's manmade attractions—and one of Ireland's greatest antiquities. The site near the base of the peninsula has been important since the early Celts used it as a place of sun worship, and was already ancient and well known when the Alexandrian geographer Ptolemy noted it in the second century AD. The circular stone cashel crowning the hill was probably erected sometime during the fifth century. Not long afterward, St. Patrick visited and baptized Eoghán, forefather of the powerful O'Neill clan, into the Christian fold.

The ring fort, with walls five metres (16 feet) high and thick, commands a stunning 360-degree panorama of distant hills and Loughs Swilly and Foyle to the west and east. The place was sacked twice, in the seventh and 12th centuries, and what you see today is a reconstruction from the 1870s.

Counties Louth and Meath

Apart from a few well-known sites, these two contiguous counties are only lightly visited by tourists. But they're nonetheless rich with passionate history and legend, and they'll amply reward the earnest explorer. There's a fine stretch of coast, for a start, with popular resorts like Blackrock and Bettystown; the magnificent megalithic tombs of the Boyne Valley; important medieval Christian remains at Kells, Mellifont and Monasterboice; Ireland's largest Anglo-Norman castle, at Trim; and the former epicentre of Gaelic rule at the Hill of Tara.

Prior to the Anglo–Norman invasion, the lands of Meath and Westmeath once formed the independent kingdom of Meath, which stretched from the Irish Sea to the Shannon. In an attempt to make this fractious domain more manageable, the English split it in two during the 16th century. Louth, formerly part of the kingdom of Ulster, is the smallest of all the Irish counties, tucked into the Republic's northeastern corner just below Northern Ireland.

Drogheda

Drogheda (pronounced "DRAW-hedda") is an ancient town and an important east-coast port on the Meath-Louth border. Though it's a busy industrial centre (population 35,000), Drogheda has managed to preserve its historical atmosphere and kept more than a few of its noteworthy buildings in good repair. The settlement was already a thousand years old when the Vikings moved in during the tenth century. Later, the Normans expanded Drogheda into twin towns on opposite sides of the River Boyne and built up encompassing fortifications. Only one of the ten original gates survives, but it's especially fine—the imposing, twin-towered **St. Laurence Gate** on Laurence Street north of the river.

In Irish memory, the name of Drogheda will always be linked with the terrible events of September 1649. After a bitterly fought siege, Cromwell and his 12,000 men took the town. For three days and nights, they rampaged in an orgy of destruction and indiscriminate killing. As historian Seumas McManus described the scene:

Only thirty men out of a garrison of three thousand escaped the sword; and it is impossible to compute what other thousands of non-combatants, men, women, and children, were butchered. They were slain in the streets, in the lanes, in the yards, in the gardens, in the cellars, on their own hearthstone.

They were slain in the church tower to which they fled for refuge, in the churches, on the altar steps, in the market-place—till the city's gutters ran with red rivulets of blood.

For a panoramic perspective over the town, walk up Millmount hill on the County Meath (south) side of the Boyne. The Normans adapted this Neolithic burial mound into their defensive scheme, and the strategic site was made into a military complex in the 18th century. A barracks building today houses the excellent **Millmount Museum**, whose collection includes extremely rare trade-guild banners and an example of a Boyne coracle, a roundish, wicker-and-hide boat that was used in these parts from prehistoric times until just a few decades ago.

The severed head of Archbishop Oliver Plunkett, displayed in a jewelled case, has made a pilgrimage centre of **St. Peter's Church** (1753) in West Street. Plunkett was canonized in 1975, the first Irishman so honoured in over seven centuries. The martyred primate, a steadfast leader during the long night of the anti-Catholic Penal Laws, was executed in London after being convicted on spurious treason charges in 1681.

Mellifont and Monasterboice

Two attractive medieval Christian establishments lie just a short distance from Drogheda. The fragmentary remains of **Mellifont**, Ireland's first Cistercian abbey, hint at a more refined and elegant religious enclave than was usual among the ascetic Irish monks in the 12th century. Indeed, Mellifont's architecture and orderly layout, reflecting the current developments on the Continent at the time, marked a clear contrast to the boxy Romanesque style then prevalent in Ireland.

St. Malachy invited the Cistercians from France to establish their order here in 1142; the peaceful site beside the River Mattock reminded Malachy of Clairvaux in Burgundy, on which the large monastery at Mellifont was patterned. Most of the abbey has been reduced to foundations over the centuries, but the remains of the unique, arched, octagonal lavabo (where the monks did their washing-up) and other buildings are still evocative even in ruin. The Cistercians founded another three dozen or so communities in Ireland after Mellifont; the most nearly complete is beautiful Jerpoint, in County Kilkenny. Mellifont is about eight kilometres (five miles) west of Drogheda.

Three gloriously carved high crosses are the centrepiece of **Monasterboice**, about eight kilometres (five miles) north of Drogheda. The monastery dates back to the sixth century, but the crosses were probably created in the tenth. Massive yet well-proportioned Muiredach's Cross, standing nearly six metres (over 17 feet) tall, is a high-water mark for artistry in scriptural crosses. Its surface is encrusted with biblical scenes as well as purely decorative panels, their details still quite legible and expressive after a thousand years. The Old and New Testament tableaux include Cain bludgeoning Abel, Adam and Eve bowered by the tempting Tree of Knowledge, the Last Judgement and Christ crucified. In their original condition, such crosses were brightly painted, the better to impress the Gospel stories on the minds of the unlettered masses. The similarly carved West Cross stands a metre taller, but the elements have been less forgiving and its motifs are more difficult to make out. Other remains at Monasterboice are its 33-metre (110-foot)-tall round tower and two ruined early churches.

The Boyne Valley

Like Drogheda, the Boyne reverberates in the Irish psyche—with pride, or with enduring bitterness, depending on one's religious and national affiliations. In July 1690, Protestant King William III's victory over his father-in-law, King James II, at the **Battle of the Boyne** turned the tide against Catholic, Gaelic Ireland. Today, Protestants across Northern Ireland mount huge celebrations each 12 July to commemorate the event. The main part of the battle was fought near the river crossing at Oldbridge, about five kilometres (three miles) west of Drogheda; a walk up a slight eminence gives a perspective over the whole battlefield, and a viewing table there explains the course of the battle.

Farther up the valley, the **Brugh na Bóinne** ("Palace of the Boyne") complex is ranged along a lazy bend of the river. A sort of Irish Valley of the Kings where a number of chieftains and other Stone Age worthies were buried, this exceedingly rich archaeological zone includes at least major 15 Neolithic passage graves (see page 20), constructed between about 3000 and 2000 BC.

Newgrange, the best known and most impressive of these monumental tombs, dates probably from around 2500 BC. This passage grave, built upon a ridge above the Boyne, consists of a mound of some 200,000 tons of stone and earth about ten metres (34 feet) high and about 80 metres (260 feet) in diameter. At the entrance and inside the grave, vibrant spirals and wave motifs were pecked out with stone tools. A ring of rough-hewn standing stones was added around the perimeter later. The passage leading into a cruciform chamber, in which the remains of three bodies were interred, was carefully designed so that, at the winter solstice, the rays of the sun illuminate the central chamber, bathing it in light for 15 to 20 minutes. (This effect is now artificially created for the tomb's thousands of annual visitors.)

These impressive monuments along the fertile Boyne Valley suggest a large population with plenty of free time on its hands. It has been estimated that a million man-days of labour went into constructing Newgrange in County Meath's Boyne River valley. Nearby Dowth, another passage grave (not open to the public), is even larger. A third important tomb in the vicinity, Knowth, is currently under excavation and will eventually be opened to visitors.

Slane is a lovely planned village on the sloping north side of the River Boyne, where the highway from Dublin (N2) meets the Drogheda–Navan road (N51). The quartet of 18th-century Georgian houses facing each other at the crossroads was reputedly built for the four spinster sisters of the Conyngham family, whose estate this is.

On the **Hill of Slane**, a short walk north of the village, there are the ruins of a 16th-century Franciscan friary and monastic school. Atop this hill St. Patrick is said to have lit his paschal fire in AD 433 to commemorate Easter, in defiance of the pagan Laoghaire, the high-king at Tara to the south. Patrick's coming had been foretold by the king's druids: "One shall arrive here", they warned, "having his head shaven in a circle, bearing a crooked staff. . . . He will seduce the people . . . and his doctrines shall reign for ever and ever".

Heeding their counsel, Laoghaire and his men intercepted Patrick at the Hill of Slane, intending to destroy the potential usurper. Patrick's power was greater, however, than the kings' soldiers or the conjury of his druids. In awe, King Laoghaire accepted conversion to Christianity, along with many others of his court, and Patrick's mission had begun.

Christianity flourished after Patrick, which meant in turn that the heyday of the pagan Gaelic chieftains was waning. The site of Tara today, about 20 kilometres (12 miles) south-

Entrance to Newgrange megalithic tomb, Co. Meath

Monasterboice round tower, Co. Louth

east of Navan, is only bare tumuli and earthworks, where once the royal capital thrived. A modern statue of Patrick erected here completes the symbolic transition.

The Cooley Peninsula

Scenically and historically, the most intriguing part of County Louth is the mountainous and beautiful **Cooley Peninsula**. Here the critical events of the first-century epic, the *Táin Bó Cuailgne* (*Cattle Raid of Cooley*), were played out. Many of the places mentioned in the *Táin*, Europe's oldest vernacular saga, are still identifiable. In the story, Connacht's Queen Maeve compared her wealth against her husband's and found it equal in all things but for his white-horned bull. Learning of a mighty brown bull which roamed the Cooley Peninsula, Maeve tried first to acquire it through cajolery; failing that, she assembled her armies and set out for Cooley to take the bull by force of arms.

In those days, Louth was a part of the province of Ulster. A curse decreed that, in the time of Ulster's greatest need, the pangs of childbirth would strike her warriors, leaving them incapacitated. As Maeve's army approached, all the Ulstermen save one—Cuchulain—were afflicted as women in labour with excruciating pain for nine days. Singlehandedly, then, Cuchulain fought the men of Connacht until the sickness passed. In the end, the two great bulls fought their own battle. The brown bull of Cooley tore the white-horned bull to pieces, but in his victory bellow his heart broke and he died.

The peninsula remains an inviting, unspoiled place, its heather-covered, hilly terrain splendid for walking and soaking up the resonances of its mythic (and real) past. After a good tramp, **Carlingford** makes an excellent destination, with no shortage of warm pubs and urbane restaurants along its narrow streets. This fishing village-cum-resort stands at the water's edge, looking across the fjordlike Carlingford Lough to County Down, "where the mountains o' Mourne sweep down to the sea", in the famous Percy French lyric. The magnificent ruined Anglo–Norman castle has stood guard above the harbourside since about 1200, another work of the ambitious fortress builder Hugh de Lacy. The three-storey "Mint" in the village centre is a well-preserved 15th-century tower house; it was reputedly chartered for the minting of coinage in 1467, though no examples are known to exist today.

Until just a few years ago, **Omeath**, eight kilometres (five miles) northwest of Carlingford, was an Irish-speaking village—the last in eastern Ireland. Alas, the language has finally faded here too. In summer, a passenger ferry crosses Carlingford Lough to Warrenspoint in County Down; the road (R173) from Omeath continues northwest over the border to Newry, and thence up to Armagh or Belfast.

Northwest of County Louth is County Monaghan, a land wrinkled by countless lumpy drumlins—the leavings from Ice Age glaciers—and dappled with scores of lakes thick with pike, bream and other rough fish that make this a popular destination for angling holidays.

Northern Ireland

> *And one read black where the other read white, his hope*
> *The other man's damnation:*
> *Up the Rebels, To Hell with the Pope.*
> *And God Save—as you prefer—the King or Ireland*
> *The land of scholars and saints:*
> *Scholars and saints my eye, the land of ambush,*
> *Purblind manifestoes, never-ending complaints.*
>
> —Louis MacNeice, from *Autumn Journal*

Although it's every bit as lovely and welcoming as the Republic, Northern Ireland's unfortunate (and misleading) reputation is one of abiding hostilities and frequent violence. The news reports out of the province are seldom happy; it's the tragic bombings and shootings and retaliations that seize the headlines and inform most people's understanding of the place.

There's tension there, and unrest, no question about it. They call it "the Troubles", a mild euphemism for what is essentially a ruthless civil war. The struggle between Catholic Nationalists (who want fair treatment and to see the island whole again) and Protestant Unionists (who'd prefer to stay British and maintain their upper hand)—though this is an oversimplification—has been simmering, and periodically boiling over, since long before six counties of Ulster were partitioned off to the United Kingdom in 1921.

And it will continue for God knows how long into the future. The conflict is complex, deeply rooted and emotionally charged. The situation is perhaps best summed up by the anonymous Belfast sage who opined, "Anyone who isn't confused here doesn't really understand what is going on". In spite of hardships and the attrition of age-old antagonisms, however, the people of Northern Ireland have demonstrated an extraordinary resilience of spirit and ability to carry on.

The spiraling violence of the 1970s and 1980s had abated for a few years but re-erupted in late 1993 with a new wave of sectarian brutality. The tragedies, however, seem only to have strengthened resolve to find a long-term solution to Ulster's dilemmas. In any case, the social strife and terrorist acts are not widespread but have been mostly confined to a handful of locales—mainly along the border and in the cities of Derry and Belfast. Outside of these areas, evidence of the Troubles is scarce, and the chance of tourists getting caught up in them anywhere in Northern Ireland is remote.

Probably the closest most visitors will come to encountering Northern Ireland's sectarian friction are the graffiti proclaiming loyalties to one faction or another, and the provocative, politically charged commemorative marches held each summer. That, and crossing the fortified checkpoints between North and South. These can be a bit unnerving, with their menacing watch-towers, coils of razor wire and machine-gun-wielding soldiers. But the experience is over in a moment, and beyond the border everything quickly returns to normal.

In the North you may notice more industrial development, that the highways have fewer potholes and that public clocks tend to tell the time more reliably. There's more order to the layout of towns, but also they often look rather drab compared to the pinks, blues, greens and whites of the South. Also, whereas in the Republic you can still see many of the original shopfronts, in Ulster, as in Great Britain, the ground floors of many of even the oldest buildings have been ripped out and replaced by characterless, modern facades. The most widespread source of colour is often the alternating red, white and blue curbstones along the roads, which mark Loyalist territory.

In Catholic communities, mostly in the cities, you may see green, gold and white versions of this, as well as the occasional tricolour flag. In such areas you will almost certainly find examples of Nationalist murals, often sophisti-cated, detailed works depicting such images as Republican hunger strikers or gunmen shown as freedom fighters. They are highly emotive, political and draw heavily on Irish cultural references: Gaelic slogans, Celtic motifs, etc. The safest place to see examples is along Belfast's Falls Road, along which you may drive freely or take a black cab from the city centre.

If you walk there, or get out to have a closer look, you will almost certainly attract local attention: someone will tell you about the last time the soldiers came and threw cans of paint at the mural (a regular occurrence) or explain the story behind a particular picture. The assumption seems to be that if you are there, and interested enough to be looking—and you will stand out for miles as a tourist—you must be sympathetic.

This, by the way, is *not* the place to get into an argument about politics. This is an excursion the Tourist Office certainly won't recommend, and the police probably wouldn't either. But there should be no problem if one is circumspect and sensible.

On both sides of the border there are nevertheless far more similarities than differences. The counties which comprise Northern Ireland—Down, Antrim, Armagh, Fermanagh, Tyrone and Derry—are made up of the same green, postcard-perfect valleys and modest farms, steely lakes, salmon-silvered rivers, windy moors, blue distant mountains. Northern Ireland has some of Europe's

Dunluce Castle, built between the 14th and 17th centuries by the MacDonnells

best fishing waters, and some 480 kilometres (300 miles) of coastline, much of it splendid and unforgettable.

Northern Ireland's bad press may have discouraged tourism some, but nevertheless many Americans arrive each year in search of their roots. Ulster's historical impact on the United States is incalculable. In the 18th century alone, a quarter of a million Ulster Irish and Scots-Irish emigrated to America. By the time of the signing of the Declaration of Independence, one-sixth of the 13 Colonies' population was of Ulster origin. Andrew Jackson, Ulysses Grant, Woodrow Wilson and nine other American presidents could trace their ancestry straight back to the northern counties. And it was a descendant of a Fermanagh family that first stepped on the moon—Neil Armstrong.

Not surprisingly, this mass emigration of the musical Irish has yielded up a great store of song. Characteristic of the genre is this verse, looking at once back at the past and forward to a new future:

> I am a rambling Irishman,
>   in Ulster I was born
> And many's the happy hour I've spent,
>   on the banks of sweet Lough Erne.
> But to live poor I could not endure,
>   as others of my station
> To Amerikay I sailed away,
>   and left this Irish nation.

Belfast

Visitors whose notions of Belfast are founded on headlines of tragic bloodshed will likely have their preconceptions shattered at first sight. They will find not a city ripped apart by war but rather a vigorous, proud and handsome capital getting on with its business. There is poverty, yes, and onerous unemployment, and the profound religious and political divisions endemic to Northern Ireland remain as yet unhealed. But recent years have at least brought relative peace and even something like optimism to Belfast, despite the bloodshed of late 1993.

Though military vehicles and armed soldiers patrolling the streets are still a jarring sight, at odds with the general normalcy of everyday life, otherwise there are few reminders of the recent incendiary past. Apart from some obviously rougher neighbourhoods, visitors here should be at least as safe as they'd be at home.

Some 400,000 people, about a third of Northern Ireland's population, call Belfast home. Like no other city in predominantly rural Ireland, the industrial revolution shaped this northern metropolis. In the 19th century, the engines of industry and commerce transformed an otherwise unremarkable Irish town into Europe's fastest-growing city, doubling in size every ten years during its heyday. Belfast's location at the head of Belfast Lough, a deep-water estuary, perfectly suited its growth as a centre for trade and manufacturing—in rope making, linen and, especially, shipbuilding. Though the industry has experienced a long decline, at one time Belfast boasted the world's largest shipyard. The unfortunate *Titanic* was built here, along with many more successful luxury liners and other vessels. To native-born poet Louis MacNeice (1907–63),

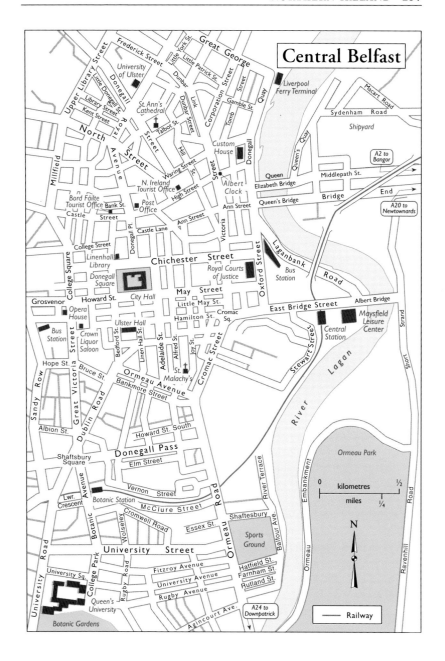

Central Belfast

Liverpool Ferry Terminal
Macart Road
Sydenham Road
Shipyard
A2 to Bangor
Middlepath St.
Queen
Elizabeth Bridge
Queen's Bridge
Bridge
End
A20 to Newtownards

Great George
Frederick Street
University of Ulster
Little York St.
Little Patrick St.
Dunbar
Upper Library Street
Little Donegall St.
Library Street
Donegall St.
Kent Street
St. Ann's Cathedral
Talbot St.
Dunbar Link
Corporation Street
Gamble St.
Tomb
Quay
Queen's Quay
North Street
Waring Street
Hill St.
Custom House
Donegall Quay
Millfield
Bord Fáilte Tourist Office
Bank St.
N. Ireland Tourist Office
Post Office
High Street
Ann Street
Albert Clock
Queen
Castle Street
Donegall Pl.
Castle Lane
Ann Street
Victoria Street
College Street
Linenhall Library
Donegall Square
Chichester Street
Royal Courts of Justice
Laganbank Road
Bus Station
College Square
City Hall
May Street
Grosvenor
Howard St.
Little May St.
Cromac Sq.
East Bridge Street
Albert Bridge
Opera House
Ulster Hall
Hamilton St.
Maysfield Leisure Center
Bus Station
Crown Liquor Saloon
Bedford St.
Linen Hall St.
Adelaide St.
Alfred St.
Joy St.
Central Station
Strand
Hope St.
Bruce St.
Ormeau Avenue
Malachy's
Cromac Street
Stewart Street
St.
Short
Sandy Row
Great Victoria Street
Bankmore Street
Lagan
Albion St.
Dublin Road
Howard St. South
River
Shaftsbury Square
Donegall Pass
Elm Street
Ormeau Park
Lwr. Crescent
Botanic Avenue
Vernon Street
Botanic Station
McClure Street
River Terrace
Embankment
Cromwell Road
Essex St.
Shaftesbury
Wolseley
Sports Ground
Balfour Ave.
University Street
University Sq.
College Park
Fitzroy Avenue
Hatfield St.
Farnham St.
Rutland St.
University Road
Rugby Road
University Avenue
Rugby Avenue
Ormeau
Ravenhill Road
Queen's University
Agincourt Ave.
A24 to Downpatrick
Botanic Gardens

0 kilometres ½
miles ¼

N

—— Railway

the shipyard's gargantuan cranes presented an unsettling profile in his 1935 poem, "Belfast":

> Down there at the end of the melancholy lough
> Against the lurid sky over stained water
> Where hammers clang murderously on the girder
> Like crucifixes the gantries stand.

After the revelation that Belfast is not an open war zone, many visitors are next surprised at the attractiveness of the city's setting, and of the city itself. A ring of green hills surrounds it, and the River Lagan runs through, spanned by three main bridges. Belfast's largely Victorian centre, full of the architectural adornments of a more gracious era, lies west of the river; there, too, are concentrated most of the interesting sights. For fear of bombs, cars have been banned from large parts of the downtown area—but this is a boon to pedestrians. The **Northern Ireland Tourist Board** office, centrally located in High Street just west of the leaning Prince Albert Memorial Clock, makes a good first stop for information. The *Belfast Telegraph* also publishes detailed listings of what's happening in the city.

The self-confident **City Hall**, built between 1896 and 1906 in a melange of styles, dominates Donegall Square and the main shopping district, lying just to the north. A guided tour conducted Wednesday morning at 10:30, the only time the building opens to the public, includes the interior murals and marble-work, and offers splendid views of the city from its central copper-sheathed dome. Just around the corner, the refurbished **Linen Hall Library**, Belfast's oldest library (established in 1788), houses an outstanding collection of Irish-interest works and rare books.

Bustling Great Victoria Street quarters some of the city's liveliest pubs, restaurants, theatres and cinemas, as well as two of Belfast's most interesting buildings. The exterior of the 1895 **Grand Opera House**, at Great Victoria and Grosvenor streets, is a remarkable collision between architectural restraint and extravagance. Classical pediments and Palladian balustrades meet whimsical curlicues and circular portholes; the overall effect, if slightly wacky, certainly catches the eye. The sumptuously rococo interior goes one step further. Pavlova has danced here, and Sarah Bernhardt graced the boards. Nowadays, the Opera House hosts a range of entertainments: ballet, rock concerts, drama and, of course, well-regarded opera performances.

Across the street is the **Crown Liquor Saloon**, no ordinary pub but a flamboyant drinking palace, "a many-colored cavern" in poet John Betjeman's words. Inside this masterpiece of High Victorian opulence you'll find richly carved Corinthian columns, polished mahogany, sparkling marble, mirrors,

A Northern Childhood

When I was in my first year at grammar school, I had a long-playing record, "The Rebel," on which the actor Michael MacLiammoir recited the works of Padraig Pearse, one of the martyrs of 1916. I thought it was great stuff, and played it over and over again, and the more I listened to it the more convinced I became that although MacLiammoir had put it over as a work of art, he had failed to convey the true emotion of a patriot saying what he felt. Anyway I learned three pieces from the record for the three heats of the talent competition, and they were all very militant. "The Rebel" ends:

> "I say to the master of my people 'Beware the risen people who will take what you would not give!'"

Another piece I chose was "The Fool," which has this passage:

> "But the fools, the fools! They have left us our Fenian dead! While Ireland holds these graves, Ireland unfree will never be at rest."

And my third and final choice was Robert Emmet's speech from the dock before his execution in 1804.

Well, off I went and recited this fighting stuff at the talent competition, and I recited it well, went through the three heats, and won first prize. Cookstown was outraged. During the three weeks of the competition, the horror grew. "Imagine a daughter of Lizzie Devlin having the cheek to go down there and say a thing like that! That comes from her father's side of the family." I believe I won on merit, but the general townspeople said I had blackmailed the judges, who were local businessmen and so forth, into awarding me first prize because I could have accused them of bigotry if they hadn't. Feeling got very high and on the last day I had to have a police escort home to protect me from the people who would otherwise have given me a cuff on the ear for my independence. My mother was delighted; she was somewhat embarrassed, but secretly glad and proud that at least I had enough of my father in me to go somewhere I was hated and look people straight in the face. This was a gift both my parents had: they never shied away uncomfortably from company they knew rejected them. As well as showing courage and defiance, I had won £10 and this too was welcome at home. To me it was like £100. I'd got the average weekly wage of a man in Northern Ireland just for standing up and saying a wee bit of prose. A year or two later, from the same feeling of defiance, I wore a tricolor pin in my coat, precisely because the Northern Ireland Flags and Emblems Act forbade it. Only once did a policeman ask me to remove it. "You remove it," I said, but as his hand came out to take the badge, I added: "If you touch me without a warrant, I'll have you in court for assault!" He just laughed and said, "Go on there, you troublemaker!" I trotted on, feeling very proud I had won, but once I'd discovered I could get away with it, I lost interest in the badge.

—Bernadette Devlin, The Price of My Soul, 1969

(following pages) Mourne Mountains, Co. Down

bright tilework, brass pipes and cozy panelled snugs for private parties. Hardly a square foot is left without some ornamental flourish. Even teetotallers should stop in for a cup of coffee and a look around.

Farther south, Great Victoria Street becomes University Road, which passes by **Queen's University**, founded in 1849, the year Herself popped over for a visit. Each November, the university hosts the **Belfast Festival at Queen's**, one of the largest cultural events in Britain and Ireland, second in scope only to the huge Edinburgh Festival. The program emphasizes classical music, but the three-week festival also offers a strong international sampling of jazz, folk music, drama, film and ballet.

The highlight of the **Botanic Gardens** is the curvilinear cast-iron-and-glass Palm House. In the grounds also is the outstanding **Ulster Museum and Art Gallery**. The collection covers 9,000 years of Irish history, and includes Northern Ireland's most extensive collection of Irish paintings, plus treasures recovered from the Spanish Armada ship *Girona*, which foundered in 1588 on the Giant's Causeway.

Another excellent Belfast museum, the **Ulster Folk and Transport Museum**, lies 13 kilometres (eight miles) east of the city centre on the Bangor road (A2). This indoor-outdoor museum includes authentic rural cottages, a forge and a mill house, among other buildings relocated here, and also chronicles 200 years of Irish passenger conveyances—pennyfarthing bicycles, carriages, vintage autos, trams and early locomotives.

A short walk from the Botanic Gardens down Stranmillis Road leads to the **Lagan Towpath**, upon which a foot traveller can follow the river upstream to Lisburn, passing woodlands, meadows and the old locks left over from the era when the Lagan was an important highway carrying waterborne goods. This 13-kilometre (eight-mile) stretch is a section of the Ulster Way, a 786-kilometre (491-mile) foot trail running all around Northern Ireland, through bogland, along spectacular coasts and over lofty granite heights.

In the 18th and 19th centuries the Lagan Valley above Belfast was an important linen-producing region. It's also the setting for one of the most haunting of all Irish love songs, "My Lagan Love". The melody is a traditional air, but it's unusual for its dirgeful, flatted notes. The lyrics, though composed early this century by Joseph Campbell, have the timelessness and age-worn beauty of true folk poetry. (The *lenanshee* referred to below means a "fairy mistress"; a man would waste away with love for her unless some other unfortunate swain could be found to take his place.)

> *Where Lagan stream sings lullaby*
> *There blows a lily fair;*

The twilight gleam is in her eye,
The night is on her hair.
And, like a love-sick lenanshee,
She hath my heart in thrall;
No life I own, nor liberty,
For Love is lord of all.

And sometimes when the beetle's call
Hath lull'd the eve to sleep
I tiptoe to her sheeling low
And through her dooreen peep.
There on a cricket's singing stone
She saves the bogwood fire
And hums in soft sweet undertones
The song of heart's desire.

The Glens of Antrim

Out of Ulster's upper right-hand corner, from Glenarm up to Ballycastle, glaciers scooped out the nine lovely green valleys known as the Glens of Antrim. Each has its own character, blending the scenic elements of steep mountain, moor, waterfall and woodland in varying proportion. In summertime, their woods and meadows grow fragrant with blooming violets, bluebells, fuchsia and honeysuckle. All are accessible now, but until the coast road was blasted out of the chalky cliffs in 1834—a marvel of engineering in its day—these glens were among the most isolated parts of Ireland, all but sealed off from the outside world. The people of the Antrim glens, consequently, were some of the last in northern Ireland to give up the Irish language and adopt English.

The coastal road, beginning in the south at the port town of Larne, squeezes between limestone cliffs and the clear green sea as it winds around the bays at the bottom of the glens. The ever-changing seascapes—jewel-green one moment, steel-grey the next under passing clouds—make this one of the prettiest drives anywhere in Ireland.

Along this eastern seaboard, the handsome port and holiday towns of **Carnlough**, **Cushendall** and **Cushendun** are convenient, enjoyable bases from which to explore the glens, and offer ample opportunity as well to try the Antrim coast's famously good fishing. Thackeray described Glenariff, the largest and

best known of the nine glens, as "Switzerland in miniature". The luxuriant forest park at the head of the valley offers delightful walks through the leafy woods, with footbridges crisscrossing the river and viewing places set up at the waterfalls. The village of **Glenariff** (also called Waterfoot), where the glen opens onto Red Bay, is the focus of the lively Feis na nGleann, a summer festival of hurling matches and music and dance competitions.

At Antrim's northeastern corner two rugged headlands, **Benmore** or **Fair Head** and **Torr Head** thrust defiantly upward. Scotland lies just 21 kilometres (13 miles) distant, and the views across the rough channel, known as the Moyle, are magnificent. This stunning coastal region figures in the legend of the Children of Lír. In ancient times King Lír, a widower with three children, took a second wife. Jealous of her stepchildren, she landed an enchantment upon them, transforming them into swans condemned to skim the seas of Ireland until the bell of St. Patrick should proclaim the advent of Christianity. Two things she granted: that they would retain their human reason, and that their song would be in their native Gaelic tongue.

For 900 years they remained swans, a third of that time spent swimming the bitter seas of the Moyle. While off the isle of Inishglora in Mayo, they at last heard the chime of Patrick's bell. Immortal they'd been as swans, but as they swam ashore, returning to human form, the centuries were still on them; there they died, withered with extreme old age. The story inspired Thomas Moore's tender "Song of Fionnuala":

> *Silent, oh Moyle, be the roar of thy water,*
> *Break not, ye breezes, your chain of repose,*
> *While, murmuring mournfully, Lír's lonely daughter*
> *Tells to the night-star her tale of woes.*
> *When shall the swan, her death-note singing,*
> *Sleep, with wings in darkness furl'd?*

The North Coast

From Fair Head all the way to the long empty strand of Magilligan Point eastward, Counties Antrim and Derry share some of Ireland's most exquisite coastline. Even this far north, the effects of the warm Gulf Stream are felt, and the sea is not too cold for swimming. In summertime, darkness is slow to descend, and the charged evening light may linger past 11 o'clock in midsummer.

"Ossian's Grave", prehistoric stone circle, Co. Antrim

The attractive market and resort town of **Ballycastle** each June hosts the Fleadh Amhrán agus Rince, the Festival of Music and Dance. The town-centre diamond is the scene of Ireland's oldest traditional fair, the Ould Lammas Fair, held every year since 1606 in late August. It's an enormous flea market revolving around sheep and pony sales and with plenty of revelry and food—including the Ulster specialties dulse, a sun-dried seaweed, and a honey-flavoured toffee called yellow man. There's even a little song about it:

> *You can take your Mary Ann*
> *For some dulse and yellow man*
> *At the oul' Lammas Fair*
> *In Ballycastle-O.*

About a hundred people and uncounted thousands of seabirds make their home on the cliffbound boomerang of **Rathlin Island**, nine kilometres (six miles) offshore from Ballycastle. In a cave at the island's eastern end, Robert the Bruce salved his wounded ego in 1306 after being defeated in battle by the English at Perth, Scotland. Legend has it that he took heart from observing a persistent spider try and try again to climb to the cave's roof before it succeeded. Robert rallied his troops and gained the Scottish throne after whipping the English at Bannockburn.

Sixty million years ago, a flow of molten basalt erupted and oozed out over the older chalk in a thick sheet. As it slowly cooled it crystallized into impressive palisades of vertical polygonal columns—the famed **Giant's Causeway**. Some of the closely packed grey-brown columns have four, five, seven or eight sides, but most of them are hexagonal.

Like a number of geological oddities in the north of Ireland, the ancient Irish credited the creation of the Giant's Causeway to Finn MacCool, the colossal Ulster warrior. When Finn fell in love with a lady in the Hebrides, one story goes, he laid these stones in a walkway to cross over to join her without wetting his toes. As proof of the legend, the same formation arises across the sea at Staffa Island, where she lived.

The clustered pillars, with little sea pinks and other flowers squeezing out from their tight interstices, spread along the wave-pounded coast over a distance of some eight kilometres (five miles). Many of the natural formations have been labelled with such fanciful descriptive names as Lord Antrim's Parlour, the Giant's Organ, the Lady's Fan and the Chimney Tops—which the Spanish Armada fired upon in 1588, mistaking them for the turrets of Dunluce Castle.

Three kilometres (two miles) inland, in the hamlet of **Bushmills**, the famed Old Bushmills Distillery has been making *uisce beatha*—the "water of life",

Irish whiskey—since 1608. In 1697, Peter the Great visited Bushmills, the world's oldest legal distiller, and declared Irish whiskey the best of all spirits. There's a free tour of the distilling process, topped off with a taste of "da pure dhrop" at the end.

West of the Giant's Causeway, the sea has separated the great chunks of rock offshore called the Skerries and sculpted the soft white-chalk cliffs into arches and caves. **Dunluce Castle**, one of the most splendidly romantic ruins in Ireland, perches on these craggy cliffs, facing the North Atlantic. From this dramatic fortress, the oldest parts of which date to about 1300, the bellicose MacDonnells ruled their corner of northeastern Ulster. In 1584, the English under Sir John Perrot captured it from the redoubtable Sorley Boy MacDonnell. After Perrot departed, MacDonnell and his men hauled themselves up the cliff in a basket to take Dunluce back from the English garrison. MacDonnell later expanded and fortified the castle, using treasure and cannon recovered from the *Girona*, a Spanish galleon which wrecked in 1588 on the nearby Giant's Causeway. In 1639, portions of the underlying cliff gave way and the castle scullery crumbled into the sea, taking with it the several unfortunate cooks and servants. Dunluce was abandoned soon afterward. A footbridge across a sea-worn chasm gives access to the gaunt ruins, and caves underneath the castle can also be explored.

The twin seaside resorts of **Portstewart** and larger **Portrush** have long been popular vacation getaways, as their sheaves of pastel-stuccoed Victorian guesthouses attest. They're crowded in summer with vacationing Irish, who come for the long beaches, amusement arcades, old-fashioned ambience and four 18-hole golf courses.

Derry City

In AD 546, the tireless missionary St. Colmcille founded a monastery here on an oak-covered hill beside the River Foyle. It came to be called Doire, the Oak Grove, of Colmcille, and he loved this place above all. "The angels of God sang in the glades of Derry", he said, and in later years he yearned to return to its then-peaceful environs:

> *My Derry, my little oak grove,*
> *My dwelling, my little cell,*
> *O eternal God in heaven above,*
> *Woe be to him who violates it.*

The city's subsequent history has been something less than idyllic, however. Following the confiscation of O'Neill and O'Donnell territories in 1608, the Guilds of the City of London were granted the towns of Derry and Coleraine and much of the land in between. They added the prefix of "London" to Derry, and in 1613 they began construction of the fortified encircling walls that would withstand assaults in 1641 and 1649, and later rebuff the army of the deposed Catholic monarch, James II.

When James's Protestant son-in-law, William of Orange, assumed the throne of England in 1685, rumours began to circulate in Ireland that Irish Catholics were again taking arms against Protestant settlers—a replay of 1641. When a Catholic regiment arrived in December 1688 at Derry to relieve the garrison in the name of King James, 13 apprentice boys slammed the city gates in their faces. In the 105-day siege which ensued, nearly a quarter of the 30,000 inhabitants died, and the beleaguered survivors were reduced to eating rats, dogs, even leather and candles. To the terms offered by the attackers, defiant Derry replied "No surrender!"—a pithy retort still seen spray-painted on walls and heard on the lips of Ulster loyalists.

Despite their grim resolve, however, Derry was preparing to submit when a British ship finally broke through the barricade on the River Foyle and relieved the city. Protestants still celebrate the shutting of the city gates each 18 December and the lifting of the siege every year on 12 August. The city walls remain virtually intact, the most nearly complete such fortifications in Britain or Ireland. Pedestrians can walk most of their circuit for good views of the city and river, and for a look at the remaining cannons set in the ramparts, including an 18-pounder affectionately tagged Roaring Meg.

The spreading River Foyle marks the divide between the hilly city's two halves—Protestant Waterside to the east, mainly Catholic Bogside to the west —linked by a single, utilitarian bridge. Its 17th-century layout, with four main streets radiating from the central diamond out to the original gates, still defines the city centre. From a distance, Derry, as it's called by most everyone, looks peaceful and little changed from the 19th century. But the city has suffered heavily from eruptions of sectarian violence since the 1960s, though the situation has calmed considerably in recent years.

With a population of about 63,000, Derry is Ireland's fourth-largest city. Most of its interesting buildings and cultural attractions are concentrated within or near the old walls. The newly reconstructed **O'Doherty Tower**, with exhibits on Derry's turbulent past, makes a good place to start exploring. Just outside the walls to the east, the 1912 neo-Gothic **Guildhall** is worth a visit for its brilliant stained-glass windows illustrating episodes from the city's history; it's also the venue for concerts and for productions of the esteemed

Field Day theatre company, which premieres new works from the likes of Brian Friel and other leading Northern Irish playwrights every autumn before they tour the country.

The **Orchard Gallery**, in Orchard Street near the Tourist Office, holds changing exhibits of modern works by local artists. Within the walls again, **St. Columb's Cathedral**, built in a regional style called "planter's Gothic" in the 1620s, is thought to occupy the site of Colmcille's little oak grove. Inside are spent cannonballs, the keys and padlocks of the gates closed by the apprentice boys in 1688 and other siege memorabilia.

By Bicycle through Northern Ireland

At 6.30 am on 15 September I left Corrymeela on its stormy clifftop and crossed Torr Head with a gale behind me. To the north-east, just above a turbulent sea, the blue-green sky was scattered with pinkish shreds. Higher, shafts of golden light came streaming towards the water from between vast, torn masses of grey and purple cloud-banks—a wild and lonely sky it was, as restless as the sea. I thought, as I sweated up Torr Head, of the Children of Lir, changed into swans by their father's jealous second wife, and swimming for centuries on the waves of the Moyle, awaiting the first ringing of a Christian bell. When they heard that sound they again became children—and died. Maybe Christianity never brought much luck in this part of the world.

My father remembered speaking a version of Scots Gaelic hereabouts, during the first world war, to the people of the Glens. From the road above the Head I could see Scotland clearly, less than thirteen miles away. Always the people of north-east Ulster have felt closer to Scotland than to the rest of Ireland. Before the coast road was built the locals brought many of their more cumbersome necessities by boat from Dunaverty, on the Scottish coast, instead of struggling overland from Carrickfergus.

At 9. am I got to Cushendall, feeling very ready for breakfast, but the entire village seemed still asleep. When I finally succeeded in rousing a hotel the astonished-looking proprietress said breakfast was never served before 9.30. Plainly north-east Ulster is in Ireland, however many affinities it may have with Scotland.

One of the loveliest roads in Europe follows the coast from Cushendall to Larne and nowadays it is almost traffic-free. With the wind helping I sped along effortlessly. The sun was bright and noisy waves leaped at the nearby rocks, drenching me with spray; and away beyond the sparkling and glinting of the blue-green sea Scotland lay clear on the horizon. During such interludes the North's tragedy seems merely a nightmare and its beauty the only reality.

—Dervla Murphy, A Place Apart, 1978

County Tyrone

Apart from Cookstown, Dungannon, Omagh and a smattering of villages, County Tyrone's small population is only thinly spread across the hilly farmland, bog and windswept moors. The south does have its fertile green valleys, but the stark, desolate Sperrin Mountains spanning the northern border with Derry are almost unpeopled. You can travel for miles and miles through parts of Tyrone and not see so much as a cottage or even a lone sheep. When potential London investors visited the region in the early 1600s, their guide was under strict orders to steer them clear of the Sperrins, for fear that the mere sight of the inhospitable, peaty hills would put them off.

But this apparent emptiness belies the county's history. A littering of prehistoric monuments, including more than a thousand standing stones, suggest an industrious prehistoric population. The **Beaghmore Stone Circles**, uncovered in the 1940s from a blanket of bog west of Cookstown, are among the county's most remarkable archaeological sites. The 12 cairns, seven stone circles and other monuments probably served ceremonial functions and show that their builders possessed at least a rudimentary knowledge of astronomy: certain alignments of the stones indicate the sunrise at the summer solstice, among other cyclical events.

To the east, Tyrone borders the marshy shore of **Lough Neagh** (pronounced "nay"). Covering about 40 square kilometres (100,000 acres), it's by far the largest lake in Ireland or the British Isles. Like the Giant's Causeway, Lough Neagh was the legendary work of Finn MacCool. Mighty Finn scooped up a great clod of earth and hurled it at a rival Scottish giant; it fell short, and landed in the Irish Sea to become the Isle of Man. Water rushed into the vast cavity left behind, and Lough Neagh was born.

Northern Ireland's finest high cross, the ninth-century **Ardboe Cross** (or Arboe), overlooks the western shore of the lough, southeast of Cookstown. It's unusually tall, standing nearly six metres (18 1/2 feet), and is carved with 22 weathered but still-decipherable panels depicting the Crucifixion, Daniel in the lion's den, the miracle of the loaves and fishes and other biblical episodes. Pilgrims formerly journeyed to Ardboe for the healing waters from Lough Neagh and to hammer coins and nails into the beech tree in the corner of the churchyard, which was believed to grant the supplicant's wishes. An old song declares:

> *In all my rakings and undertakings*
> *Arboe, your equal I ne'er did see.*

The barren hills and bogland north of Ardboe infuse many of the evocative poems of Seamus Heaney, who grew up within sight of Slieve Gallion (elevation 529 metres, or 1,799 feet), the big peak at the eastern end of the Sperrin Mountains.

In the 17th century, the Irish of Tyrone vigorously resisted the English invasion, but with only temporary success; by the 1700s, the area was well "planted" with Scottish settlers. A curious legacy of those turbulent times is the peppering of the local dialect with archaic turns of phrase, many of them throwbacks to Elizabethan English.

By the end of the 18th century, some quarter of a million people had left Ulster in search of fresh opportunity in America. An excellent place for getting a sense of the Ulster emigrants' experience—both what they left behind and what they encountered in the New World—is at the **Ulster-American Folk Park**, between Omagh and Newtownstewart. In 1818, five-year-old Thomas Mellon left here with his family and moved to America. His grandson, the financier Andrew Mellon, would make a fortune for himself in the States and become one of the world's richest men.

In addition to the thatch-roofed Mellon home, the two sections of this park re-create the buildings and milieu of both a 19th-century Ulster village, with a school, farrier's forge, Presbyterian meetinghouse, shop, etc., and their frontier American counterparts. Weavers, blacksmiths, candlemakers and others garbed in traditional costumes ply their trades under historically authentic conditions. Just to the east, the long-distance Ulster Way foot trail passes through **Gortin Glen Forest Park**, which also has nature trails and good vistas.

Strabane is a predominantly Catholic enclave in a mostly Protestant region. This border town has suffered from sectarian violence in recent years and has been ravaged by ruinous unemployment—among the worst in Western Europe. One relic of better times is Georgian-fronted **Gray's Printing Shop**, in Main Street, which houses a museum of early printing machines. One of the shop's 18th-century apprentices, John Dunlap, emigrated to America, where he founded America's first daily newspaper, the *Pennsylvania Packet,* and printed the first copies of the Declaration of Independence. James Wilson, grandfather of President Woodrow Wilson, also apprenticed here. The white-washed, two-storey Wilson family farmhouse, at Dergalt three kilometres (two miles) southeast of town, is open to the public. The wickedly satirical Brian O'Nolan (the writer behind the aliases Flann O'Brien and Myles na gCopaleen), was another notable native son, born in Strabane in 1911.

Something about Tyrone seems to have nurtured the writing impulse in others, as well, and the county has contributed an impressive pantheon of writers to Irish literature. The prolific William Carleton (1794–1869),

sometimes called the Irish Dickens, was born in the south near Augher; the modern poet John Montague, who was born in America but raised on his aunt's Tyrone farm; and the widely popular playwright Brian Friel, author of *Translations* and *Dancing at Lughnasa*, was born in Omagh in 1929.

The Fermanagh Lakeland

Though it's a landlocked county, water is Fermanagh's defining element. Upper and Lower **Lough Erne** cover a third of the county, dividing it into two halves. On a map, Lower Lough Erne, the more northerly of the pair, looks something like a leaping dolphin, with its nose making for the open water of Donegal Bay and its island-dappled tail slapping the narrows at Enniskillen. Upper Lough Erne is a different story altogether, a lacework of reticulated shoreline and islands so confusing that boaters need navigational charts to find their way through. Similar drumlin topography—formed by glacial leavings pushed into knolls and ridges—continues south into County Cavan, making a maze of the River Erne.

Outstanding trout and salmon fishing, as well as record-setting catches of bream, pike, perch, rudd and other rough fish, make Fermanagh a favoured destination for anglers. The county is well set up to accommodate them as well as the flotilla of inland sailors who come to explore the loughs. Companies in the lakeside villages of Carry Bridge, Kesh and Killadeas rent out cruise boats (the Tourist Office on Shore Road, Enniskillen, has a complete list).

A number of Lower Lough Erne's dozens of green, low-lying islands are famed, too, for their early Christian ruins and curious stone effigies. In the Caldragh Cemetery on **Boa Island**, connected by bridges to the mainland at the north end of the lake, a squat statue stands among the buttercups, ferns and headstones. This famous figure is comprised of two neckless men back to back—a sort of Irish Janus—primitively carved with triangular heads, staring almond eyes and mouths agape as if frozen in midsentence.

Several such two-faced (and occasionally three-faced) carvings have been discovered around Fermanagh and Cavan. The Boa Island figure dates from perhaps the seventh century—after the arrival of Christianity in the region— yet there's a lingering pagan feeling to it. Perhaps the carver, whoever he was, remained under the spell of his unconverted forebears.

Bringing in the cows, Co. Kerry

Forested **White Island**, near the eastern shore in Castle Archdale Bay, is accessible by ferry. Inside its roofless 12th-century Romanesque church, eight stone figures dating from the seventh to tenth centuries have been assembled in an otherworldly chorus line. One of them has been identified as a *sheila-na-gig*, an ancient female fertility symbol; she makes a startling contrast to the others, most of which have been interpreted as representing pilgrims or early clerics. A final figure was roughed out but left blank and unfinished by the sculptor, perhaps because of a flaw in the stone.

Despite their frank expressions, there is a brooding, enigmatic quality about all of them. The crosier and bell and other Christian paraphernalia notwithstanding, the inscrutable faces seem to have been caught, like the Boa Island statue, in some transitional twilight between the advent of the Gospel and earthier civilization of the pre-Christian Celts.

In the sixth century, St. Molaise founded a monastery on **Devenish Island** which remained active for over a thousand years. The remains of his community—the most extensive early-to-medieval Christian settlement extant in Northern Ireland—include two roofless medieval churches, 15th-century St. Mary's Abbey and a perfect round tower. A small museum exhibits artifacts found on the island.

As with most of the early saints, volumes of miraculous happenings have come to be attributed to Molaise. One legend relates that, while concentrating on the song of a bird (in which he could hear the voice of God), the holy man lapsed into a reverie that lasted a hundred years. Only when he came to did he realize that a stone church had been built up around him.

In spring and summer Devenish can be reached by a short ferry ride from Trory; the tour boat *Kestrel* from Enniskillen, three kilometres (two miles) south, also stops at the island on its two-hour cruise around the lake.

Enniskillen and Thereabouts

The county's main town (population about 12,000), occupies the strategic narrow crossing between the two great lakes. This has always been an important bridge between the provinces of Ulster and Connacht, and Enniskillen was key to Ulster's resistance against Norman and Tudor incursions. Enniskillen Castle, the stronghold of the powerful Maguire clan, stands on an island in the middle of the old town. After the "Flight of the Earls" in 1607, the castle passed into English hands. The new owner, William Cole, added the water gate with its two round corner bartizans—unusual features in Irish fortifications.

The well-preserved castle houses both the county museum and the Regimental Museum, with uniforms, faded banners and battle trophies of the Waterloo veterans, the Royal Inniskilling Fusiliers and Inniskilling Dragoons. George Sigerson commemorated them with a song:

> *They were all dressed out like gentlemen's sons*
> *With their bright shining swords and carbine guns*
> *With their silver-mounted pistols, she observed them full soon*
> *Because that she loved her Enniskillen Dragoon.*

With an abundance of tackle shops, Enniskillen is a handy provisioning centre for fishermen heading out to the region's many rivers and lakes. If you're shopping for gifts, the town is also a good place to look for handmade lace, Irish knitwear and the delicate, ivory-coloured Belleek china. You can watch the craftsmen make the famous latticework parianware at the pottery in **Belleek**, near the Donegal border west of Lower Lough Erne.

Samuel Beckett attended the hilltop Portora Royal School in Enniskillen, as did Oscar Wilde. Young Oscar was unhappy with his experience here, but he did well enough at his Greek studies to earn himself a scholarship to Trinity College.

Once the English finally wrested possession of Fermanagh from the Irish Maguires, they found themselves obliged to build a series of castles to maintain control. As the colonists began to feel more secure, they commissioned grand mansions for their estates. Two of the finest are near Enniskillen and open to the public. The first earl of Belmore spared no expense in building and furnishing his **Castle Coole**, three kilometres (two miles) southeast of Enniskillen, in the 1790s; in the process, he exhausted his fortune but created an elegant masterpiece of Palladian architecture. The Cole family, eventually to become the earls of Enniskillen, began **Florence Court** in the 1760s, 13 kilometres (eight miles) southwest of Enniskillen. The three-storey mansion is known for its lavish rococo plasterwork, fine furnishings, landscaped gardens and extensive wooded grounds. Just down the road are the **Marble Arch Caves**, part of a vast limestone cavern system recently developed for tourism.

> *May we have the grace of God, and die in Ireland.*
> —Irish blessing

Practical Information

Useful Addresses

Irish Tourist Board Offices

The Irish Tourist Board (Bord Fáilte) maintains some two dozen offices year-round in main towns throughout the country, and another 65 or so offices are open seasonally.

REPUBLIC OF IRELAND
Irish Tourist Board
Baggot Street Bridge
P.O. Box 273 (for postal inquiries)
Tel. 01-676-5871
Fax 01-676-4764
Dublin 8, Ireland

UNITED STATES
Irish Tourist Board
345 Park Ave.
New York, NY 10154
Tel. 212-418-0800, 800-223-6470
Fax 212-371-9052

CANADA
Irish Tourist Board
160 Bloor St. East, Suite 934
Toronto, Ontario M4W 1B9
Tel. 416-929-2777
Fax 416-929-6783

UNITED KINGDOM
Irish Tourist Board
150 New Bond St.
London W1Y 0AQ
Tel. 071-493-3201
Fax 071-493-9065

NORTHERN IRELAND
Irish Tourist Board
53 Castle St.
Belfast BT1 1GH
Tel. 0232-327888
Fax 0232-240201

FRANCE
Irish Tourist Board
9 rue de Miromesnil
75008 Paris
Tel. 1-47 42 03 36

GERMANY
Irish Tourist Board
6000 Frankfurt am Main
Untermainanlage 7
Tel. 069-236492
Fax 069-234-626

Northern Ireland Tourist Board Offices

NORTHERN IRELAND
Northern Ireland Tourist Board
59 North St.
Belfast BT1 1ND
Tel. 0232-231221/246609
Fax 0232-240960

UNITED STATES
Northern Ireland Tourist Board
276 Fifth Ave., Suite 500
New York, NY 10001-4509
Tel. 212-686-6250
Fax 212-686-8061

British Tourist Authority
625 North Michigan Ave., Suite 1510
Chicago, IL 60611
Tel. 312-787-0490
Fax 312-787-7746

British Tourist Authority
World Trade Center
350 South Figueroa St.
Los Angeles, CA 90071-1203
Tel. 213-628-3525
Fax 213-687-6621

CANADA
British Tourist Authority
94 Cumberland St., Suite 600
Toronto, Ontario M5R 3N3
Tel. 416-925-6326
Fax 416-961-2175

REPUBLIC OF IRELAND
Northern Ireland Tourist Board
16 Nassau St.
Dublin 2
Tel. 01-6791851/6791977
Fax 01-6791853

UNITED KINGDOM
Northern Ireland Tourist Board
11 Berkeley St.
London W1X 5AD
Tel. 071-493-0601
Fax 071-499-3731

FRANCE
Northern Ireland Tourist Board
3 rue Pontoise
78100 St. Germain-en-Laye
Tel. 39 21 93 80
Fax 39 21 93 90

GERMANY
Northern Ireland Tourist Board
Taunusstrasse 52-60
6000 Frankfurt/Main
Tel. 069-23 45 04
Fax 069-238-0717

Accommodations

Camping is, of course, the cheapest way to stay in Ireland, but the wet, change-able weather makes it a risky proposition, and a few nights of rain can dampen anyone's enthusiasm. A reliably waterproof tent is a must. Ireland has hundreds of organized campgrounds, most of them concentrated along the coast. Many hostels, too, allow camping and use of their facilities for £2–3 per person. In a pinch, a farmer might well allow you to pitch your tent in his field for a night; do ask permission first.

An Óige, the Irish Youth Hostel Association, maintains about 40 **hostels** throughout the Republic, many of them in rather remote and picturesque locations. Membership or a supplemental fee is required for a stay in most of them, and restrictions such as a nighttime curfew and daytime closure are usually in effect. Beds are in segregated dormitories. The overnight fee ranges from about £3 to £9, depending on the location and facilities. The Youth Hostel Association of Northern Ireland runs the official hostel network in the North.

Over the past several years, alternatives to these official hostels have sprouted like mushrooms, mostly clustered throughout the western counties and with a few in Northern Ireland. Independent Hostel Owners and the smaller Irish Budget Hostels are the two main organizations, with more than 120 member hostels between them. These run the gamut from warm and quite comfortable to downright tatty; other travellers are a good source for recommendations. No membership is required, they stay open throughout the day, and there is generally no curfew. Independent hostels are comparable in price to the official hostels, with the exception that, in addition to dorm beds, private rooms are often available for a few pounds more.

In the Republic, **bed-and-breakfast** accommodations, or B&Bs, are ubiquitous throughout town and country, somewhat less widespread in the North. Irish B&Bs generally are housed within private homes; bathrooms often are shared among guests, and meals are taken in a common dining room. A night's stay, with a typical, filling Irish breakfast (tea, toast, cereal, eggs, bacon, sausage—vegetarians beware!), averages £8–16 per person, though it's possible to find plenty of B&Bs for a few pounds less or several pounds more. Many also offer high tea or full evening meals for an additional fee. The tourist offices offer reservations services and publications detailing hundreds of B&Bs throughout the island.

Hotels and **guesthouses**, at the bottom end of their scale, overlap B&Bs in price and go up from there; it's possible to get a perfectly decent room for £10 or so, and it's just as easy to spend ten times that for something more atmospheric or luxurious. The variety is enormous: from small, humble but cozy village hotels to more opulent Georgian town or country houses to extravagant renovated castles.

The accommodations below have restaurants on the premises. Price ranges are per person sharing:

Inexpensive: £20 or less	Expensive: £35–60
Moderate: £20–35	Luxury: £60 and above

COUNTY ANTRIM

Camera House, 44 Wellington Park, Belfast. Tel. 0232-660026. A plush B&B. Moderate.

Bushmills Inn, Main Street, Bushmills. Tel. 02657-32339. Pleasing location, good food. Moderate.

Londonderry Arms, 20 Harbour Road, Carnlough. Tel. 574-885255/885458, fax 574-885263. Small, old-fashioned. Moderate.

The Wellington Park Hotel, 21 Malone Road, Belfast. Modern hotel in nice neighbourhood, close to Botanic Gardens. Tel. 0232-381111. Expensive.

Ballygally Castle, 274 Coast Road, Ballygally. Tel. 574-583212, fax 574-583681. A 17th-century manor house with lovely views of Ballygally Bay. Expensive.

Europa, Great Victoria Street, Belfast. Tel. 327000, fax 327800. Modern high-rise, close to Opera House. Luxury.

COUNTY ARMAGH

The Charlemont Arms Hotel, 63 English Street, Armagh. Tel. 0861-522028. Small, centrally located. Moderate.

COUNTY CARLOW

Royal Hotel, Dublin Street, Carlow Town. Tel. 0503-31621, fax 0503-31621. Moderate.

COUNTY CAVAN

Park Hotel "Deerpark" Lodge, Virginia. Tel. 049-47235, fax 049-47203. Eighteenth-century hunting lodge with its own nine-hole golf course. Moderate.

Cabra Castle, Kingscourt. Tel. 042-67030, fax 042-67039. A Norman-style castle with 88-acre park grounds and nine-hole golf course. Expensive.

COUNTY CLARE

Mungovan's Guesthouse, 78 Parnell Street, Ennis. Tel. 065-24608, fax 065-20982. Small, intimate. Inexpensive.

Ballinalacken Castle Guesthouse, Lisdoonvarna. Tel. 065-74025. Built in 1840, beside a 15th-century O'Brien castle. Views of the Atlantic, the Aran Islands, Connemara. Inexpensive.

The Falls Hotel, Ennistymon. Tel. 065-71004, fax 065-71367. Georgian house in wooded setting overlooking cascading River Inagh. Inexpensive–Moderate.

Halpin's Hotel, 2 Erin Street, Kilkee. Tel. 065-56032, fax 065-56317. Built in 1880. Inexpensive–Moderate.

Aran View House Hotel, Coast Road, Doolin. Tel. 065-74061, fax 065-74061. Refurbished Georgian house, good views. Moderate.

Hylands Hotel, Ballyvaughan. Tel. 065-77037/15, fax 065-77131. Moderate.

Gregans Castle Hotel, Ballyvaughan. Tel. 065-77005, fax 065-77111. Comfortably furnished manor house in the centre of the Burren, excellent restaurant. Expensive.

COUNTY CORK

Garnish House, Western Road, Cork. Tel. 021-275111, fax 021-273872. Cheery, nicely appointed. Inexpensive.

Vickery's Inn, New Street, Bantry. Tel. 027-50006, fax 027-50006. Nineteenth-century coaching inn, in the centre of Bantry. Inexpensive.

O'Donovan's Hotel, Pearse Street, Clonakilty. Tel. 023-33250/33883, fax 023-34393. Pleasant and old-fashioned. Inexpensive.

Arbutus Lodge Hotel, Montenotte, Cork City. Tel. 021-501237, fax 021-502893. Elegant early 18th-century town house, famous for its fine restaurant. Moderate.

Ashley Hotel, Coburg Street, Cork. Tel. 021-501518, fax 021-275158. Centrally located on north side of Lee. Moderate.

Commodore Hotel, Cobh. Tel. 021-811277, fax 021-811672. Overlooks Cobh Harbour. Moderate.

The Castle Guesthouse, Castletownshend, near Skibbereen. Tel. 028-36100. Overlooking lovely harbour in private, wooded grounds. Moderate.

Devonshire Arms Hotel, Pearse Square, Youghal. Tel. 024-92018/92827, fax 024-92900. Good restaurant. Moderate.

Dromkeal Lodge Hotel, Ballylickey, Bantry. Tel. 027-51519, fax 027-51519. Georgian country house with gardens. Moderate–expensive.

Blue Haven Hotel, Pearse Street, Kinsale. Tel. 021-772209, fax 021-774268. Cozy small hotel, excellent seafood. Moderate–expensive.

Metropole Hotel, MacCurtain Street, Cork City. Tel. 021-508122, fax 021-506450. Beautiful Victorian hotel in city centre. Expensive.

Ballymaloe House, Shanagarry, near Midleton. Tel. 021-652531, fax 021-652021. Charming ivy-twined farmhouse. Renowned restaurant serves outstanding food, much of it grown on the surrounding family farm. Expensive.

Fitzpatrick Silver Springs Hotel, Tivoli, Cork City. Tel. 021-507533, fax 021-507641. Modern high-rise overlooking river, with nine-hole golf course and leisure centre. Expensive–luxury.

Longueville House, Mallow. Tel. 022-47156, fax 022-47459. Stately Palladian mansion on large estate, outstanding food. Expensive–luxury.

COUNTY DERRY

Clarence House, 15 Northland Road, Derry City. Tel. 265342. Comfortable guesthouse close to city centre. Inexpensive.

Everglades, Prehen Road, Derry City. Tel. 0504-46722/44414, fax 0504-748005. Modern hotel overlooking River Foyle three kilometres (two miles) south of the city. Expensive.

COUNTY DONEGAL

The Lone Star, Bridge Street, Killybegs. Tel. 073-31518, fax 073-31664. Good value, with fresh seafood in the restaurant. Inexpensive.

Danby House, Rossnowlagh Road, Ballyshannon. Tel. 072-51138. Fine 1820 country house surrounded by farm and woodland. Inexpensive–moderate.

St. Ernan's House Hotel, St. Ernan's, Donegal Town. Tel. 073-21065, fax 073-22098. Located on its own wooded islet outside Donegal Town. Moderate–expensive.

Rathmullan House, Rathmullan, Lough Swilly. Tel. 074-58188, fax 074-58200. Sprawling old country house on the shore of Lough Swilly. Moderate–expensive.

COUNTY DOWN

Portaferry Hotel, 10 The Strand, Portaferry. Tel. 02477-28231. Terrific seafood, right on the harbour. Moderate.

COUNTY DUBLIN

Dergvale Hotel, 4 Gardiner Place, Dublin 1. Tel. 01-744753/743361. Good-value, northside hotel. Inexpensive–moderate.

Clifton Court Hotel, 11 Eden Quay, O'Connell Bridge, Dublin 1. Tel. 01-743535, fax 01-786698. In the city centre overlooking the Liffey at O'Connell Bridge. Moderate.

Maple Hotel, 75 Lower Gardiner Street, Dublin 1. Tel. 01-745239, fax 01-745239. Moderate.

Georgian House, 20/21 Baggot Street Lower, Dublin 2. Tel. 01-618832, fax 01-618834. Very central 18th-century town house, a stone's throw from Stephen's Green. Moderate–expensive.

Powers Hotel, Kildare Street, Dublin 2. Tel. 01-6794388, fax 01-6794914. In the heart of Dublin city centre. Moderate–expensive.

Longfield's Hotel, Fitzwilliam Street Lower, Dublin 2. Tel. 01-761367, fax 01-761542. Beautiful Georgian red-brick house, beside Merrion Square. Expensive.

The Shelbourne Hotel, 27 St. Stephen's Green, Dublin 2. Tel. 01-766471, fax 01-616006. An elegant matron overlooking St. Stephen's Green, where Dublin's elite meet. Luxury.

Fitzpatrick Castle Hotel, Killiney. Tel. 01-2840700, fax 01-2850207. In 300 acres of woodlands and gardens overlooking Dublin Bay. Expensive–luxury.

COUNTY GALWAY

The Boat Inn, The Square, Oughterard. Tel. 091-82196, fax 091-82694. Cheerful place in village centre. Inexpensive.

American Hotel, Eyre Square, Galway. Tel. 091-61300, fax 091-66252. Moderate.

Great Southern Hotel Galway, Eyre Square, Galway. Tel. 091-64041, fax 091-66704. Comfortable old dowager and social crossroads of central Galway, built in 1845. Expensive–luxury.

Alcock and Brown Hotel, Clifden. Tel. 095-21086, fax 095-21842. Moderate.

Ballynahinch Castle Hotel, Recess, Connemara. Tel. 095-31006/31086, fax 095-31085. A much-storied retreat, ancestral seat of eccentric Martin family, in a gorgeous setting at the foot of the Twelve Bens. Expensive–luxury.

Cashel House Hotel, Cashel. Tel. 095-31001, fax 095-31077. Splendid gardens and location, horseback riding, private beach. Luxury.

COUNTY KERRY

The Bianconi, Annadale Road, Killorglin. Tel. 066-61146, fax 066-61950. Small and affordable, with good meals. Inexpensive.

Herlihy Accommodations, Binn Bán, Dingle. Tel. 066-51611. Family-run B&B, close to Dingle; spectacular sea views. Inexpensive.

Doyle's Seafood Bar & Townhouse, John Street, Dingle. Tel. 066-51174, fax 066-51816. Homey, tastefully furnished rooms, superb seafood meals. Moderate.

Arbutus Hotel, College Street, Killarney. Tel. 064-31037, fax 064-34033. Central, quiet atmosphere. Moderate.

Eviston House Hotel, New Street, Killarney. Tel. 064-31640, fax 064-33685. Reasonably priced, in the centre of Killarney. Moderate.

Great Southern Hotel Killarney, Killarney. Tel. 064-31262, fax 064-31642. Sumptuous hotel constructed in 1854, spacious grounds and all the amenities; feel like splurging? Expensive–luxury.

The Park Hotel Kenmare, Kenmare. Tel. 064-41200, fax 064-41402. A grand Victorian hotel amid private gardens, one of Ireland's finest hotels. Luxury.

The Grand Hotel, Tralee. Tel. 066-21499, fax 066-22877. Moderate.

COUNTY KILDARE

Curryhills House Hotel, Prosperous, Naas. Tel. 045-68150, fax 045-68805. Congenial Georgian farmhouse. Moderate.

COUNTY KILKENNY

Butler House, 15/16 Patrick Street, Kilkenny City. Tel. 056-65707/22828, fax 056-65626. Former home of the duchess of Ormonde, central yet secluded. Moderate.

Club House Hotel, Patrick Street, Kilkenny City. Tel. 056-21994, fax 056-21994. Retains the sporting ambience from its days as headquarters of Foxhound Club. Moderate.

Mount Juliet, Thomastown. Tel. 056-24455, fax 056-24522. Eighteenth-century country estate on 37 square kilometres (1,500 acres) of parkland, 18-hole golf course. Luxury.

COUNTY LAOIS
Roundwood House, Mountrath. Tel. 0502-32120. A charming, family-run guesthouse in a faithfully restored Georgian mansion. Inexpensive.

COUNTY LEITRIM
County Hotel, Carrick-on-Shannon. Tel. 078-20042, fax 078-21180. Moderate.

COUNTY LIMERICK
Railway Hotel, Parnell Street, Limerick City. Tel. 061-413653/414250, fax 061-419762. Attractive and personable, right in the heart of Limerick. Inexpensive–moderate.

Fitzpatrick Bunratty Shamrock Hotel, Bunratty. Tel 061-361177, fax 061-471252. Modern comfortable hotel in wooded grounds adjacent to Bunratty Castle. Luxury.

Dunraven Arms Hotel, Adare. Tel. 061-396209, fax 061-396541. Two-hundred-dred-year-old inn, excellent restaurant. Moderate–luxury.

COUNTY LOUTH
Boyne Valley Hotel, Drogheda. Tel. 041-37737, fax 041-39188. Peaceful gardens and grounds. Moderate.

Derryhale Hotel, Carrick Road, Dundalk. Tel. 042-35471, fax 042-35471. Moderate.

COUNTY MAYO
Grand Central Hotel, The Octagon, Westport. Tel. 098-25027, fax 098-26316. Friendly small hotel in centre of town. Moderate.

Mount Falcon Castle, Ballina. Tel. 096-21172, fax 096-21172. Imposing grey-stone Gothic manor, roaring log fires, private fishing waters. Expensive.

Newport House, Newport. Tel. 098-41222, fax 098-41613. Magnificent ivy-clad Georgian house in forested riverside grounds. Expensive–luxury.

COUNTY MEATH
Old Mill Hotel, Julianstown. Tel. 041-29133. Converted riverside mill, private fishing. Inexpensive–moderate.

COUNTY OFFALY
Dooly's Hotel, Emmet Square, Birr. Tel. 0509-20032, fax 0509-21332. Eighteenth-century coaching inn, pleasant atmosphere. Moderate.

COUNTY ROSCOMMON
Royal Hotel, Castle Street, Roscommon. Tel. 0903-26297/26317, fax 0903-26225. Moderate.
Royal Hotel, Bridge Street, Boyle. Tel. 079-62016, fax 079-62016. Riverside, 250-year-old building, hearty menu. Moderate.

COUNTY SLIGO
Clarence Hotel, Wine Street, Sligo Town. Tel. 071-42211. Centre of Sligo town. Moderate.
Hotel Silver Swan, Hyde Bridge, Sligo Town. Tel 071-43231, fax 071-42232. Central, perched right above the River Garavogue, excellent restaurant. Moderate–expensive.

COUNTY TIPPERARY
Baileys of Cashel, Main Street, Cashel. Tel. 062-61937, fax 062-62038. Very good value in nearly 300-year-old town house. Inexpensive.
Castle Court Hotel, Cahir. Tel. 052-41210/41227. Inexpensive–moderate.

COUNTY TYRONE
The Royal Arms, 51 High Street, Omagh. Tel. 0662-243262, fax 0662-245011. In town centre. Moderate.

COUNTY WATERFORD
Candlelight Inn, Dunmore East. Tel. 051-83215/83239, fax 051-83289. Appealing, friendly ambience, with well-prepared meals. Moderate.
O'Shea's Hotel, Strand Street, Tramore. Tel. 051-81246. Small, family-run hotel close to beach. Moderate.
Granville Hotel, Waterford. Tel. 051-55111, fax 051-70307. Gracious and sophisticated. Moderate–expensive.
The Bridge Hotel, The Quay, Waterford. Tel. 051-77222, fax 051-77229. Luxury.

COUNTY WESTMEATH
Village Hotel, Tyrrellspass. Tel. 044-23171, fax 044-23491. Family-run, affable town house on village green, good food. Moderate.
Prince of Wales Hotel, Church Street, Athlone. Tel. 0902-72626, fax 0902-75658. Expensive.

COUNTY WEXFORD
Devereux Hotel, Rosslare Harbour. Tel. 053-33216/33180, fax 053-33301. Convenient to Rosslare ferry port. Moderate.

White's Hotel, George's Street, Wexford Town. Tel. 053-22311, fax 053-45000. Popular, tony establishment, with two quite cosmopolitan restaurants. Expensive.

COUNTY WICKLOW
Grand Hotel, Wicklow. Tel. 0404-67337, fax 0404-69181. Moderate.

The Old Rectory Country House and Restaurant, Wicklow. Tel. 0404-67048, fax 0404-69181. Intimate lodgings, delightful gourmet and vegetarian cuisine. Expensive.

Holidays and Events

JANUARY
1: New Year's Day, national holiday

MARCH
Arklow Music Festival, Arklow, Co. Wicklow
17: St. Patrick's Day, national holiday

APRIL
Good Friday, national holiday
Easter Monday, national holiday

MAY
May Day (first Monday in May), national holiday—Northern Ireland only
Pan Celtic Festival, Killarney, Co. Kerry
Spring Holiday (last Monday in May), national holiday—Northern Ireland only
Fleadh Nua, Ennis, Co. Clare

MAY–JUNE
Listowel Writers' Week, Listowel, Co. Kerry

JUNE
June Holiday (first Monday in June), national holiday—Republic only
GPA Festival of Music in Great Irish Houses, various locations

JULY
12: Orange Day or Battle of the Boyne Holiday, national holiday—Northern Ireland only
West Cork Festival, Clonakilty, Co. Cork
Cobh International Folk Dance Festival, Cobh, Co. Cork
Dublin Horse Show
Galway Arts Festival, Galway City
"Lady of the Lake" Festival, Irvinestown, Co. Fermanagh

JULY–AUGUST
Galway Races, Galway City
Ballyshannon Folk and Traditional Music Festival, Ballyshannon, Co. Donegal
O'Carolan Harp and Traditional Irish Music Festival, Keadue, Co. Roscommon
City of Belfast International Rose Trials, Belfast

AUGUST
August Bank Holiday (first Monday in August), national holiday—Republic only
Granard Harp Festival, Granard, County Longford
Puck Fair, Killorglin, Co. Kerry
Cobh People's Regatta, Cobh, Co. Cork
Kilkenny Arts Week, Kilkenny Town
Sligo Arts Festival, Sligo Town
Connemara Pony Show, Clifden, Co. Galway
Rose of Tralee International Festival, Tralee, Co. Kerry
Fleadh Ceoil na hÉireann, changing location
Summer Bank Holiday (last Monday in August), national holiday—Northern Ireland only

Ould Lammas Fair, Ballycastle,
Co. Antrim
Letterkenny Festival of Music and
Dance, Letterkenny, Co. Donegal
Galway Arts Festival, Galway City

SEPTEMBER
Belfast Folk Festival
Galway Oyster Festival, Galway City

SEPTEMBER–OCTOBER
Clifden Community Arts Week,
Clifden, Co. Galway
Westport Arts Festival, Westport,
Co. Mayo
Waterford International Festval of
Light Opera, Waterford City
Dublin Theatre Festival

OCTOBER
Ireland's Matchmaking Festival,
Lisdoonvarna, Co. Clare

October Holiday (last Monday in
October), national holiday—
Republic only
Kinsale Gourmet Festival, Kinsale,
Co. Cork
Cork Jazz Festival, Cork City

OCTOBER–NOVEMBER
Wexford Opera Festival, Wexford
Town

NOVEMBER
Belfast Festival at Queen's University

DECEMBER
25: Christmas Day, national holiday
26: St. Stephen's Day, national
holiday—Republic only
26: Boxing Day, national Holiday—
Northern Ireland only

Irish Vocabulary

It's impossible to briefly summarize all of the rules and sounds of Irish. Dialectal differences and the effects of sounds upon one another present complex variations that are beyond the scope of this guide. But while your chances of encountering someone who speaks no English are slender, knowing and using a few words in Irish will likely surprise your Irish acquaintances and warm your welcome in the Gaeltacht.

NUMBERS / PRONUNCIATION

aon—one	ain	aon déag—eleven	ain jeg
dó—two	doe	dó dhéag—twelve	doe yaig
trí—three	tree	trí déag—thirteen	tree jeg
ceathair—four	KEH-har	ceathair déag—fourteen	KEH-har jeg
cúig—five	KOO-ig	cúig déag—fifteen	KOO-ig jeg
sé—six	shay	sé déag—sixteen	shay jeg
seacht—seven	shockht	seacht déag—seventeen	shockht jeg
ocht—eight	ockht	ocht déag—eighteen	ockht jeg
naoi—nine	nee	naoi déag—nineteen	nee jeg
deich—ten	jeykh	fiche—twenty	FEE-hah

DAYS, MONTHS, AND TIME

Dé Domhnaigh—Sunday	je DOW-nee
Dé Luain—Monday	je LOO-in
Dé Máirt—Tuesday	je MARTCH
Dé Céadaoin—Wednesday	je KAY-deen
Déardaoin—Thursday	JARE-deen
Dé hAoine—Friday	je HEEN-ya
Dé Sathairn—Saturday	je SA-hurn
inniu—today	in-YOO
anocht—tonight	uh-nukht
amárach—tomorrow	um-AWR-uck
oíche amárach—tomorrow night	EE-hah MAW-ruckh
inné—yesterday	in-YAY
aréir—last night	a-RARE
mí—month	mee
Mí Eanáir—January	mee ANN-ar
Mí Feabhra—February	mee FYOW-rah
Márta—March	MAR-tah

Aibreán—April ah-BRON
Mí na Bealtaine—May mee nah BAL-tenna
Meitheamh—June MEE-hev
Mí Iúil—July mee OOH-ill
Mí Lúnasa—August mee LOO-nassa
Meán Fómhair—September man fowar
Deireadh Fómhair—October JERR-ah fowar
Mí na Samhna—November mee nah SOW-nah
Mí na Nollag—December mee nah NULL-ug
Cad é an t-am?—What time is it? cod ay un TOWM
Tá sé a cúig a chlog.—It is five o'clock. taw shay a koo-ig a khlug

FOOD AND DRINK

óstán—hotel ow-STAWN
teach tabhairne—pub chock towern-yah
tae—tea tay
caife—coffee kaffay
arán—bread a-RON
bainne—milk bonn-ya
siúcra—sugar shook-ra
fíon—wine fee-un
uisce beatha—whiskey ishk-ya BA-ha
beoir—beer byore
dinnéar—dinner dinyayr
lón—lunch loan
bricfeasta—breakfast brick-FAS-ta

CONVERSATION

tá—yes thaw
níl—no neel
Dia duit—hello JEE-uh gwitch
Dia's Muire duit—hello (in reply) JEE-uss MORRA gwitch
Dia dhuit ar maidin—good morning JEE-uh gwitch ar MOD-jin
oíche mhaith dhuit—good night EE-hah woy-hitch
slán—goodbye slawn
Conas tá tú?—How are you? CUNN-us taw too
Tá mé go maith—I'm fine. taw may guh MAH
Go raibh maith agat—Thank you. GRA-mah HUGG-ut
Tá fáilte romhat—You're welcome. taw FALTCHA ROW-ut

Tá an aimsir go h-álainn.
—The weather is beautiful.

taw un AM-shur guh HALL-in

Tá an aimsir go fliuch.
—The weather is wet.

taw un AM-shur flookh

sláinte—cheers

slawn-cha

Gabh mo leithscéal—Excuse me.

go muh LESH-kayle

Cad is ainm duit? —What is your name?

cod iss ONNEM ditch

... is ainm dom. —My name is . . . .

... iss ONNEM dum

An bhfuil Gaeilge agat?
—Do you speak Irish?

un will GWAYL-ga UGGUT

Tá, beagáinín.—Yes, a little.

thaw, byug-AWN-yeen

Cad é seo?—What is this?

cod ay SHUH

Cad é sin?—What is that?

cod ay SHIN

Cá bhfuil an seomra na mban?
—Where is the women's toilet?

caw will an SHOAM-rah nah mon

... seomra na bfear?—men's toilet?

SHOAM-rah nah var

Ar mhaith leat deoch?
—Would you like a drink?

ur wall lat JYUCK

Ba mhaith liom gloine beoir.
—I would like a glass of beer.

buh WALL-um glinya be-yore

Cá mhéad sin?—How much is it?

kay-VAY-ud shin

Iryſhe,	Latten,	Engliſhe,
Conerʒa ʒu.	Quomodo habes.	How doe you.
Ʒaɪm ʒo maɪh.	Bene ſum.	I am well,
Ʒo ʃo maɪh aʒaɪ,	Habeo gratias,	I thancke you,
In ʒolʊɣʒ ʒealaʒ	Poſſis ne~ ~ ~ʒ	Cann you ~ ~

Recommended Reading

More than a thousand years ago, an anonymous Irish poet praised "a clever verse" as an "accomplishment well regarded in Ireland". He went on to expound:

> *Three excellent qualities in narration: a good flow, depth of thought, conciseness.*
> *Three dislikeable qualities in the same: stiffness, obscurity, bad delivery.*

Those guidelines have served well. English was foisted on the native Irish, but over the centuries Irish writers have taken the language and gotten a delicious revenge, creating a marvellous body of literature that expresses, often brilliantly, the full span of Irish—and human—experience, in a myriad of voices that are by turns lyrical, playful, tender, bitter, scaldingly sardonic and frequently fired by genius. The playwright Denis Johnston noted the irony:

> *How odd it is that over the past three centuries—from Swift to Sheridan to Shaw and Joyce—this ragbag of misplaced persons, this Seventh City of Christendom, built by fair strangers in one of Europe's backyards—has consistently taught the Englishman how to write in his own tongue.*

The very brief list below suggests a few points of entry into good writing by and about the Irish.

HISTORY AND CULTURE

Bell, J. Bowyer. *The Irish Troubles: A Generation of Violence 1967–1992.* St. Martin's Press, 1993. A good contemporary overview.

Breathnach, Breandán. *Folk Music and Dances of Ireland.* The Mercier Press, 1971. A somewhat specialized and advanced introduction to the subject, but full of interesting information for the non-musicologist as well.

Crowl, Phillip A. *The Intelligent Traveller's Guide to Historic Ireland.* Contemporary Books, 1990. Combines an authoritatively told history with meticulous descriptions of mansions, castles, museums, monasteries, prehistoric sites, etc., in Northern Ireland and the Republic.

de Breffny, Brian. *In the Steps of St. Patrick.* Thames and Hudson, 1982. Well-written attempt to disentangle the myths surrounding St. Patrick from the man and his times.

de Breffny, Brian, editor. *The Irish World: The History and Cultural Achievements of the Irish People.* Thames and Hudson, 1977. Excellent, lucid account weaves history and politics with Irish architecture, literature, painting, crafts, etc.

FitzGibbon, Constantine. *The Irish in Ireland.* David & Charles, 1983.

Flood, W.H. Grattan. *A History of Irish Music.* Praeger, 1970.

Harbison, Peter. *Pilgrimage in Ireland: The Monuments and the People.* Barrie and Jenkins, 1991. A scholarly yet quite accessible examination of early to modern Christianity in Ireland and its holy places and people.

Hull, Roger H. *The Irish Triangle: Conflict in Northern Ireland.* Princeton University Press, 1976.

Joyce, P.W. *A Social History of Ancient Ireland.* Longmans, Green and Co., 1903. Remarkably detailed, two-volume survey of ancient Irish society, customs, economy, crafts, personal adornment, etc.

Macardle, Dorothy. *The Irish Republic.* Farrar, Straus and Giroux, 1965. Thick with telling detail, concentrates on the events of 1916–1923, leading to Irish independence.

MacManus, Seumas. *The Story of the Irish Race: A Popular History of Ireland.* Revised edition. The Devin-Adair Co., 1978. Particularly strong chapters on mythology and pre-Christian Ireland. Ends, unfortunately, in 1938.

Mason, Redfern. *The Song Lore of Ireland.* Wessels & Bissell, 1910. As much about Irish music and song as about the historical milieu which produced them.

Murphy, Frank. *The Bog Irish.* Penguin, 1987. A look at the lives of the dispossessed Irish from the 17th through 19th centuries, told through eyewitness accounts, diary entries, poems, anecdotes.

Newby, Eric, and Diana Petry. *The Wonders of Ireland.* Stein and Day, 1969. Relates the histories and legends of interesting sites throughout Ireland, both man-made and natural, well-known and obscure.

Newman, Peter R. *Companion to Irish History: From the Submission of Tyrone to Partition 1603–1921.* Facts on File, 1991. An extremely helpful reference with concise entries on significant people, organizations and events, arranged alphabetically.

O'Brien, Máire and Conor Cruise. *A Concise History of Ireland.* Thames and Hudson, 1972. Balanced but rather sketchy overview.

Ranelagh, John. *Ireland: An Illustrated History.* Oxford University Press, 1981.

Robinson, Tim. *Stones of Aran: Pilgrimage.* New York: Viking, 1986. A thoroughly fascinating, detailed account of the history, folklore, archaeology and geography of Inishmore, largest of the Aran islands.

Scherman, Katharine. *The Flowering of Ireland: Saints, Scholars and Kings.* Little, Brown, and Co., 1981. Absorbing reading, Scherman breathes life into the personages and events of medieval Ireland.

Woodham Smith, Cecil. *The Great Hunger.* Hamish Hamilton, 1962. A riveting history of the Great Famine of the 1840s and the social and political milieu of the times.

General

Cahill, Susan and Thomas. *A Literary Guide to Ireland.* New York: Charles Scribner's Sons, 1973. An affectionate ramble through the varied literary landscapes of Ireland, deftly interweaving the words of Joyce, Moore, Swift, Yeats, et al.

Dorris, Paul. *Pocket Irish Phrasebook.* Appletree Press, 1983. A good start on the language, with a bit of grammar thrown in to keep things confusing.

Morris, Jan. *Ireland: Your Only Place.* Clarkson N. Potter, 1990. Lyrical text complemented by brooding, unusual colour photos by Paul Wakefield.

Ryan, Kathleen Jo, and Bernard Share, editors. *Irish Traditions.* Harry N. Abrams, Inc., 1985. Essays on varied aspects of Ireland and Irishness by John B. Keane, Peter Somerville-Large, Máire de Paor and others, vividly illustrated with Ryan's colour photos.

Shaw-Smith, David. *Ireland's Traditional Crafts.* Thames and Hudson, 1984. Well-illustrated, large-format volume describes boatbuilding, instrument-making, weaving, basketry, woodwork, stone carving, ceramics and other crafts.

Travelogue and Memoir

Bulfin, William. *Rambles in Eirinn.* 2 vols. Sphere Books, 1981. The author bicycled over 3,000 miles around Ireland in the early 1900s, and produced this personal and opinionated account of his adventures, first published as a series of newspaper articles.

Devlin, Bernadette. *The Price of My Soul.* Vintage Books, 1969. Devlin, elected in 1969 to the British Parliament at the age of 21, recalls the hard knocks and small joys of growing up Catholic in Northern Ireland and describes her views on the byzantine politics at work in Northern Ireland.

Gibbings, Robert. *Lovely Is the Lee.* E.P. Dutton & Co., 1945. An easygoing memoir of the author's travels through Connacht and his native Cork in the 1940s, illustrated with his own beautiful woodcuts.

Love, Deborah. *Annaghkeen.* Random House, 1970. Love's intimate, contemplative journal of a summer spent in Ireland with her husband (writer Peter Matthiessen) and children.

Murphy, Dervla. *A Place Apart*. The Devin-Adair Co., 1978. Inveterate traveller and tireless observer Murphy roved around Northern Ireland by bicycle in the mid-1970s, living among and talking with people of all persuasions involved in (or trying to stay out of) the "Troubles".

O'Brien, Kate. *My Ireland*. Hastings House, 1962. Highly personal observations and ruminations from the great Limerick novelist.

Synge, J.M. *The Aran Islands*. John W. Luce and Company, 1911. Recounts Synge's experiences among a remarkable island people in transition, patiently observed and beautifully recounted.

Synge, J.M. *In Wicklow, West Kerry and Connemara*. Rowman and Littlefield, 1980. A collection of 14 lyrical essays written by Synge about Ireland's country folk in the early 1900s. With helpful modern commentary by George Gmelch and Ann Saddlemyer and photos by Saddlemyer.

FICTION AND LITERATURE

Deane, Seamus, editor. *The Field Day Anthology of Irish Writing*. 3 vols. Field Day Publications, 1991. A magnum opus survey of Ireland's literature in both Irish and English, from the earliest records up to 1990: prose, poetry, plays, criticism, political writings, etc. Extremely well edited and annotated—the footnotes alone constitute a course in Irish culture.

Gregory, Lady Isabella Augusta. *A Treasury of Irish Myth, Legend, and Folklore*. Avenal Books, 1986.

Joyce, James. *The Portable James Joyce*. Viking Press, 1981. One-volume collection includes complete *Dubliners*, *Portrait of the Artist*, *Collected Poems*, *Exiles* and excerpts from *Ulysses* and *Finnegans Wake*.

Macken, Walter. *Seek the Fair Land*. Macmillan, 1959. An enjoyable, flavourful historical novel dealing with Ireland in the bloody decade of the 1640s.

Montague, John, editor. *The Book of Irish Verse*. Macmillan, 1976. A representative anthology covering the sixth through 20th centuries.

O'Brien, Edna. *A Fanatic Heart*. Farrar Straus Giroux, 1984. A fine sampling of 29 stories from a supple, sensitive writer.

O'Brien, Flann. *Stories and Plays*. The Viking Press, 1973. A brief assortment from the quirky satirical genius of Irish letters.

O'Connor, Frank. *Traveller's Samples: Stories and Tales*. Alfred A. Knopf, 1951. Fourteen short stories from one of Ireland's best-loved writers.

O'Faoláin, Seán. *Selected Stories of Seán O'Faoláin.* Little, Brown & Co., 1978. A well-rounded introduction to the subtle, evocative prose of one of Ireland's finest story-tellers.

MacNeice, Louis. *Collected Poems.* Faber and Faber, 1966.

Plunkett, James. *Strumpet City.* Delacorte Press, 1969. Richly textured historical novel centred on labour leader Jim Larkin and a panoply of fictional supporting characters in early 20th-century Dublin.

Somerville, Edith, and Martin Ross. *The Real Charlotte.* Rutgers University Press, 1986. A portrait of Irish manners, ambitions and social strata in the 1890s, the twilight of the Anglo-Irish Ascendancy.

Somerville, Edith, and Martin Ross. *Some Experience of an Irish R.M.* R.S. Surtees Society, 1983. The first of a trio of breezy, appealing novels concerning the interplay between various levels of 1890s Irish society.

Williams, Niall, and Christine Breen. *O Come Ye Back to Ireland: Our First Year in County Clare.* Soho Press, 1987. Memoirs of a husband and wife who chucked their New York City careers and moved to a farm in Clare.

Yeats, W.B. *Collected Poems.* Macmillan, 1956.

Index